The School Choice Wars

John Merrifield

The Scarecrow Press, Inc.
A Scarecrow Education Book
Lanham, Maryland, and London
2001

SCARECROW PRESS, INC.
A Scarecrow Education Book

Published in the United States of America
by Scarecrow Press, Inc.
4720 Boston Way, Lanham, Maryland 20706
www.scarecroweducation.com

4 Pleydell Gardens, Folkestone
Kent CT20 2DN, England

British Library Cataloguing in Publication Information Available

Library of Congress Cataloging-in-Publication Data

Merrifield, John, 1955–
    The school choice wars / John Merrifield.
        p. cm.
    Includes bibliographical references and index.
    ISBN 0-8108-3953-9 (alk. paper) — ISBN 0-8108-3956-3 (paper : alk. paper)
        1. School choice—United States. 2. Education—Parent participation—United States.
    I. Title.
    LB1027.9 .M47 2001
    379.1'11'0973—dc21   00-049659

♾ ™ The paper used in this publication meets the minimum requirements of
American National Standard for Information Sciences—Permanence of
Paper for Printed Library Materials, ANSI/NISO Z39.48–1992.
Manufactured in the United States of America.

To Milton Friedman, Myron Lieberman, and Quentin Quade,
the three intellectual giants of parental choice advocacy.

CONTENTS

Foreword

I have no doubt that when future historians write about the post–World War II era, they will say a great deal about how educational reform became a matter of public policy as never before in our national history. I have several fears about what they will write. The first is that they will concentrate on the ways the reform movement was a manifestation of the political-ideological battles long a feature of our national history, which indeed it is. The second is how intractable to change our educational system was, which (again) it is. The third is the historians' bewilderment that the reform movement continues to have little to show that is a source of encouragement or optimism. The fourth is that being historians they will fall prey to a superficial comprehension of the language and logic of the reform movement. More correctly, they will pay more attention to the labels attached to this or that program than to the fact that these labels in practice were predictably a source of confusion and failure. It is my opinion that this last fear is the most bothersome because unless the language and logic of reform are classified and clarified, there will be further confirmation of the maxim that the more things change the more they will remain the same. If the future historians should have the good sense to read Professor Merrifield's book, they are likely to avoid superficiality.

Professor Merrifield asks this question: what is meant by and what is the intended consequence of reforms bearing such labels as vouchers, school choice, charter schools, privatization, and competition? This book brilliantly and clearly exposes the superficiality and extraordinary fuzziness of those labels. It also makes plain that partisans for these nostrums will, at best, have very little effect on changing our existing school systems. The author is a passionate supporter of public education. He is no nihilistic critic. Quite the contrary, he is a sober, clear, logical thinker who has illuminated how the means and ends of educational reform require more than adherence to virtuous sounding labels that generate heat, but no light. (So what else is new in the arena of educational reform?) Logic, respect for data, calling a spade a spade are distinguishing characteristics of this book.

The Federal Food and Drug Administration was created to prevent the use of drugs that had not gone through certain tests and passed prescribed standards demonstrating truth in labeling. The school choice wars needs analogous labeling tests and standards. What this book does is to demonstrate that if the labels that are the rallying cries for changing our educational system, and no one denies that that is the goal of those in the school choice wars, then that change will never be achieved; the educational Tower of Babel will still produce Babel. Passion, power, political clout, and hype are no substitute for clarity of goal, methods to reach them, and data to substantiate them.

This book is not a polemic. It will not sit well with those who believe, usually unreflectively so, that there is only one way, the present way, that public education can be conceptually organized and provided. That belief is understandable if only because the great bulk of people grew up in the system and cannot even imagine alternatives. Well, when you are faced with a problem that has been intractable to change and you can conceive of no alternatives to the system of which that intractability is a feature, you are part of the problem and not of the solution. But that is also the case of the partisans in the school choice wars who have come up with an alternative, but in becoming a combatant in the wars forgot what they were fighting for: To change the existing system.

I have expressed my fears about what future historians will write. I have and continue to have similar fears about what economists are writing and will write. Professor Merrifield is an economist, the only one who has made a seminal contribution to explaining why the current school choice wars cannot change our educational system.

Seymour B. Sarason, Ph.D.
Professor Emeritus of Psychology
Yale University
December 5, 2000

Preface

Because system transformation is what "a nation at risk" needs, much of what is said to advocate and oppose parental choice is wrong, misleading, or irrelevant. Assertions to the contrary notwithstanding, very few of the prominent parental choice proposals can change the system. Most of the public debate is about policies that can only move a few children within a virtually unchanged system. This book discusses choice advocates' policy and political strategy mistakes, suggests corrections, and describes the key elements of the school choice wars, including the views of nonexperts. What the American people believe about parental choice will determine the nature of K–12 reform and the future of our country.

This book defines and argues for a particular view of parental choice as a reform catalyst. In the process, the book is highly critical of strategies, tactics, processes, assumptions, constraints, and incentive systems. Since parental choice advocates have accomplished a lot, I want to apologize for the unavoidable linkage between names and criticisms.

I hope this perspective from behind the front line will reorient America's most important movement, not alienate its key field generals and foot soldiers. After all, regardless of this book's impact, the parental choice advocates of the recent past will be the most prominent advocates for the foreseeable future. The same thing is true of educators. Any reformed system will depend on most of the educators collectively producing unacceptable results now. I believe that this book can help current parental choice advocates and educators produce much better results, and that the future will be much brighter if they do.

Acknowledgments

This book evolved from Dr. Myron Lieberman's realization that the specific parental choice programs supported and analyzed by choice advocates hardly ever had any relevance to their professed goal of reforming K–12 education. Likewise, there was much talk about competition, but little apparent understanding of what competition entailed, or what could be expected from it. Dr. Lieberman, Senior Research Scholar at the Social Philosophy and Policy Center and Chairman of the Education Policy Institute, first raised those issues in his book, *Public Education: An Autopsy* (Harvard University Press, 1993), and subsequently in "The School Choice Fiasco" (*The Public Interest* [Winter, 1994]: 17–34). Meanwhile, although I was quite new to the issues of K–12 reform and parental choice, I was reaching some of the same conclusions as Dr. Lieberman. That's where things stood in March, 1997 when similar critiques of alleged experiments caused Dr. Lieberman to appear with me in a *School Reform News* article. A letter I wrote to Dr. Lieberman eventually produced an invitation to join him at an October 1997 conference at the Dallas Federal Reserve Bank headquarters. That meeting kicked off the work that became this book.

Initially, the book was to be coauthored, but it eventually became clear that Dr. Lieberman's schedule would not permit that level of work-sharing. Still, he did much more than emphasize the need for a book on the issues that concerned both of us. He provided many helpful suggestions, materials, and contacts, and commented on each chapter draft at least once. In short, Dr. Lieberman's help was invaluable, and he deserves much of the credit for whatever impact the book eventually has. Of course, he is not responsible for the shortcomings that survived his critical comments. I did all of the research and made all of the final judgments about content and style.

While Dr. Lieberman deserves by far the largest "thank you," several other people made significant contributions to the final product. Again, they deserve credit for some of the book's virtues but none of the blame for its shortcomings. Vincent DiMartino, my colleague at the University of Texas at San Antonio, commented on all 15 chapters. His suggestions prompted many essential clarifications. Darcy Olsen of the Cato Institute read the entire manuscript and provided some helpful comments; one in particular, greatly improved chapter 15. RosaLynda "Gina" Vormelker did the copyediting, allowing this to become publisher-friendly enough to see the light of day. None of the hundreds of students who has seen a semester's worth of my exams and assignments would list editing as one of my strengths.

1 Overview

CHAPTER 1

Introduction

> "When you're fighting from the trenches ...
> your point of view is distorted by the fog of war."
> — Ken Elias, letter to the editor, *Wall Street Journal* (October 11, 1994)

This book was written because the vagueness of the term *school choice* has led to widespread confusion about the desirability of parental choice as public policy. Parental choice plans differ with respect to grade level coverage, whether they include private schools, the financing method, how many children can participate, and the payment process (direct payment, vouchers, tax credits, etc). The list of potential variations is endless. All such plans are labeled *school choice* plans, so the public understandably is confused.

This book is partisan in that it strongly favors parental choice. Since it argues for specific versions of parental choice, it rejects much of the alleged evidence and many of the common arguments responsible for the confusing school choice wars. The nearly universal failure to distinguish different versions of parental choice is a major problem because generalizations are drawn from claims and evidence that are relevant only to some versions. Outcomes of "choice" under some conditions do not demonstrate that parental choice is a good (or bad) idea under all conditions. Naturally, both sides emphasize the outcomes that support their point of view.

The numerous mistaken inferences that effects of noncompetitive situations— often incorrectly alleged to be competitive—are good indicators of the effects of competitive situations decrease the political feasibility of parental choice plans that would establish a competitive education industry. This book focuses on the competitive education industry version because it:

- Forces others to define clearly what they mean when they support or criticize "school choice" or "parental choice."
- Makes it possible to analyze the issues from a consistently held concept of choice.
- Allows assessment of the single most critical argument for parental choice, that the benefits of a competitive education industry outweigh the transition costs.

CONFUSION ABOUT PARENTAL CHOICE

There are many versions of parental choice, in part because there are several reasons why choice advocates think society will benefit. Each reason places different demands on the specifics of a choice policy. The strategy of doing whatever is politically feasible in the short run also underlies parental choice variety and the confusion about what parental choice entails.

In 1955 and 1962, Milton Friedman proposed universal choice through vouchers so that competition would invigorate the delivery of K–12 education services.[1] Unfortunately, early voucher programs were not universal,[2] and they reduced only slightly the public funding bias against private school users. That's still true of most choice proposals. They only allow a tiny fraction of families to participate, and always with much less public funding per child than public school users. Choice advocates' practice of not publicly protesting major restrictions helped choice opponents convince people that vouchers divert public funds to benefit a few children at the expense of the vast majority that must stay in public schools. *Voucher* became "the V word;"[3] the scarlet letter of the school choice wars. Most choice advocates reacted to the stigma by replacing *voucher* with the general terms *school choice* and *parental choice*. Choice opponents reintroduced the term voucher as much as possible. The multiple electoral defeats of voucher proposals also lowered expectations and produced the incrementalism strategy. Some choice advocates are "frustrated by the piecemeal nature of the moves that have been made toward increasing choice,"[4] but incrementalism is the accepted practice.

Many choice advocates switched to the term *scholarship*.[5] They apparently agree with John Miller's remark that "scholarship sounds so much more appealing than voucher."[6] Unfortunately, scholarship is a bad label. Universal choice is a key element of a competitive education industry, but a universal scholarship program is a contradiction. The scholarship label reinforces the perception that only a relatively few students will qualify. Scholarship programs available to, even targeted at, low achievers are, likewise, contradictions. Use of scholarship in place of voucher deters potential applicants who expect eligibility criteria to include a strong academic background.

Concern for religious freedom is the dominant motivating factor of many parental choice advocates. According to that rationale, parents who cannot afford private school tuition must send their children to public schools that do not give religious instruction, and that promote concepts like evolution, which some parents regard as antireligious. Low-income families don't like having to send their children to schools that contradict their family values. Forcing them to do so contradicts our education traditions, and it creates social tensions and political hostilities.

Equity concerns are another widely cited justification of parental choice.[7] Economically disadvantaged families cannot afford to live near the better public schools or send their children to private schools. From that perspective, parental choice reduces the advantages of affluence. Equity benefits probably will prove to be the biggest political asset of competitive education industry versions of parental choice. Some analysts cite the equity rationale to argue for means testing public support, a position opposed in chapter 10.

CONFUSING TERMINOLOGY

The confusion does not end with politically driven substitutions like scholarship for voucher. It begins with the basics. *Public education* and *public school system* mean the same thing to most people, even though the former is a goal and the latter is a delivery system. For example, Frederick Wirt and Michael Kirst's politics of education text equates a demise of public schools with "an end of American commitment to public education,"[8] even though a public commitment to schooling doesn't require that the government operate schools, or the denial of public funds to families that prefer the education services of private entities. Jack Kemp, the 1996 Republican vice presidential nominee, and Erskine Bowles, a former Clinton Administration chief of staff, put it very nicely: "the current model—a noncompetitive monopoly—is not the only way to deliver public education."[9] Not nearly enough people make the distinction between the goal and the delivery mechanism.

Except when quoting people who use "public education" to refer to the public school delivery system—a practice that inhibits communication and clear thinking—this book uses the term *public education* only in chapter 9's more detailed discussion of this source of confusion. This book's opposition to the public school monopoly on public funding is perfectly consistent with its support for the public education goal of universal education opportunity and shared core values. This book argues that a competitive education industry is the best way to deliver education services. This book will use "school system" to refer to the entire K–12 education system, including the private sector.

The terms *public school* and *private school* are also somewhat misleading. The former adequately conveys the public ownership of education facilities, but the exclusive attendance zones of most public schools make them among the least public of government facilities. Private sounds very exclusive, but private schools do not have formal attendance zones. Many private schools have their own significant enrollment barriers, in particular high tuition for students who don't qualify for scholarships and entrance requirements, but many private schools are more widely accessible (more public) than public schools.

Since the public school system is a government agency—funded by taxpayers, staffed by government employees, and accountable to politicians—"government school" is more accurate than "public" school. Indeed, "one of the truly remarkable features of the education literature is that schools are rarely treated as the government agencies they are."[10] Use of "government" school is growing, and truth in labeling is a major guiding principle of this book, but the familiarity of the term *public school* trumps the more accurate *government school*. "Public" school in quotations will remind the reader of the relative exclusivity of each school, and that attendance zones make "public" schools the least public of government facilities.[11]

DISSATISFACTION WITH K–12 EDUCATION

Widespread dissatisfaction with K–12 academic gains is a major reason why this book was written. The causes of dissatisfaction include low test scores, "public" and private school differences, comparisons with students in other countries, school district differences, and the skill deficits of entry-level job applicants. Those deficiencies get your attention, but none of the causes establish an appropriate standard. Many of the countries that top the United States in international comparisons are deeply dissatisfied with their schools. Suburban "public" schools and private schools generally have higher test scores than urban "public" schools, but none of the groups performs acceptably. For example, former Assistant Secretary of Education Chester Finn said that the states with the best test scores "are at the top of the cellar stairs."[12] Virtually everywhere, a large proportion of students score below the basic skills level, and a majority are below proficient.

THE CASE FOR A COMPETITIVE EDUCATION INDUSTRY

Promises to spread the best existing practices, match the performance of schools in other places, or regain past achievements are not reasons to implement a competitive education industry. A business that said that its ultimate goal was to match the competition, or match past achievements, probably would vanish quickly and deservedly so.

Shocking academic deficiencies raise interest in reform, but the case for a competitive education industry does not hinge on attention-getting evidence of student shortcomings. The case for a competitive education industry rests on the choiceworthiness imperative. In a competitive setting, producers must specialize . and pursue improvement relentlessly to survive. The contrast between competitive markets and other delivery systems is overwhelming evidence that market systems—though not perfect—are superior to politically driven delivery systems. K–12 education is not an exception to that generalization. A competitive education industry should generate better services at a lower cost than any alternative, including foreign systems that rank above the current U.S. school system in widely publicized international comparisons. It is true that hardly anyone cares about competition per se,[13] but marketable objectives like equity, academic improvement, and social harmony won't be realized without it.

There are many good reasons to believe that a competitive education industry will perform better than most markets. Traditional sources of market problems—poorly informed buyers (mistakes and fraud), society or negative neighborhood effects (often called *negative externalities* or *spillover costs*), not enough competition—are likely to be rare. Political control is not required to realize the spillover benefits of K–12 education. The recurrent, expensive nature of education purchases rewards informed consumers and raises the value of a good reputation. Producers cannot rely on deceptive practices to maintain long-term relationships with well-informed parents. They must offer substantive alternatives to all parents, even though all of them may not choose carefully. The low value of education resources (physical assets and the skills of education professionals) in noneducation uses also strengthens educators' incentives to pursue continuous improvement and develop long-term customer relationships. Those factors minimize the fast-buck potential that underlies the fraudulent behavior and shoddy service that exist in some industries.

HOW THE DISCUSSION PROCEEDS

Part 1, the overview, resumes with chapter 2's discussion of what competitive education industry means. The competitive education industry discussion follows a brief discussion of monopoly and the applicability of that term to our current school system. Chapter 3 shows that much of the widely cited evidence and research—favorable and unfavorable—is essentially irrelevant to the merits of a competitive education industry. Chapter 4 discusses the evidence that does help to evaluate the desirability of a competitive education industry.

Part 2 addresses the issues that dominate the parental choice debate. Chapter 5 shows that supporters and opponents of parental choice rely on arguments they reject in other contexts. Although no policy conclusions are drawn from those inconsistencies, they help to illustrate the confused state of the school choice wars, governing and funding systems' resistance to change, and the importance of improved parental choice analyses. Chapter 6 describes the fallacies that pervade the school choice wars, especially arguments that don't apply to a competitive education industry. Chapters 7 through 11 discuss regulation and cost issues, confusion between education goals and procedures, equity and equality, and diversity and unity issues. The discussion of these issues is in the context of a competitive education industry, and there are frequent comparisons with existing parental choice analyses.

The third section of the book deals with strategic and tactical issues. Chapter 12 discusses strategic/tactical fallacies, many of which parallel the substantive fallacies discussed in chapter 6. Chapter 13 analyzes the private voucher movement and its implications for a competitive education industry. It explains how privately funded vouchers might lead to a major political breakthrough, but it concludes that it is too early to tell whether private vouchers will help or hinder the emergence of a competitive education industry.

Chapter 14 compares the current school system, very limited versions of parental choice, and a competitive education industry from teachers' perspective. Even though market forces contain a large dose of unpredictability, there are still numerous reasons to believe that many teachers will prefer a competitive education industry to the current system, and to the very limited versions of parental choice adamantly opposed by teachers' unions. Identifying gainers and losers is much more complicated than defining good and bad teachers. Chapter 15 summarizes the outlook for a competitive education industry, and includes ways to overcome significant political roadblocks and the key policy issues that will arise.

NOTES

1. Milton Friedman, *Capitalism and Freedom* (Chicago: University of Chicago Press, 1962); Milton Friedman, "The Role of Government in Education" in Solo, R. A. (ed.) *Economics and the Public Interest* (New Brunswick, N.J.: Rutgers University Press, 1955).

2. Joseph Viteritti, *Choosing Equality* (Washington: Brookings Institution, 1999), p. 55.

3. Michael Fox, "Remarks of Ohio State Representative Michael Fox," *State Legislator Guide to Teacher Empowerment* (American Legislative Exchange Council, February 1997), p. 17; *Wall Street Journal* editors, "School Reform Blooms," *Wall Street Journal* (May 5, 1999); "The presidential and vice-presidential candidates have run from the "V" word this [2000] campaign," June Kronholz, "In Michigan, Amway Chief and Wife Give School Vouchers a Higher Profile," *Wall Street Journal* (October 25, 2000).

4. Douglas J. Lamdin and Michael Mintrom, "School Choice in Theory and Practice: Taking Stock and Looking Ahead," *Education Economics* 5(3) (1997): p. 235.

5. John Coons and Stephen Sugarman, *Education by Choice* (Troy, N.Y.: Educator's International Press, 1999).

6. John Miller, "Why School Choice Lost," *Wall Street Journal* (November 4, 1993).

7. Coons and Sugarman, 1999; Viteritti.

8. Frederick Wirt and Michael Kirst, *The Political Dynamics of American Education* (Berkeley, Calif.: McCutchan, 1997), p. 51.

9. Erskine Bowles and Jack Kemp, "An Offer Bush and Gore Can't Refuse," *Wall Street Journal* (June 15, 2000).

10. Frederick Hess. *Spinning Wheels: The Politics of Urban School Reform* (Washington: Brookings Institution, 1999).

11. Defense facilities and jails are exceptions.

12. Barbara Kantrowitz and Pat Wingert, "A Dismal Report Card," *Newsweek* (June 17, 1991): 65.

13. Frank Luntz and Bob Castro, "Dollars to Classrooms and Parental Choice in Education" Memorandum (April 14, 1998).

CHAPTER 2

Elements of a Competitive Education Industry

This chapter clarifies the concept of a competitive education industry; however, it begins with a discussion of monopoly. A direct comparison with monopoly—the existing situation in K–12 education everywhere in the United States—gives the key elements of a competitive education industry more meaning.

MONOPOLY

Whenever competitiveness is an issue, market area is a key issue. The market for some goods and services is local. For others it is regional, national, or international. Plumbing repair is a locally provided service. It may be supplied competitively in some areas, but not in others. Automaking is a global business. The number of auto producers worldwide is important. The number in each specific place is nearly irrelevant. The reverse is true of plumbing repair. A one-plumber town is a monopoly, even if there are many plumbers elsewhere. By itself, however, the one-plumber situation is not a major problem. If the plumber performs poorly, charges extraordinary rates, or just can't keep up with the demand, the monopoly probably will vanish. Migration and training programs can deliver new plumbers. Except for natural monopolies (defined below), monopolies survive only if shielded by high entry barriers.

Some commentators claim that the "public" school system is not a monopoly because there are nearly 15,000 diverse school districts.[1] Because education markets are local, the large number of districts nationwide is as irrelevant to the competitiveness of a K–12 service area as the number of independent water purveyors (often monopolies) nationwide.

Though the single-provider feature seems clear-cut—monopoly literally means "single seller"—practically speaking, monopoly is a matter of degree. The government has an 88 percent market share of K–12 education. That market share is much closer to the single-seller case than virtually every alleged monopoly; 88 percent far exceeds the level that usually triggers a government antitrust lawsuit.

There are four kinds of barriers to market entry:

- government policy,
- economies of scale—unit production costs are sometimes much lower for larger firms,

- patents—temporary rights to an exclusive franchise, and
- control over resources required to make a product.

Only the first two are relevant to K–12 education. Government policy is the most important cause of the "public" school monopoly. The most critical barrier is the government policy of offering a K–12 education to families at no additional charge beyond the taxes they must pay. The "public" school system has an almost airtight monopoly on public funding. In addition, state governments typically regulate the physical facilities, teacher qualifications, pupil age limits, curriculum, school day and school year, pupil transportation standards, and a host of other matters. Entrepreneurs theoretically are free to enter the market for K–12 services, but it is very difficult to beat a zero-tuition competitor.

Economies of scale exist in sparsely populated areas. There, K–12 education is a natural monopoly. Low enrollments make it too expensive to operate tiny competing schools in place of one larger one. Some sparsely settled areas have no schools. Children go to schools in larger, nearby communities. Parts of Maine and Vermont have longstanding examples of that practice. Outside sparsely populated areas, K–12 education is not a natural monopoly.

Monopolies lack direct, intense competition, which leads to higher prices and inefficiencies, and the "public" school monopoly does charge taxpayers a high and ever-rising sum. The "public" school system's administrative overhead is one example of inefficiency. According to an international comparison by the Organization for Economic Cooperation and Development (OECD),[2] the United States is the only country with fewer teachers than nonteaching staff (a 3:4 ratio, compared with a 5:2 average ratio for the other countries in the OECD study).

Dynamic inefficiency—insufficient improvement—is evident in the school system's failure to pursue research and development systematically, and implement innovations.[3] In addition, while change in "public" schools is undeniable, technological backwardness is the norm, and there is complacency about success and failure. There is no discernible propensity to identify and spread effective practices, or to root out unproductive practices and practitioners.[4] According to a Dale Ballou and Michael Podgursky study,[5] "public" schools give little weight to the quality of teachers' credentials. Unproductive teachers are rarely terminated.

GENERAL REQUIREMENTS OF COMPETITIVE INDUSTRIES

Chapter 1 pointed out that parental or school choice doesn't mean the same thing to everyone, and that the absence of a commonly accepted definition causes widespread confusion over its desirability. A clear definition will not eliminate controversies, but it might prevent the ones that result from failure to clarify what is meant by parental or school choice.

A parental choice policy produces a "competitive education industry," if it contains four key elements. These elements are:

1. *Free entry and exit in the long run.*
On the supply side of the market, the long run is the time it takes to set up a competing business. In the long run, the number of sellers changes in response to changes in profitability. Increased profitability attracts additional sellers, thus making the market more competitive, and decreased profitability does the opposite. Therefore, changes in the number of sellers keep the profitability of competitive industries comparable.

On the demand side, the long run is the time it takes to become a new purchaser of a product. Population is the primary determinant of the number of buyers. However, the number of buyers also changes in the long run if the price trend differs (holding quality constant) significantly from the overall rate of inflation.

Since universally tiny market shares—so small that no one can influence the market price by themselves—maximize the benefits of competition,[6] economics texts consistently list "many buyers and sellers" as a key feature of a competitive industry. When consumers have more options, sellers cannot survive complacency, inefficiency, and inattention to constantly changing consumer desires as easily. Unpopular sellers lose resources and they must improve or perish. However, a large number of sellers is not an indispensable factor. Contestability—new firms can contest market share easily—is the critical element. Economists have shown that contestability with only a few sellers at any one time, though not as good as many buyers and sellers, still produces reasonably competitive behavior.[7]

2. *Well-informed and mobile buyers and sellers.*
Competitive pressures are adequate—that is, they establish producer accountability to consumers—when there are enough mobile, well-informed buyers to affect the financial viability of the sellers, and establish accountability.[8] So, competitive industries can contain many poorly informed, low-mobility participants. High-fixed-cost industries require very few mobile, well-informed buyers. Financial viability hinges on a relatively small number of informed and mobile buyers. For example, consider the airline industry: a high-fixed-cost industry because of the money tied up in aircraft and because depreciation and administrative costs vary little with ticket sales. American Airlines once earned a significant profit equal to just one passenger per flight. Since ticket prices must reflect airlines' large fixed costs, but the number of passengers per flight has little impact on costs, a small change in the number of passengers has a large effect on airlines' net revenues. Schools also have high fixed costs, so their financial condition is also quite sensitive to small enrollment changes.

3. *Producer survival depends on ability to satisfy consumers.*

4. *Price changes reflect market pressures.*

Nobel Prize winner Frederich Hayek summarized the critical features as follows: "The parties in the market should be free to sell and buy at any price at which they can find a partner to the transaction, and that anybody should be free to produce, sell, and buy anything that may be produced at all."[9] It was the main point of Hayek's influential *The Road to Serfdom*, whose title aptly describes what happens to societies when they eliminate those market features, or miss opportunities to create them.

APPLICATION TO EDUCATION

The foregoing discussion means that an education system is competitive if it contains the following characteristics.

1. No significant barriers to the entry or exit of education producers. Such barriers are absent only if parents are free to enroll their children in another school without any change in the publicly funded tuition subsidy they receive, if any, and families can enter the education market by relocating, or by ending/starting home schooling, without suffering significant financial penalties.
2. The survival of each school depends on its ability to attract enough parents willing to pay a price that will enable the school to stay in business.
3. The number of parents willing and able to transfer their children to another school is large enough to affect the financial viability of schools.
4. Schools charge whatever they want without jeopardizing the parents' eligibility for direct government support, or indirect support through vouchers or tax credits.
5. Schools can refuse to serve someone if they don't violate antidiscrimination laws. Government regulation predominantly addresses the health, safety, and fraud issues that apply to all businesses and nonprofit producers.

1. Free Entry and Exit

The best possible situation from a competitive perspective is a large number of independent competitors—parents as buyers and independent producers as educators—with no one large enough to affect the market price by themselves. The number of producers is the number of independent school owners, such as the government, individual business firms, and religious organizations, not the number of schools. For example, if a region has 200 "public" schools, 20 Catholic schools, and 10 private, nondenominational schools operated by one company, the region has 230 schools, but just three education producers. If the school board decides to privatize management of some schools by contracting it out to a private firm, the number of producers stays the same. The region may have another school manager, but the attendance area boundaries keep children from acquiring additional options.

Differences between private management of a "public" school and private ownership create other problems. Managers face uncertainty about contract renewal, which creates the temptation to maximize short-run profits by cutting corners, and underinvestment because the management contract might not survive long enough to recoup investment outlays. While the profit motive enhances competitive forces considerably, it can be counterproductive in the absence of competition; a privately managed "public" school is still a local monopoly.

Free entry also demands a high degree of certainty about underlying authority and demand. Entrepreneurs are much less likely to enter an education market if the political support for the key elements of the market is shaky, or if key policies face a credible legal challenge. Pilot voucher programs, and some privately funded voucher programs, will not stimulate major new investments. For example, a ten-year, privately funded, full-tuition voucher program in the Edgewood District of San Antonio, Texas, filled up existing space in private schools, but expansions have been modest, and so far there hasn't been significant new construction. Shaky or explicitly temporary programs also diminish parental participation. Parents value continuity. They are less likely to choose a new school if its survival could depend on political decisions that have no relationship to school quality or parent preferences.

The ideal "many buyer, many seller" case is the most likely outcome in most places. In places that can support only one school, free entry and exit will still create competitive pressure by making markets contestable. Examples created by actual rivalry in large markets will increase the pressure to behave competitively in the small markets.

Tuition increases attract competition, so free entry and exit will keep tuition levels low. Even if there are entry barriers or fixed prices, rivalry will dissipate at least partially above normal profits through service upgrades and by creating excess capacity. The prederegulation airline industry was a good example of that profit dissipation process. Before deregulation of airline fares, most of the fares set by the Civil Aeronautics Board (CAB) were very attractive to the airlines. The CAB protected the regulated airlines from competition from new airlines, so rivalry for passengers among the existing airlines occurred through promises of better service, including more attractive flight attendants, better meals, and more frequent flights.

Service upgrade rivalry and excess capacity will arise to the extent that policy makers overreact to the efficiency or fairness rationales with excessive education subsidies. The efficiency argument is that the profitable level of education is below the efficient level because members of society other than children benefit when children learn more. For example, society benefits when children learn citizenship skills, but some parents may only be shopping for vocational education. Some low-income families cannot even afford that. In both cases, the efficiency argument is that the tuition subsidy necessary to rectify those deficiencies costs society less than the deficiencies. There is also the fairness argument. Society will probably continue to insist on guaranteeing some access to education for every child.

Free entry and exit does not exist if parents suffer a significant financial penalty when they transfer a child to another school. Because of the status quo's large penalty for choosing a private school, the status quo is quite hostile to them. It is very difficult to compete with free services. Private schools must charge parents a significantly higher price for a service that is usually more cheaply made[10] than what "public" schools offer. The difficulty of that feat is what keeps private schools' market share extremely low. That any nonelite, nonsectarian private schools can survive is quite remarkable. Consequently, free entry and exit means equal or nearly equal government funding of mainstream students;[11] no differences in the government support of "public" and private school students.

Free entry and exit will also act as a primary agent of the geographic expansion of a competitive education industry. Consider the situation of an area with a competitive education industry surrounded by areas without one. Parents suffer no penalty for moving there, and if they prefer private schools, they realize a large financial gain, or large losses if they leave the area. Those rewards and penalties exist even in the absence of convincing 'evidence' that competitive pressures improve educational outcomes. The development of such evidence will attract parents who prefer government-run schools. Local governments compete for residents and tax base,[12] so the authorities in adjacent areas probably will react. Many responses are possible. They could establish their own competitive education industry.

While free entry does mean some imitation of successful sellers, it does not mean greater homogeneity. Markets involve individual decisions, so competition reduces the differences among sellers only when buyers become more similar.[13] For example, higher profit margins for Chinese restaurants would increase their size and numbers, but specialization within the restaurant industry would remain the same.

Specialization is a critical element of markets and the entry-exit process. Since buyers are usually quite diverse, sellers must specialize to capture a share of the market. Specialization increases productivity because then each educator concentrates on what he or she does best. Educators will specialize in different subject matters,[14] aptitude levels, and teaching styles, including use of technology. Contrast that to the status quo. We stifle specialization by assigning the diverse children of each attendance area to neighborhood "public" schools.[15] In the absence of free entry and specialization, educators must struggle to be "all things to all people."[16] That means one size fits all for required classes and lots of elective courses and extracurricular programs. Within the severe constraints of the current system, specialization is already a common denominator of success. Principals of high-performing, high poverty schools "design their curriculum around the unique strengths and expertise of their staff."[17]

2. Survival

In a competitive industry, customer preferences determine the difference between financial trouble, and eventual extinction through liquidation or bankruptcy, and success. The survival of each school depends on its ability to recruit students.

The likely demise of slow-to-change, unpopular schools raises the issue of bankruptcy, a political liability without some careful explanation. Bankruptcy is an easily monitored, relatively objective indicator of failure, and the possibility of bankruptcy strengthens the incentive to pay attention to customers and make decisions carefully. Bankruptcy is rare in the public sector, which is a major reason why so many government programs are allegedly obsolete. In the private sector, bankruptcy performs the critical task of shifting resources from obsolete and inefficient producers to new and growing businesses.

Bankruptcy does not always force a change in the ownership of school assets. The Legal Information Institute points out that: "Under Chapters 11, 12, and 13 [of the Federal Bankruptcy Law], a bankruptcy proceeding involves the rehabilitation of the debtor to allow him to use his future earnings to pay off his creditors."[18] Debtors get time to restructure, and customers may not notice changes.

In a competitive education industry, bankruptcies probably would not cause many abrupt shutdowns. Children would move to a new school on short notice only in the most extreme circumstances. Bankruptcies that require more than restructuring would still usually only shift the physical assets of the school to new managers. Ownership changes, even sudden mid-year changes, will not necessarily disrupt classrooms. New owners have strong incentives to cater to the existing student body's capabilities and desires. That means that new owners are unlikely to abandon the existing faculty and staff, or subject and methodological specialty areas, except where there is an obvious link to the cause of the bankruptcy problem.

The public can establish safeguards against abrupt mid-year shutdowns, and parents will avoid financially shaky schools if the authorities publish critical financial data. An analog to bank deposit insurance is an option. The authorities can protect parents and children from mid-year shutdowns by requiring schools to post a bond or buy insurance sufficient to run the school until the current school year ends. Insurance companies would audit schools and signal which ones are risky through refusal to issue a policy or by demanding high premiums.

Unhappy parents do not yet threaten the survival of "public" schools. Most stay because moving children to another school is costly, and alternatives are often scarce, unattractive (religion mismatch), or expensive. Furthermore, when children leave "public" schools, the school only loses the state government allocation. Since the tax money raised locally is not lost, departures raise a district's per pupil funding, and they can help growing districts avoid new construction. Districts suffer only if the state's payment exceeds the cost avoided by having fewer students. If there is population growth anywhere in the district, district authorities can avoid budget cuts at any school by reconfiguring the district's attendance areas.

The connection between customer satisfaction and funding level is also minimal when funding comes from sources other than clients—for example, endowment funds, legislative appropriations, or management contracts. In the current system, parents can reward good service, or punish poor service, only through an organized political movement. Educators frequently ignore calls for change unless parents first convince their representatives—the people who actually pay educators' salaries—that parent demands are politically significant.

3. Well-Informed Parents Willing to Transfer Their Children

Since K–12 education entails significant fixed costs, a few active, mobile parents can affect school finances greatly. Parents who are unaware of school differences, or indifferent to them, will benefit from the efforts to please informed, mobile parents. For example, all car buyers benefit from safety features that appeal to safety-conscious buyers. The benefits of competition do not depend on most parents being motivated and able to choose the best school for their children.

4. No Price Controls, Flexible Prices

Price movement is a primary source of information and incentives and is an indispensable component of market forces. Price changes are the main reason for net exit or entry. Customers signal increased demand by driving up prices, which increases industry profitability and motivates entry. As more services become available, prices drop, industry output stabilizes, and inefficient producers go out of business. Only the best firms continue to earn above-normal profits. That process performs the crucial function of allocating resources to competing uses, and it helps motivate continuous service improvement. Each resource is put to its most valuable use when market prices are flexible and comprehensive and, therefore, reflect changes in market conditions quickly. Prices are comprehensive when they reflect all of the costs of producing and consuming a product.

Comprehensive, market-determined, flexible prices do not exist in the current system, or in public school choice programs, including charter schools. "Public" school tuition stays at zero even after major changes in key underlying demand and supply factors. The political process drives resource allocation decisions and performance evaluations. Most voucher and tax credit programs[19] would not establish market-determined prices either. The programs are too small, and some prohibit private schools from charging more than the voucher amount.

Requiring private schools to accept the voucher amount as full payment (banning privately funded "add-ons") will narrow school choices greatly. Except for the survival of expensive, elite private schools, a universal program with a ban on add-ons would have the same effect as a price ceiling at the voucher amount. Participation limits like those in Florida and Milwaukee, Wisconsin wouldn't lessen the price ceiling effect very much. Consider the following example. Say a voucher is worth $3,000. Then, a $3,000 per year private school would cost families only the school taxes they pay. However, if "add-ons" are banned, families cannot use the voucher to help pay tuition of $3,001. An extra $1 worth of services would cost them $3,001. Few families will pay thousands more for a few dollars' worth of additional services. A $3,000 voucher combined with a ban on add-ons would eliminate school choices costing somewhat more than $3,000, and greatly reduce the demand for school choices costing significantly more than $3,000. For example, there probably wouldn't be any $4,000 services, and very few $7,000 services. Many of the families that would be willing to buy the $7,000 services by supplementing the $3,000 voucher with $4,000 of their own money probably would not pay the full $7,000 themselves if add-ons were not allowed. Instead of paying an extra $7,000 for an additional $4,000 worth of schooling, many parents would use the voucher at a school that would accept it as full payment, and then pursue additional education informally by investing in tutoring, summer programs, and home education tools, such as games and software.

5. Regulation Issues

Though competitive pressures create accountability (consequences proportional to service quality), people who don't trust the market may seek regulation of tuition, discipline policies, input (including personnel) characteristics, and subject matter content and the like. Such regulation limits the scope of specialization and potential avenues of innovation, and it can become an entry barrier. Therefore, only the regulations that apply nearly uniformly throughout the economy (health, safety, fraud, discrimination by race, creed, gender, or national origin) should apply to the producers of K–12 education.

A modest minimum size restriction will probably preclude establishment of extremist schools at taxpayer expense.[20] Note, however, that such a restriction is just insurance against an extremely unlikely event. There is no evidence that private school students are more likely to engage in extremist behavior.

Since the critical elements discussed in this chapter are widely neglected, the school choice wars have yet to tell us much about the desirability of a competitive education industry. Few parental choice policies that would establish a competitive education industry have even been on a political radar screen.[21] Getting the key participants in the school choice wars, and the public, to link choice, competition, and the critical elements discussed in this chapter must begin with an assessment of the alleged evidence. The next chapter critiques the development and frequent use of inappropriate assumptions, misleading studies, and misinterpretations of facts.

NOTES

1. Robert Lowe and Barbara Miner interview in Robert Lowe and Barbara Miner (eds.), *Selling Out Our Schools* (Milwaukee, Wisc.: Rethinking Schools, 1996).
2. OECD, *Education at a Glance: OECD Indicators* (Paris: Author, 1995).
3. D. W. Miller, "The Black Hole of Education Research," *Chronicle of Higher Education* (August 6, 1999).
4. Myron Lieberman, *Public Education: An Autopsy* (Cambridge, Mass.: Harvard University Press, 1993) summarizes the evidence on those issues.
5. Dale Ballou and Michael Podgursky, *Teacher Pay and Teacher Quality* (Kalamazoo, Mich.: W.E. Upjohn Institute for Employment and Training, 1997).
6. For example, see Robert B. Ekelund, and Robert D. Tollison, *Microeconomics: Private Markets and Public Choice*, 5th edition (Reading, Mass.: Addison Wesley Longman, Inc., 1997), p. 206; Robert A. Collinge and Ronald M. Ayers, *Economics by Design* (Upper Saddle River, N.J.: Prentice Hall, 1997); p. 241.
7. Steven A. Morrison and Clifford Winston, "Empirical Implications and Tests of the Contestability Hypothesis," *Journal of Law and Economics* 30 (April 1987): 53–66; Severin Borenstein, "The Evolution of U.S. Airline Competition," *Journal of Economic Perspectives* 6 (Spring 1992): 45–74; William J. Baumol, John C. Panzar, and Robert D. Willig, *Contestable Markets and the Theory of Industry Structure* (New York: Harcourt Brace Jovanovich, Inc., 1982).
8. Note that political accountability is much weaker than competitive market accountability. Low-quality services do not jeopardize government agencies' financial viability. And, as Eric Hanushek aptly states: "Nobody's career is really dependent upon the children doing well." ("Incentives: the fundamental problem in education," *School Reform News* [January, 2000]: 17).
9. Frederich A. Hayek, *The Road to Serfdom* (Chicago: The University of Chicago Press, 1994), p. 42.
10. Per pupil spending of private schools—about $3,116 (1993–94 data), according to the National Center for Education Statistics—was much lower than "public' schools" per pupil expenditures. Both "public" and private schools underestimate their costs, but the underestimates are much larger for public schools (see Myron Lieberman and Charlene Haar, *The Real Cost of Public Education* [in press]).
11. I define mainstream child more broadly than just lacking any learning disabilities. If a student can find appropriate education services for the dollar value of public per student support, or close to that amount if some private contribution to tuition payments is expected, the student is mainstream. That will be the vast majority. Public law 94-142 assures nonmainstream students—children with especially severe disabilities—sufficient taxpayer support to implement an Individual Education Plan.
12. Charles Tiebout, "A Pure Theory of Local Expenditures," *Journal of Political Economy* 64 (October 1956): 416–24.
13. In contrast, the political arena is about collective choices. Therefore, competition in the political arena reduces differences among the choices.

14. There is some subject area specialization by "public" schools, mostly by so-called magnet schools that children are not assigned to.

15. According to 1993 data from the National Center for Education Statistics (NCES), 80 percent of the Grade 3–12 student population attends the public school they are assigned to. NCES did not say why its data excluded grades K–2, but the percentage will be higher at those grade levels.

16. Frank C. Nelsen, "Parental Choice: Will Vouchers Solve the School Crisis?" *Christianity Today* (August 19, 1991): 29.

17. Samuel C. Carter, *No Excuses: Lessons from 21 High-Performing, High Poverty Schools* (Washington: Heritage Foundation, 2000), p. 27.

18. The Legal Information Institute Web page (*www.law.cornell.edu/topics/bankruptcy.htm*) quotation refers to the chapters of the Federal Bankruptcy Statute (Title 11 of the U.S. Code).

19. True of most actual and proposed past and current programs. There are some exceptions— for example, California's Proposition 174 (defeated in 1993), the November 2000 Voucher2000 proposition (California Proposition 38), and New Mexico Governor Gary Johnson's universal voucher proposals.

20. Myron Lieberman, *Public Education: An Autopsy* (Cambridge, Mass.: Harvard University Press, 1993), p. 290–92.

21. The statewide universal voucher proposals (for example, California's 1993 and 2000 ballot initiatives and New Mexico Governor Johnson's proposal) still left private schools at a considerable disadvantage. Private school users would receive thousands less in public support than "public" school users.

CHAPTER 3

Experiments

"Every time we don't tell the truth,
we play a part in destroying kids' lives.

— Howard Fuller, "The Case for Radical Reform," Monthly Letter to
Friends of the Center for Education Reform 49 & 50
(December 1998–January 1999): 3

Major changes can seem risky even when the status quo is terrible. Even when a major transformation seems necessary, many people still prefer limited trials. After all, an experiment can expose critical design issues, or it may indicate which reform mechanisms are the best choice. The potential counterarguments are that trials would produce unacceptable delays, enough data already exist so that the proposed reform is not that risky, and the experiment is potentially risky. Poorly designed experiments won't yield useful insights, and they may jeopardize potential reforms by misrepresenting the effects of those reforms. Experiments are especially risky when politicians, not scientists, have the final say on experiment design issues.

All three counterarguments apply to the current parental choice programs widely called "experiments."

- Delay is very costly. We are "a nation at risk"; probably even more than when a 1983 presidential panel coined that phrase. Since then, another cohort of children has passed through a system that is so badly broken that it is the nation's number one political issue.
- Economic theory is sufficient to design parental choice programs that would unleash market forces, and there is abundant evidence that market forces can transform industries, including evidence specific to K–12 education (see chapter 4).
- The alleged experiments, including many programs not enacted for that purpose,[1] are badly designed. There is a severe mismatch between the conditions of the alleged experiments and the conditions outlined in the original Milton Friedman proposal. The extensive debate of the parental choice "experiments" that are just limited escape conduits from one part of the current system to another badly misrepresents the potential effects of parental choice as a reform catalyst.

LARGELY IRRELEVANT AND DANGEROUSLY MISLEADING

Current parental choice programs help a few children, but the programs are too small and contain too many debilitating restrictions to provide any insight into the effects of a competitive education industry. Since the current programs lack the critical elements of a competitive education industry, those programs cannot tell us if a such an industry is a desirable reform.

Parental choice programs, including "public" school choice (as well as charter schools), privately funded partial tuition vouchers, and the Cleveland and Milwaukee publicly funded voucher programs[2] are not "experiments." *Webster's Dictionary* defines "experiment" as "test: trial" and "tentative procedure or policy." In "a nation at risk,"[3] programs limited to a few students are not "tentative [reform] policies." School system change, not the academic gains of a few transferees, is the critical issue. Therefore, but for the groundless political hype, existing parental choice programs would be irrelevant to everyone but the few who participate in them.

Because of price controls,[4] the absence of a profit motive,[5] and eligibility limits, existing parental choice programs cannot change the school system significantly. They can only tell us what happens when a few children move to existing private schools. Cash from a few small vouchers will not enhance private school capabilities or prompt much new school formation, because even excellent schools cannot expect significant increases in funding per student. There won't even be much additional rivalry in the private sector. Without significantly greater numbers of private schools, only a few choice participants will be near more than one.

Confusing tiny escape valves with reform is politically risky. A perception of failure may tarnish much more than the limited conditions that were actually present, and a perceived success may only spread restriction-laden programs. Furthermore, the alleged experiments lack the clearly stated hypothesis that is a key ingredient of any experiment, and the implied hypothesis is believable without empirical evidence. It is an intuitive proposition.

IMPLIED HYPOTHESES

Current parental choice programs lack clearly stated hypotheses, but virtually identical implied hypotheses are evident in statements, such as: "In every experiment where a child has transferred from a public to a private school . . ."[6] The fate of relatively few transferees is their focus. Prominent choice advocate Daniel McGroarty states the inappropriate focus of the alleged experiments very clearly: "For many observers, the success or failure of school choice hinges on hard statistical data: Are choice students' test scores higher than those of their public school peers?"[7] The implied hypothesis is that voucher students will do better than similar students who are left behind. That hypothesis matches the program conditions, but the focus on transferees neglects the issue of school reform—that is, how different degrees of parental choice can affect school systems.

Test score comparisons only indicate whether choice participants are good judges of education alternatives. Applicants compete for limited vouchers and limited private school space because they are confident that a voucher will secure access to a better school. Even if test score data reflect the factors that parents valued the most, the alleged "experiment" will produce no significant insight. Since most thoughtful people already believe that active parents can tell which school will achieve the best results for their children, choice opponents can attribute positive outcomes to selection bias—voucher applicants are the most active, informed parents—or declare the results irrelevant because the program involves too few children.

Since test score data may not reflect the reasons parents preferred a private school, and analytical errors can easily misrepresent effects, something called "choice" can end up appearing ineffective. Since positive-sounding results are easily dismissed, and negative-sounding results are possible, experiments with restriction-laden parental choice pose real political risks without any potential gain. Media hype and overblown rhetoric from choice advocates then combines to help choice opponents generalize apparent negative outcomes of restriction-laden parental choice to parental choice generally. Each general reference to a restriction-laden parental choice program as a "choice experiment" threatens the competitive education industry cause.

An incremental change hypothesis also underlies much choice advocacy. The hope is that any extra freedom will initiate irresistible pressure to expand choice. According to that hypothesis, politicians will steadily loosen restrictions, and restriction-laden choice for a few will gradually change into universal choice with few restrictions. Supposedly there is no danger of stalling or lengthy detours. Any extra choice supposedly moves us closer to "full school choice,"[8] a competitive education industry to some choice advocates, but not very many.[9]

So far, there is little evidence to support the incremental hypothesis. The key original restrictions persist in essentially their original form in nearly every program.[10] Perhaps with fewer initial restrictions, most of the remaining ones would wither away more quickly, but so far the incremental hypothesis is just wishful thinking.

CONFUSION

The mismatch between the restrictions on parental choice and the rhetoric about competition creates considerable confusion.[11] Much of the controversy about parental choice is about conflicting interpretations of data that have little or no relevance to K–12 reform efforts. Competing studies and interpretations of studies usually overlook the critical issue of school system change. Choice advocates are responsible for much of the confusion that the opponents of competition exploit to defeat parental choice proposals.

How the public defines "school choice," "parental choice," and "voucher program" depends mainly on what choice advocates support. Their enthusiastic support for programs limited to relatively few low-income families fosters the perception that parental choice is just a way to allow disadvantaged children to leave the worst "public" schools. Even the newsletters of parental choice organizations rarely, if ever, support universal choice, meaning that taxpayer support of each child does not depend on the school they attend. Virtually every article is about restriction-laden programs. Since such programs only help relatively few students, many people believe that voucher programs inherently neglect, even harm, "public" school students, and other people believe the programs' modest scope renders them irrelevant to reform efforts.

Virtually everyone bases sweeping generalizations on unsupportive, limited data. Choice opponents exploit choice advocates' enthusiastic support for restriction-laden programs. At least six publications[12] claim that the effects of those programs prove that parental choice is an unproductive reform. In one of the six, Kevin Smith and Kenneth Meier assert that experience with restriction-laden choice justifies a sweeping condemnation of choice because "there is no such [less restrictive] system to test" (p. 32). Similar, though more softly spoken, claims are common.[13] Typically, they dismiss 'less restrictive systems' as lacking empirical support. Such claims are intellectually dishonest and disingenuous. Choice opponents fiercely resist every attempt to increase parental choice significantly.

POLITICAL JEOPARDY

Statistically significant support for the implied hypothesis that voucher users will outperform their "public" school peers means that choice "works" as an escape mechanism, not as a reform catalyst. After all, the implied hypothesis is not about changes in the school system. Equating gains by transferees with school reform is risky, even when the intellectual dishonesty is accidental. High risk is often an inevitable partner of a potentially high return. Unfortunately, that is not the case here. The focus on transferees compromises potential benefits.

Gains by transferees improve the political feasibility of a competitive education industry only if: 1) Studies document large gains by transferees; and 2) The incremental hypothesis that restrictions will wither away gradually is correct; limited programs progressively shed restrictions until a competitive education industry exists, or choice advocates convince enough of the electorate that the findings from restriction-laden programs hint at equal or better outcomes from a competitive education industry.

No evidence, only wishful thinking, underlies the second requirement. Even the first requirement is quite demanding. The key issue underlying the implied hypothesis—can voucher applicants identify the best school for their children?—is an intuitive proposition, but that doesn't mean analysts can transform available data into convincing documentation. The smaller budgets of private schools, and failure to create significant competitive pressures, hinder generation of statistically significant gains. Test scores may not reflect parents' primary choice criteria, and opportunities to contest the choice of education, social, and demographic factors that influence test scores, and debate statistical issues and data deficiencies, are nearly endless.[14]

Restriction-laden programs don't affect many people directly, and they fail to create the benefits of genuine competition, so they cannot generate the market contestability or political pressure required for steady, incremental change. Restriction-laden programs only threaten the government-run system with tiny market share losses, so they may not cause any reaction. If there is a reaction, it's not the relentless pursuit of improvement that epitomizes competitive markets. Largely beneficial one-time changes, such as policy reviews, personnel changes, and advertising, may occur, but dirty tricks like "intimidation and misinformation"[15] are also possible. The initial Milwaukee Public School (MPS) reaction to vouchers wasn't positive, and many would argue that it still isn't. Rather than outcompete private schools that spend much less per student, MPS authorities resolved "to strangle the choice experiment in its crib."[16]

The MPS reaction is not surprising. Monopolies can benefit from underhanded behavior because they will pick up most of their victim's lost customers. Dirty tricks would be pointless in a competitive education industry, because credible slander would benefit all of the victim's competitors, not just the perpetrator.

THE MILWAUKEE PARENTAL CHOICE PROGRAM

Severe Restrictions

Until recently, only 1 percent to 1.5 percent of Milwaukee "Public" School (MPS) students could participate, and voucher users couldn't attend church-run schools. At first, voucher users could not exceed 49 percent of enrollment. Those restrictions disqualified all but six of Milwaukee's private schools, and over 80 percent of the voucher students attended just three of them.[17] The space limitations of those schools, and the legal cloud that engulfed the program during its first year, kept voucher use from reaching the 1 percent cap right away. A subsequent change in the voucher enrollment limit from 49 percent to 65 percent helped the number of eligible schools rise to 23, with enough combined space for all voucher recipients. Even though the participation cap also rose to 1.5 percent, most of the voucher students still attended just a few of the eligible schools.

The private schools have to admit voucher-supported students randomly and accept the voucher equal to the state share of MPS funding—just over 50 percent in 1996–97—as full payment. A program expansion delayed by a court challenge materialized in 1998–99, but the published studies of the Milwaukee voucher program used data that predate that expansion.

Weak Incentives and Wishful Thinking

Once the voucher applicants exceeded voucher availability, there was no financial incentive to pursue gradual improvement. Small improvements would only cut the number of unsuccessful voucher applicants. Since gradual improvement would not change the number of voucher users, increased media attention was the only new incentive for MPS leaders to pursue improvement. With so few participating private schools, most voucher recipients probably had access to only one of them, and because the number of vouchers initially exceeded the available space, there wasn't even much rivalry among the private schools. The much needed additional resources and a key incentive for private school improvement were cut off by a ban on add-ons.

As the continued unsatisfactory performance of the MPS attests (the governor threatened a June 2000 state takeover), improvements in MPS, if any, were slight. However, despite the small scale of the voucher program and the persistently unacceptable conditions of MPS, there are periodic claims that the program forced productive changes in MPS. Only one included supporting "evidence."[18] Nina Rees of the Heritage Foundation said the proof that the Milwaukee voucher program produced change in MPS was that all nine MPS school board members signed a fund-raising letter for a private scholarship program. No academic data were cited. Rees said "it is too soon to assess [MPS] academic outcomes;" an odd claim since choice advocates, including Rees, often approvingly cite studies of voucher student performance. MPS academic data is the benchmark that defines voucher student progress.

After the Rees article went to press, Superintendent Alan Brown promised that MPS students would read at grade level, even if it took personalized summer instruction. Joe Williams, education reporter for the *Milwaukee Journal Sentinel,* said it was "one of the strongest signs to date that Milwaukee Public Schools *may* [emphasis in the original] be stepping up to make its schools more competitive."[19] Williams emphasized "may" because results often do not follow promises. Many choice advocates did not wait for results. To them, just the promise was a major achievement. They[20] credited the voucher program for causing it, even though there were several possible causes for the MPS promise, and there was no evidence of linkage with the voucher program.

The promise to provide personalized summer reading instruction at taxpayer expense also illustrates an important difference between settings that promote limited rivalry and competitive market settings. Personalized reading instruction may not be a cost-effective expenditure, or there may be better uses for the money. MPS can fund inefficient programs because people have to pay taxes. Without competing choices, inefficient programs are much more difficult to identify and eliminate. Genuine competition purges inefficient programs by offering customers better buys.

Someone needs to carefully document the voucher program's impact on the Milwaukee school system, including the private schools. To avoid the looming political fallout that could result from the hype created by choice advocates, the study needs to show that the program's small size and debilitating restrictions were the reason that there was no significant school system improvement. Otherwise, there will be more assertions like the Carnegie Foundation report's claim that parental choice is a pointless reform because "Milwaukee's plan has failed to demonstrate that vouchers can . . . spark school improvement."[21]

Inappropriate, Misleading Evaluation Criteria

The performance of the voucher recipients—a maximum of 1.5 percent of MPS in the published studies—receives a lot of publicity. The debate includes detail-intensive discussions of the nuances of the voucher student data, the meaning of statistics, and which factors to include in the study.[22] The possible effect on the remaining MPS children, and nonvoucher private school students, receives little attention. The net effect of adding money, along with low-performing MPS transferees to private schools, is a key issue that deserves careful study.

The performance of the children of unsuccessful voucher applicants was the benchmark that defined voucher students' academic gains. That benchmark is inconsistent with claims that the voucher program caused MPS improvements because employing such a benchmark amounts to an implicit assumption that the voucher program does not affect MPS students. The research procedures implicitly assume away system reforms, but John Dilulio,[23] Paul Peterson, and Jay Greene believe that the Milwaukee program is "a randomized experiment with school choice"; a general test of parental choice. They make that assertion even though they quietly acknowledge that the conditions "depart only marginally from past practice," and that it is "a highly compromised choice plan."[24] Herbert Walberg calls it a "true experiment."[25]

In effect, the hypothesis that voucher children would learn more than their MPS peers was that successful voucher applicants could identify a private, non-religious school able to teach their children more—as measured by standardized tests—than their assigned, wealthier MPS (>$8,000 per student in 1996–97). Greene et al. found that voucher users outperformed comparable, unsuccessful voucher applicants by their third year in the program.[26] In other words, parents found better learning environments, which probably surprises only the scholars aware of the daunting data and statistical issues that can obscure underlying facts. They found better learning environments even though academics were not the primary concern of most parents. Most of them said they were motivated by nonacademic concerns like safety.[27] That's fortunate, because they probably would not have waited three years to realize significant benefits. Because of the political focus on the voucher users' test scores, it is also fortunate for the parental choice cause that test scores eventually rose.

The problems of the participating private schools created another source of risk. The physical conditions and staffing constraints of the three schools that initially enrolled over 80 percent of the voucher students[28] reflected the fact that they were on the brink of financial collapse. A fourth school did collapse despite the infusion of voucher funds. Even so, hundreds of low-income families preferred them to their assigned, much better-funded MPS School.

If choice advocates believe the Milwaukee 'experiment' is an "exciting *reform* [emphasis added],"[29] they should not look for differences in test scores between voucher students and their former MPS peers. Differences in scores mean that some children were helped, not that reform occurred. Choice advocates who expect the voucher program to cause noticeable reform of the Milwaukee school system should not compare transferees and their MPS peers.

A comparison of transferees and their MPS peers makes parental choice look better, the less effective as a reform it actually is, and vice versa. For example, if MPS students are not affected at all, but voucher students improve a lot, no reform has occurred, but the voucher program will seem effective. If MPS students improve as much or more than the voucher students, comparisons will not reveal relative gains by voucher students. Therefore, if the voucher program motivates improvements in the Milwaukee schools, the test score comparison will cause the voucher program to seem ineffective.

Since competition has a great track record, the failure to produce insightful information about a competitive education industry is not a major problem. The major threat is the possible political fallout from the likely misunderstandings and misinterpretations of irrelevant data. Claims that a potential reform was tested can have catastrophic political consequences if the public cannot tell that the test was invalid. Because of its small size (especially pre-1998) and its major restrictions, the program can only tell us if voucher applicants knew when an eligible private school was better for their child.

Even though the expanded Milwaukee program still does not approach the conditions of a competitive education industry, the inclusion of church-run schools and 15 percent of MPS children could prompt some MPS improvements. The greater chance of some beneficial reactions by MPS greatly increases the potential political cost of another comparison of MPS and voucher students. One hopes that analysts will recognize that tests of a potential reform demand different data and different hypotheses from policies that just facilitate some transfers to existing private schools.

The comparison that underlies most of the choice "experiments" is misleading for another reason. What can we hope to learn by comparing 90-pound weaklings (typical low-budget private schools) and 500-pound gorillas (wealthier "public"

schools)? The 500-pound gorillas are in a political straitjacket and poorly motivated (they don't have to be choiceworthy), but it remains a mystery what such a
bizarre contest can actually demonstrate. The constraints, incentives, and schools'
resources will be very different in a competitive education industry. Still, analysts
on both sides see inconclusive student achievement comparisons as evidence of
parental choice ineffectiveness, even though such results at least indicate that the
private schools achieved similar results for less money.

Parent satisfaction and Peterson's findings of academic gains after three years
led to increased participation in the restriction-laden program, and it increased
interest in the Milwaukee version of parental choice. In 1999, New York City
Mayor Rudolph Giuliani proposed a Milwaukee-style low-income voucher program for New York.[30] Howard Fuller said the positive results from Milwaukee and
Cleveland indicate that their programs "should be expanded to other cities."[31]
Clint Bolick said the "Milwaukee Plan should be exported."[32] According to Nina
Rees of the Heritage Foundation, "conservative lawmakers and minority activists
in Colorado plan to promote a Milwaukee-style pilot program for Denver."[33]
While the positive results of the Milwaukee program did encourage imitation,
they did not result in movement toward a competitive education industry.

Hype and Unrealistic Expectations

Even though the underlying issue (do voucher applicants know if a nearby eligible private school is better for their child?) is an intuitive proposition, the academic and public debate is intense.[34] Exaggerations, distorted perceptions of
parental choice uses, and unrealistic expectations of restriction-laden programs
are commonplace. The heated discussion about voucher student achievements
threatens to render competitive education industries politically infeasible. Analysts have not had time to publish studies of the expanded program, but even the
expanded program would not justify general headlines like Paul Peterson's, "A Report Card on School Choice."[35] Choice opponents "spin" the same results into a
general conclusion that parental choice is a failed reform.[36] Both sides ignore dis-
claimers like John Witte's statement that "this program should not be used as evidence for evaluating more inclusive choice programs."[37] Witte eventually ignored
it himself. In 2000, Witte published a book about the Milwaukee program inappropriately titled *The Market Approach to Education.*

The media spread and amplify the exaggerations. Analyses of Milwaukee's
voucher students appear as general evidence of parental choice effects. "School
Vouchers on Trial in Milwaukee and Cleveland" is a typical headline.[38] Rene Sanchez
of the *Washington Post* said, "researchers are still feuding over a bottom-line
question—whether [voucher] students do substantially better."[39] Similar headlines
appeared in major publications like the *Wall Street Journal* (10/11/96), and *Education Week* (8/5/98). Bob Davis's *Wall Street Journal* article said "Education scholars

were hoping the Milwaukee experiment would finally settle whether vouchers help poor kids academically." a recurring plea that speaks volumes about persistent, deeply ingrained misperceptions of voucher uses and school system deficiencies.[40] Milton Friedman said parental choice through a universal voucher system should *replace* the "public" school monopoly on taxpayer funding. But as Davis's comment illustrates, voucher systems are just widely seen as additions to the current funding system; a way to allow a few low-income children to attend private schools.

The marginalization of voucher programs, the controversy over the voucher students' academic progress, and the small scale of the highly restricted Milwaukee program have not dampened the enthusiasm of the *Wall Street Journal*'s editors. They opined that the original Milwaukee program was a "pathbreaking voucher program,"[41] and that the Wisconsin Supreme Court decision to allow the modest expansion of the Milwaukee program was a "thunderclap," "a huge boost to the school choice movement," and that the "Choice Debate is Over."[42] In the continuing triumph of hope over reason and experience, choice advocates, including Wisconsin's Governor Tommy Thompson, "contend that [this time] competition for students will force [significant] improvements in the MPS."[43]

Because the Milwaukee "experiment" cannot generate valid generalizations about parental choice, the attention given to its impact on voucher students should be a cause for considerable concern by advocates of market-based reforms. However, prominent choice advocates rarely, if ever, raise such concerns. Choice advocates' newsletters describe the alleged evidence of the benefits of choice without any caveats. The debilitating impact of the restrictions, the absence of competition, and the mistaken focus on helping a few children, rather than improving the entire school system, are rarely, if ever, mentioned.

Greene's report acknowledged the Milwaukee program's severe restrictions, but did not recognize that they precluded all but limited rivalry. He said his controversial findings[44] demonstrated the benefits of competition. Daniel McGroarty casually noted[45] the "small size and short duration" of Milwaukee's program, and the huge political stakes, but didn't explain that there was no basis for a high-stakes research battle or what a valid test would require. Instead, McGroarty complained that choice advocates were at a disadvantage because, at the time, only John Witte had access to the achievement data. After Witte published the data, McGroarty mistakenly asserted that choice advocates (disciples of "theoretical models that borrow from free market economics") could "test their theories against the reality of the one city [Milwaukee] where it [competition] exists."[46]

Jeanne Allen,[47] President of the Center for School Reform, said "if these things [charges that the Milwaukee program with its minimal choice and limited rivalry, hadn't helped students academically or created more equity for racial minorities] were true, two of the key arguments of choice proponents would be refuted." The Milwaukee program cannot demonstrate what Allen says it must. Moving relatively few children within the current system won't affect equity or achievement noticeably. Such an impact requires the genuine competition that would improve schools significantly. To make matters worse, statements like Allen's include specific ways to discredit the parental choice cause, including unqualified support for "experiments" like the Milwaukee program that provide opportunities for choice opponents to do just that.

Incrementalism in Action?

An adequate evaluation of the incrementalism hypothesis that restrictions will wither away gradually does not exist for Milwaukee or any other parental choice program. Only the Milwaukee program—because of its expansion from 1 percent to 1.5 percent, and now 15 percent, the recent inclusion of church-run schools, and some slight easing of other restrictions—constitutes limited support for the incrementalism hypothesis. However, the 1998 expansion to 15 percent of MPS enrollment and inclusion of church-run schools still leaves it far short of a competitive education industry, and it might not get any closer. That, and the stagnation of other choice programs, offers little basis for optimism that current programs will expand quickly, if ever, to the point where a competitive education industry exists.

If our extensive experience with competition in other settings, including the history of competitive education industries that once existed in some other countries,[48] isn't enough to elicit voter support for a competitive education industry, syndicated columnist William Raspberry, a supporter of limited parental choice, is right: "It's time for some serious [emphasis added] experimentation."[49] The appropriate parental choice "randomized experiment" is for all of the children in some regions to exercise parental choice without financial penalty, while the status quo survives as the "control" in other, similar regions.

PRIVATELY FUNDED VOUCHER PROGRAMS

The Milwaukee voucher program is the best example of a politically risky, pseudoexperiment, but there are others. Privately funded voucher programs are also often touted as voucher experiments. Like the publicly funded Milwaukee program, it is not the private programs that are regrettable, but the attempt to generalize from their modest effects. Like the Milwaukee program, the privately funded programs weren't capable of transforming the system. They can only transfer a few children to better, but still academically deficient schools.

The *Wall Street Journal*'s Amity Shlaes said a privately funded $1,400 voucher for 1,200 New York children[50] was a good test of vouchers because analysts could easily define and monitor an appropriate control group, and thereby readily assess voucher students' academic gains. Studies of the New York program and the other privately funded programs test only whether voucher students gain academically relative to their "public" school peers. None of the key elements of a competitive education industry is present.

Like the Milwaukee and Cleveland publicly funded programs, privately funded programs award small amounts to just a few families. There are two additional reasons why privately funded programs probably will not establish a competitive education industry. First, most private programs only award partial tuition vouchers to low-income families.[51] The parents' share still represents a large financial penalty for choosing a more cheaply produced private education. That reduces what parents will pay, which reduces the quality of private school programs. That reduces the demand for vouchers and private school services, but at current funding levels, it only reduces the waiting list. Second, the uncertain, sometimes explicitly temporary nature of philanthropic support discourages the entry of school entrepreneurs. Many investments will not pay off in the time frame that entrepreneurs are relatively sure the voucher program will exist at or above current funding levels. The problem is especially acute when programs derive a large share of their funds from a small number of donors.

The privately funded program in the Edgewood School District in San Antonio, Texas is a partial exception to those caveats about privately funded programs. Because the Edgewood program is a ten-year commitment to full-tuition vouchers to every low-income family applicant from the district (virtually every family is eligible), it has the best chance of evoking a competitive response from the district authorities and the private sector.

FLORIDA'S VOUCHER PROGRAM AND TEXAS'S PROPOSED PROGRAM

A voucher proposal was a hot topic of the 1995, 1997, and 1999 biennial sessions of the Texas legislature. Low-income children in selected regions qualify for a voucher if the government decides their assigned school is low-performing. If the government decides that a school is unsatisfactory, children who have suffered years of education malpractice can attend a private school with public funding. Private schools cannot charge more than the voucher amount. As in the public and private programs discussed above, the proposed evaluation criterion was the effect on transferees' academic progress.

Choice advocacy organizations celebrated[52] when retiring Lieutenant Governor of Texas Bob Bullock, a powerful Democrat, announced his support for the 1997 proposal: "Let's see if it works, and let that be the report card to Texans about its value—or if it doesn't work, about its demise."[53] The program's major restrictions meant that it could not reveal the benefits of a competitive education industry. Bullock may not have realized that, or he recognized that a small, so-called pilot program that cannot harness competitive forces to any great extent is a potential ally of choice opponents. Voucher program implementation and evaluation takes a long time, so a pilot program can help proponents of the "public" school monopoly delay some reforms. For the voucher program to be deemed successful, voucher students enrolled in resource-starved private schools must decisively outperform a clearly comparable control group. Under those demanding circumstances, controversial results, even apparent failures, that could easily destroy the political feasibility of parental choice of any kind are quite possible. Choice opponents' skillful spin doctors always exploit opportunities for deception.

In 1999, Florida enacted such a voucher program. If the program survives a legal challenge, it will allow children to use a voucher if their assigned "public" school was officially graded "F" in at least two out of four years. Choice advocates widely applauded the program, even though children only gain access to vouchers after they become so academically deficient that they might not be able to use them. In Texas, many Edgewood voucher students had to return to their assigned "public" school because they were too academically deficient to keep up with the private school curriculum. In addition, though every state has about 40 percent of its children below the National Assessment of Educational Progress (NAEP) definition of basic ("half of Florida's fourth-graders can't read at a basic level"[54]), the share of Florida's schools that will receive an F is not expected to exceed 6 percent.[55]

As was the case with the perceived success of the Milwaukee program in boosting the test scores of its participants, Florida's political success with restriction-laden parental choice could spread such programs, but not improve the political feasibility of parental choice that would transform the system. In a front-page article in *Education Week*, Darcia Bowman said that, "more policymakers are borrowing a page from Florida's book and linking their choice plans to the performance of public schools."[56] Because such programs create the public image of "parental choice," Florida clones would probably reduce the probability of system transformation through universal parental choice and competition.

CHARTER SCHOOLS

Charter schools are generating evidence, but of what? Since the appeal of charter schools is their exemption from some of the rules applicable to "public" schools, the concept is certainly evidence of strong concerns about political/bureaucratic management. When elected officials seriously consider it, they are admitting that the political process is a likely source of education problems. Within the groups seeking the authority to operate a charter school, it is more than a concern; it is a strong conviction. They would not undertake the arduous pursuit of charter status unless they thought the avoided rules were counterproductive.

Charter school achievements can indicate whether insulation from politics is possible in a government institution. Several scholars have concluded that the prospects are poor. Sheldon Richman argued that "autonomous public school is an oxymoron."[57] In effect, Caroline Hoxby also reached the conclusion that politics will remain a major factor. She said charter schools just amount to new school districts.[58] In New Jersey, "the state has defined each charter school as a kind of district unto itself."[59] Sarah Tantillo, founder of the Charter School Resource Center, said, "I have yet to meet a regulation that charters are free from."[60]

Though school district names often include the word *independent*, insulation from political pressures is an illusion. Charter schools and traditional districts are in a similar political position, hence Hoxby's conclusion. Will charter schools be able to teach controversial subject matter or adopt textbooks that are politically incorrect?[61] I doubt it. Charter schools may avoid some old rules whose constituency has faded, but what about new political causes? Supporters of a new rule will surely believe it is beneficial for all schools to comply with it.

Government institutions like the Federal Reserve that are relatively "independent" have their own source of funds. They don't have to compete for funds in the ordinary budget process. Charter schools are not so lucky. Even if funds don't have explicit strings attached, the competitive appropriation process creates unwritten rules. In addition, state education officials often try to exercise oversight that charter schools thought didn't apply to them.

The preliminary evidence supports the view that an autonomous "public" school is a fantasy.[62] It's a fantasy even in states like Arizona and Michigan, which have the "strongest" charter school laws. For that reason, and because such strong charter school laws are not the norm, there is little hope that charter school legislation will capture the benefits of a competitive education industry, or even change the school system significantly.

Charter analysts debate "to what degree should market forces determine success."[63] Many do not trust market forces to produce quality control. The lack of trust exists despite the assumed presence of market forces, but their absence is a better reason. A family is lucky to have a charter alternative to its assigned school, an option that is also government-controlled and lacks many of the critical freedoms and pressures of markets. Relatively few firms run extremely rare for-profit charters, and opportunities to adjust prices are nonexistent. Charter schools don't even have to outperform traditional "public" schools. A popular specialty area will attract students. However, charter schools often appear to outperform "public" schools, even though charters have to fund capital expenses out of operating funds. According to *U.S. News & World Report*, charter schools with significant problems were able to stay in business.[64]

Politics and bureaucracy are still significant factors. Their effects exist even in states with the strongest charter school laws, such as Arizona and Michigan, which account for about half of the nation's charter schools. If those effects weren't evident in Michigan and Arizona, there would be little mention of them.

Charter sponsors are government institutions subject to political pressures. For example, sponsors have closed some popular charter schools.[65] Test score gains by charter school students are the official performance measures, though the best measures of an alleged reform are parental satisfaction and improvements in the school system. The additional uncertainty that results from vulnerability to political pressures, and the importance of test scores regardless of parental satisfaction, has made it harder for charter schools to secure financial support for start-ups or expansions. Only the few for-profit charter schools have access to venture capital.

There are complicated accountability formulas, and some charter schools don't control their finances. Charter schools must have an open admissions policy, despite the recognition, even by some choice opponents, that some selectivity in admissions is essential.[66] Since some students cost more—sometimes a lot more—an open admissions policy creates financial uncertainty. Open admissions also inhibit specialization, a key element of a market system.

If autonomous public schools are illusions, what about the academic gains that charter students may achieve, and what if rivalry with charter schools improves traditional "public" schools? The academic gains will reflect the effects of the rules that charter schools avoid. Some analysts already attribute changes in traditional "public" schools to the mere presence of charter schools,[67] though the changes—spend more money, personnel changes, advertise—seem more defensive than competitive. It will take more time to measure achievement effects.[68]

Even if charter school availability does cause improvements in traditional "public" schools, the improvements will only hint at the potential short- or long-run effects of real competition. The profit motive, flexible prices, and lower entry barriers of a competitive education industry would create much stronger market forces. Under most charter school laws, school owners cannot earn a profit. Therefore, there is no reason for most charter operators to try to cut per pupil expenses. The general absence of the profit motive also greatly weakens the incentive to improve through research and experimentation. Tuition changes cannot reward innovation or signal the unit costs of charter schools or traditional "public" schools. There is no market entry mechanism to force down high unit costs, or to tell policy makers, through overcapacity, that school taxes are too high.

Charter schools will harm the private sector. The private sector's primary shortcoming is unequal access to resources, a problem that charter schools exacerbate by recruiting some of the children who would have attended private schools.[69] In the *Wall Street Journal*, Hugh Pearson described the "transformation of black private schools into charter schools."[70] The November 1998 issue of *School Reform News* (p. 12) reported that charter schools are "killing private schools."[71] Edgar J. Huffman of Phoenix said his school faced a financial disaster three years ago after he lost half of his students, a year after passage of charter school legislation." Huffman converted his school to a charter: "We basically had no choice but to go charter."

Like other versions of choice that create few, if any, market conditions, charter schools could reduce the political feasibility of a competitive education industry. Though certainly an improvement over the status quo, charter schools are much more likely to be a major, perhaps permanent detour than a step in the right direction. Quentin Quade was right again: Charter schools "can be a detour, and a devastatingly bad one."[72]

MORE EXAMPLES OF FAULTY ANALYSIS AND WISHFUL THINKING

As noted previously, it is common for analysts to acknowledge that too few people have choice to create much competitive behavior,[73] but then ignore that limitation. Even economists—scholars who study market systems—sometimes use the term *experiment* carelessly. They sometimes state what the so-called experiments cannot tell us, but then fail to recognize that there isn't much left that they can tell us. One especially shocking example of careless analysis appeared in an academic journal article written and peer reviewed by economists. The 1997 article surveyed parental choice studies. Even though there is virtually no resemblance between the universal voucher plan Milton Friedman proposed as a replacement for "public" schools' monopoly on public funds, and the privately financed, partial-tuition vouchers available in a few cities to a few low-income families, the authors equated them! "The nature of some of these [privately financed vouchers] programs allows for studies of essentially Friedman-like voucher arrangements."[74]

When Schools Compete[75] is another shocking example. Economist Helen Ladd co-authored the study of New Zealand's policy of universal choice among the government-operated schools. There are no profits, no market-determined prices, and 96.5 percent of the children attend government-owned schools. New Zealand definitely does not have a competitive education industry. The central government strictly controls the supply of schools. Space shortages persist because the government refuses to "invest in new school facilities while others [schools] remain under-utilized" (p. 250). Space shortages at popular schools force parents to patronize unpopular schools that might otherwise be forced to close, and the shortages forced the authorities to partially reimpose attendance zones. Specialization is minimal because "local goals were secondary to those imposed from the center in the form of the National Education Guidelines" (p. 298). Enrollment is only one determinant of each school's funding. Despite the near total absence of market forces, Ladd and her coauthor repeatedly make such statements as: 1) "New Zealand's foray into the realm of *full parental choice and competition* [emphasis added]" (p. 250); 2) "a system of parental choice and *market competition* [emphasis added]" (p. 292); 3) "self-governing schools functioning in a competitive environment" (p. 297).

Economist Scott Milliman coauthored an article claiming that Arizona's char-

ter school law had "initiated a free market in public education,"[76] even though
market entry is regulated; charters and their "competitors" have the same owner;
and a dominant "producer"—traditional district "public" schools—has a nearly
90 percent market share. Milliman reached the conclusion that charter schools are
"market-driven," even though charter schools are largely nonprofit operations
that cannot turn away customers or even decide the price of their services.

Journals, talk shows, and the popular press report countless mistakes, including many by choice advocates, and few, if any, subsequent rebuttals or corrections.
The misstatements indicate what many activists believe and the misinformation
policy makers and the general public learn from them. Here are a few[77] examples:

- Though the opportunity to transfer to another district does not establish any
  of the key elements described in chapter 2, David Armor wrote a report titled,
  Competition in Education: A Case Study of Interdistrict Choice.[78]
- G. Carl Ball used phrases like "market-driven," "the competitive way," and
  "provide the customer the opportunity to evaluate the competition" to describe "public" school choice; choice among different branches of the same
  producer.[79] The socialist countries proved that consumers' ability to shop at any
  state-owned store did not produce competition or improve the quality of their
  goods and services.
- A right to attend another "public" school does not establish any of the key elements of markets, but Tom Peters said that "public" school choice is "a surro-
  gate for competition."[80]
- "In 1986, the National Governors Conference issued a statement endorsing the
  concept of public school choice as a way to 'unlock the values of competition
  in the marketplace.'"[81]

A Joe Nathan book[82] describes more misrepresentation of "public" school
choice, including "public" school choice that the authorities can veto.

- Nathan and Edward Fiske (p. 5) applaud what Cambridge, Massachusetts, calls
  "controlled competition." Parents exercise "public" school choice as long as
  their choices advance racial diversity goals. The authorities vetoed all three top
  choices of 15 percent of Cambridge parents. Since Cambridge's limited "public" school choice is even further from a competitive education industry than
  ordinary "public" school choice, Tony Wagner's opinion of the Cambridge
  schools is no surprise. Wagner, a Cambridge resident, and prominent educator,
  said, "school choice has not produced significant improvements in the schools.
  The majority of the 13 [Cambridge K–8 schools] seem virtually interchangeable and are mediocre."[83]
- Adam Urbanski (p. 228): "Competition among public schools would be more
  fair and more productive than competition between public and private
  schools."

- Herbert Walberg (p. 69) complains about bureaucracies "unsubjected to market competition," and then says choice limited to the schools owned and run by the government education bureaucracy will solve that problem. Even strong critics of the status quo take its key elements for granted.

- John Chubb and Terry Moe said "district- or state-wide open enrollment systems and magnet schools" would achieve meaningful competition. Their controversial book, *Politics, Markets, and America's Schools*,[84] demonstrates in great detail that bureaucracy significantly inhibits educational achievement, and that bureaucracy is an inherent part of democratic control.[85] Then, in their final chapter, Chubb and Moe lobby for a choice program run by a bureau[86] of a democratically elected government. They believe a "market system" is perfectly consistent with bureaucratic control of the choices, including price controls.

- John Witte and Mark Rigdon claim that the Chubb and Moe plan would mean "complete autonomy for all schools."[87] Witte said that the original, restriction-laden Milwaukee program was "the market approach to education."[88]

- The fallacy that a little bit of choice is enough to create meaningful competition took center stage in the Utah governor's boardroom.[89] The February 17, 1997, meeting included education experts, activists, and Utah lawmakers.

- Dr. David Salisbury, president of the Sutherland Institute, described some choice programs, including the Milwaukee and Cleveland voucher programs, and said: "These educational choice initiatives are based on the free market principle that competition and consumer choice produce excellence in educational services."

- According to Alan Bonsteel,[90] the Milwaukee Voucher Program provided America with "one of its first experiments in a system of open competition and freedom of choice in education, modeled after the highly successful GI Bill of Rights." The Milwaukee program lacks all of the characteristics of a competitive market, and there's not much of anything "open" about it. The GI Bill was not limited to secular schools like the Milwaukee program was at the time of Bonsteel's remark. The GI Bill's target population of military veterans was not nearly as narrow as the 1.5 percent cap in effect in 1997.

- Chester Finn and Diane Ravitch[91] are choice advocates and former high officials in the Reagan and Bush Education Departments, respectively. They labeled the Cleveland and Milwaukee low-income voucher programs "the most exciting reform," and charter schools the next most exciting, yet they admit that neither has changed the schools attended by the vast majority of children.

- Helen Ladd, Ted Fiske, and Joseph Viteritti say that charter schools are "a market-based reform strategy,"[92] and that "real competition"[93] exists with unlimited charter schools. Lewis Solmon, Michael Block, and Mary Gifford characterize charter schools as "a market-based education system in the making."[94]

- Jerry Hume said the Milwaukee program was "a big step in the direction" of producer accountability to education consumers.[95]
- Market-oriented education reform was not even in a prominent proposal, but George Clowes, managing editor of *School Reform News*, said, "1997 was a breakthrough year for market-oriented education reform."[96] 1998 received a similar designation.

Intellectual Prisoners of the Status Quo

Many debilitating elements of the status quo are challenged very rarely. For example, choice advocates usually assume the permanence of school cartels called districts[97] and district office bureaucracies. Such carelessness is a major problem. Many choice advocates champion competition in market settings with their rhetoric and publications, but then undermine competition with analytical and political mistakes, including enthusiastic support for restriction-laden proposals.

The common misstatements of choice opponents are also harmful. Deliberate distortions and competition-defeating restrictions are a predictable result of choice opponents' determination to preserve the current funding and governance system, but not all of their mistakes are intentional. Many choice opponents are also unaware of the essential features of competitive settings, and they instinctively assume the permanence or indispensability of key elements of the status quo. For example, consider the following statement by longtime American Federation of Teachers' President Albert Shanker: "Education is a public good that communities have provided for all children because they are our future citizens."[98] Shanker implied that communities could only offer all children an education if the government operates a school system. Shanker and many others equate universal access to education services with the "public" school delivery mechanism. Chapter 9 discusses this fallacy in more detail.

Sometimes compromise or appeasement is the reason choice advocates support proposals that lack every essential feature of a competitive education industry. However, carelessness and inertia are probably the most common reasons. Even when choice advocates know they are accepting harmful restrictions, their support is usually still enthusiastic and unqualified. When prominent choice advocates have concerns about debilitating restrictions, they only rarely voice them publicly.

CONCLUSION

There is confusion about how to evaluate the effects of parental choice as a reform catalyst, and about what kinds of facts are relevant evidence. The next chapter identifies and discusses the evidence relevant to the competitive education industry issue.

NOTES

1. For example, Polly Williams did not propose the original Milwaukee program to test the effects of parental choice. She proposed parental choice so that a few low-income families, including her own, could afford to leave the Milwaukee Public Schools.

2. The unfortunate use of the term *experiment* has spread from Milwaukee (Jay P. Greene, Paul Peterson, and Jiangtao Du, *The Effectiveness of School Choice: The Milwaukee Experiment* [Cambridge, Mass.: Program in Education Policy and Governance, Harvard University, 1997]) to the more recent Cleveland low-income voucher program (Jay P. Greene, Paul Peterson, and William Howell. *Test Scores from the Cleveland Voucher Experiment* [Cambridge, Mass.: Program in Education Policy and Governance, Harvard University, 1997]), and some privately funded voucher programs, like the one in Indianapolis (David J. Weinschrott, and Sally B. Kilgore, *Educational Choice Charitable Trust: An Experiment in School* (Hudson Institute Briefing Paper #189, 1998]).

3. National Commission on Excellence in Education, *A Nation at Risk: The Imperative for Educational Reform* (Washington: U.S. Department of Education, 1983).

4. Actual (like Milwaukee and Florida) and proposed programs typically, though not universally, prohibit privately funded voucher add-ons. That means that private schools cannot charge voucher students more than the value of the voucher; a requirement that amounts to a price control.

5. The vast majority of private schools are nonprofit.

6. Jeanne Allen, "Benefits of Choice," Letter to the Editor of the *New York Times* (November 8, 1993). Note that Allen is president of the Center for Education Reform, a vocal supporter of "school choice."

7. Daniel McGroarty, *Break These Chains* (Rocklin, Calif.: ICS Press, Prima Publishing, 1996).

8. George A. Clowes, "Five Steps to Full School Choice," *School Reform News* (September 1998): 10–11.

9. The rhetoric of competition is commonplace, but most parental choice advocates are not aware of the requirements explained in chapter 2. Many are quite willing to accept a noncompetitive system of limited parental choice. Most parental choice advocates' definition of "full school choice" falls far short of a competitive education industry.

10. For example, the Cleveland low-income voucher program, the Minnesota "public" school choice plan, Cambridge's "controlled" public school choice, and to a lesser extent, the Milwaukee program, discussed in more detail shortly.

11. C. W. Cobb, *Responsive Schools, Renewed Communities* (San Francisco, Calif.: The ICS Press, 1992).

12. Economic Policy Institute. *School Choice: Examining the Evidence* (Washington: author, 1993); Carnegie Foundation for the Advancement of Teaching, *School Choice: A Special Report* (Princeton, N.J.: Author, 1992); TSTA/NEA, *Our Public Schools: The Best Choice for Texas* (Austin: Mimeographed, 1994); Richard Elmore, Gary Orfield, and Bruce Fuller, *School Choice: The Cultural Logic of Families, the Political Rationality of Institutions* (New York: Teachers College Press, 1995); Kevin B. Smith, and Kenneth J. Meier, *The Case Against School Choice* (New York: M. E. Sharpe, 1995); Darrel W. Drury, "Vouchers and Student Achievement," *Policy Research* (Summer 2000).

13. See, for example: Joseph Viteritti, *Choosing Equality* (Washington: Brookings Institution, 2000), p. 114.

14. For example, see Drury, Summer 2000.

15. Frederick Hess, Robert Maranto, and Scott Milliman, "Coping with Competition: How School Systems Respond to School Choice," Working Paper (1999); More on this issue later in the chapter.

16. Daniel McGroarty, *Break These Chains* (Rocklin, Calif.: ICS Press, Prima Publishing, 1996), p. 85.

17. Jay P. Greene, Paul Peterson, and Jiangtao Du, *The Effectiveness of School Choice: The Milwaukee Experiment* (Cambridge, Mass.: Program in Education Policy and Governance, Harvard University, 1997).

18. Nina S. Rees, "Public School Benefits of Private School Vouchers," *Policy Review* (Jan/Feb 1999): 16–19.

19. Joe Williams, "MPS Guarantees Help for Poor Readers," *Milwaukee Journal Sentinel* (December 23, 1998).

20. *School Reform News*, "Lessons on Vouchers from Milwaukee;" and Bruce R. Thompson interview, "School Choice: Changing the Vision for Public Education" (May 1999). At least one prominent choice advocacy organization e-mailed the news of the MPS promise to prominent choice advocates under the heading "choice works."

21. Carnegie Foundation for the Advancement of Teaching. *School Choice: A Special Report* (Princeton, N.J.: 1992).

22. For example, see Joy Kiviat, "Vouchers Improve Academic Outcomes," *School Reform News* (April 2000); 6–7; McGroarty, 1996, pp. 177–87 for a detailed discussion of the Milwaukee voucher program.

23. John J. Dilulio, Jr., "My School Choice: Literacy First," *The Weekly Standard* (October 19, 1998): 26. The statement by Paul Peterson appeared in the September/October 1998 *Philanthropy* (the title was not cited).

24. Paul E. Peterson, Jay P. Greene, and Chad Noyes, "School Choice in Milwaukee," *The Public Interest* (Fall 1996): 38–56.

25. Herbert J. Walberg, "Market Theory of School Choice," *Education Week* (July 12, 2000): 49.

26. Greene, Peterson, and Du, 1997.

27. "Seventy-four percent of the parents who chose to use vouchers did so because of the disciplinary guidelines and general atmosphere of private schools," Nina H. Shokraii and John S. Barry, "Two Cheers for S. 1: The Safe and Affordable Schools Act of 1997," *The Heritage Foundation Issue Bulletin* 232 (May 14, 1997): 5.

28. Greene, Peterson, and Du, 1997.

29. Chester Finn and Diane Ravitch, *Wall Street Journal* (September 7, 1995).

30. Mark Walsh, "Giuliani Proposes a Voucher Program for New York," *Education Week* (January 27, 1999): 3.

31. Howard Fuller, "A Research Update on School Choice," *Marquette University Current Education Issues* 97, no. 3 (October, 1997): 1.

32. *Church and State*, "Voucher Advocate Says 'Milwaukee Plan' Should be Exported" (May, 1992): 16–17.

33. Nina S. Rees, *School Choice 2000 Annual Report* (Washington: Heritage Foundation, 2000).

34. Howard L. Fuller. "The *Real* Evidence: An Honest Research Update on School Choice Experiments," *Wisconsin Interest* (Fall/Winter 1997); Cecilia E. Rouse, *Private School Vouchers and Student Achievement: An Evaluation of the Milwaukee Parental Choice Program* (Washington: National Bureau of Economic Research, 1996); Cosmo Wenman, "Choice Cuts: The Real Impact of Milwaukee's Vouchers," *Reason* (December 1996); Daniel McGroarty, "Hope for Milwaukee," *Report Card* (May–June 1996); Howard L. Fuller and Sammis B. White. *Expanded*

School Choice in Milwaukee: A Profile of Eligible Students and Schools (Thiensville, Wisc.: Wisconsin Policy Research Institute, 1995); Greene, Peterson, and Du, 1997; Drury, Summer, 2000; John F. Witte, Andrea B. Bailey, and Christopher A. Thorn, *Third-Year Report, Milwaukee Parental Choice Program* (Madison, Wisc.: Department of Political Science and The Robert La Follette Institute of Public Affairs, University of Wisconsin, [December, 1993]).

35. Paul E. Peterson, "A Report Card on School Choice," *Commentary* (October 1997): 29–33.

36. Drury, Summer, 2000.

37. Witte, Bailey, and Thorn, 1993, p. 29. See also William A. Testa and Surya Sen, "School Choice and Competition (A Conference Summary), *Chicago Fed Letter* #143a (July 1999).

38. *Mobilization for Equity* newsletter, February 1998.

39. Rene Sanchez, "Riley Launches Attack on School Vouchers," *Washington Post* (September 24, 1997): A6.

40. Chapter 6 discusses the fallacy that school system problems are limited to the inner city schools of low-income families.

41. *Wall Street Journal* Editorial Board, "Choice Thunderclap" (June 11, 1998): A22.

42. *Wall Street Journal* Editorial Board, "Choice Debate Is Over" (April 6, 2000).

43. June Kronholz, "School Voucher Drive Bolstered by Court Action," *Wall Street Journal* (June 11, 1998): A24.

44. Greene, Peterson, and Du, 1997. It's controversial because it contradicted some of the findings of a John Witte study described by Bob Davis, "Dueling Professors Have Milwaukee Dazed over School Vouchers," *Wall Street Journal* (October 11, 1996): A1. Likewise, there are competing research results for the Cleveland low-income voucher program: A Kim Metclaf study summarized by Mark Walsh, "Vouchers Yield Mixed Results, Report Says," *Education Week* (December 2, 1998): 3 versus Jay P. Greene, Paul Peterson, and William Howell. *Test Scores from the Cleveland Voucher Experiment* (Cambridge, Mass.: Program in Education Policy and Governance, Harvard University, 1997).

45. Daniel McGroarty, "School Choice Slandered," *Public Interest* (Fall 1994): 95–96.

46. McGroarty, 1996, xx.

47. *Washington Times*, 11/10/93.

48. Andrew J. Coulson, *Market Education* (New Brunswick, N.J.: Transaction Publishers, 1999).

49. William Raspberry, "Let's at Least Experiment with School Choice," *Washington Post* (June 16, 1997).

50. Amity Shlaes, "Voucher Program Passes Its Test," *Wall Street Journal* (October 30, 1998).

51. The program located in the Edgewood School District of San Antonio, Texas, pays the entire private school tuition of nearly every available private school. The remaining privately funded programs pay around half of most private schools' tuition.

52. "Texas Vouchers Gain Democratic Support," *School Reform News* (January 1998).

53. Peggy Fikac, "Bullock Defends Pro-Voucher Role," *Austin American-Statesman* (November 12, 1997).

54. "Victory in Florida," *School Reform News* (June, 1999): 1, 4.

55. Fourth and eighth grade math, reading, and science NAEP scores reported in *Education Week*, 1/11/99.

56. Darcia H. Bowman, "States Giving Choice Bills Closer Look," *Education Week* (March 1, 2000): 1, 24.

57. Sheldon Richman, *Separating School and State* (Fairfax, Va.: The Future of Freedom Foundation, 1994).

58. Caroline Hoxby, "What Do America's Traditional Forms of School Choice Teach Us about School Choice Reforms," FRBNY *Economic Policy Review* 4 (March 1998): 47–59.

59. Leslie G. Pfaff, "The Right to Choose," *The New Jersey Monthly* (September 15, 2000).

60. Ibid.

61. The special interest group gauntlet that confronts textbook publishers is a major, inherent flaw of a politically driven education policy. For revealing examples, see Charles J. Sykes *Dumbing Down Our Kids* (New York: St. Martins Press, 1995).

62. Chester E. Finn, Bruno V. Manno, Louann A. Bierlein, and Gregg Vanourek, *Charter Schools in America Project: Final Report, Part 2* (Indianapolis: Hudson Institute, 1997); Lynn Schnaiberg, "Charter Schools Struggle with Accountability," *Education Week* (June 10, 1998): 1, 14; Thomas Toch, "The New Education Bazaar," *U.S. News & World Report* (April 27, 1998): 34–36; James N. Goenner, "Charter Schools: The Revitalization of Public Education," *Phi Delta Kappan* 78, no. 1 (September, 1996): 32–34; Lynn Schnaiberg, "Firms Hoping to Turn Profit from Charters," *Education Week* (December 10, 1997): 14.

63. Schnaiberg, June 10, 1998.

64. Toch, April 27, 1998.

65. Robert Maranto and Scott Milliman, "In Arizona, Charter Schools Work," *Washington Post* (October 11, 1999): A25.

66. Barry McGhan, "Choice and Compulsion," *Phi Delta Kappan* 79, no. 8 (April 1998): 610–15.

67. *School Reform News* (February 1998) and Maranto and Milliman, October 11, 1999.

68. Achievement gains by students in all types of schools is evidence of effective competition. Gains by charter school students relative to students in traditional "public" schools is the signature of a rescue, not a school system reform.

69. Chester E. Finn, Jr., Bruno Manno, and Gregg Vanourek. *Charter Schools in Action: Renewing Public Education* (Princeton: Princeton University Press, 2000).

70. Hugh Pearson, "An Urban Push for Self-Reliance," *Wall Street Journal* (February 7, 1996).

71. *School Reform News* (November 1998): 12.

72. Quentin Quade, *Financing Education* (New Brunswick, N.J.: Transaction Publishers, 1996), p. 158.

73. Isabel V. Sawhill and Shannon L. Smith, "Vouchers for Elementary and Secondary Education" in *Vouchers and Related Delivery Mechanisms: Consumer Choice in the Provision of Public Services* (Washington: Brookings Institution Conference, October 2–3, 1998): 150–154. Even Milton Friedman refers to the Milwaukee and Cleveland programs as experiments: "Freedom and School Vouchers," *Chronicles* (December 1998).

74. Douglas J. Lamdin and Michael Mintrom, "School Choice in Theory and Practice: Taking Stock and Looking Ahead," *Education Economics* 5, no. 3 (1997): 235.

75. Edward B. Fiske and Helen F. Ladd, *When Schools Compete: A Cautionary Tale* (Washington: Brookings Institution Press, 2000).

76. Maranto and Milliman, October 11, 1999.

77. Some additional examples are discussed in greater detail in chapters 6 and 12.

78. David Armor, *"Competition in Education: A Case Study of Interdistrict Choice"* (Boston: Pioneer Institute for Public Policy, 1997).

79. G. Carl Ball, "In Search of Educational Excellence," *Policy Review* (Fall 1990): 54–55.

80. Tom Peters, "In Search of Educational Excellence," *Policy Review* (Fall 1990): 57–58.

81. Joseph Viteritti, *Choosing Equality* (Washington: Brookings Institution, 2000), p. 57.

82. Joe Nathan (ed.), *Public Schools by Choice* (St. Paul, Minn.: The Institute for Learning and Teaching, 1989).

83. Tony Wagner, "School Choice: To What End?" *Phi Delta Kappan* 78, no. 1 (September 1996): 71.

84. John Chubb and Terry Moe, *Politics, Markets, and America's Schools* (Washington: Brookings Institution, 1990).

85. John Chubb and Terry Moe, *Educational Choice* (San Antonio: Texas Public Policy Foundation, 1990), p. 21.

86. For a detailed discussion of the inconsistency between the findings and policy recommendations of Chubb and Moe, see E. G. West, "Autonomy in School Provision: Meanings and Implications," *Economics of Education Review* 11, no. 4 (1992): 417–25.

87. John F. Witte and Mark E. Rigdon, "Education Choice Reforms: Will They Change American Schools?" *Publius: The Journal of Federalism* (Summer 1993): 95–114.

88. John F. Witte, *The Market Approach to Education: An Analysis of America's First Voucher Program* (Princeton: Princeton University Press, 2000).

89. "Free to Choose: a Legislative Briefing on Education Reform and School Choice," *Sutherland Speeches* 8 (November 1997): 1–17.

90. Alan Bonsteel and Carlos A. Bonilla (eds.), *A Choice for Our Children* (San Francisco: ICS Press, 1997), p. 5.

91. *Wall Street Journal* editorial, 9/7/95.

92. Statement by Helen Ladd at a Brookings Institution Panel Discussion (February 24, 2000) based on her book: Fiske and Ladd, 2000.

93. Viteritti, 2000, p. 221.

94. Lewis C. Solmon, Michael K. Block, and Mary Gifford, *A Market-Based Education System in the Making* (Phoenix, Ariz.: Goldwater Institute, 2000).

95. Jerry Hume, "In Search of Educational Excellence," *Policy Review* (Fall 1990): 55.

96. *Intellectual Ammunition* (Feb/March 1998): 5.

97. School districts satisfy the definition of a cartel: an association of producers that eliminates or significantly reduces competition. A school district is a much more stable anticompetitive institution than any cartel of private firms, or even a cartel of nations, like the OPEC oil cartel. See, for example, J. Chrys Dougherty and Stephen L. Becker, *An Analysis of Public-Private School Choice in Texas* (San Antonio: Texas Public Policy Foundation, 1995).

98. Edith Rasell and Richard Rothstein (eds.), *School Choice: Examining the Evidence* (Washington: Economic Policy Institute, 1993), p. xii.

CHAPTER 4

Real Evidence about Competition

"The first step in school reform ... is putting
ideology aside and doing what works in education."

— Sandra Feldman, president, American Federation of Teachers,
"Not All Credit to Bush," *Wall Street Journal* letter (August 11, 2000)

Competitive industries have an impressive track record, and K–12 education should respond to competition at least as well as the rest of the economy. The evidence includes the education system of pre-1840 United States,[1] and experience with competitive education industries in other countries. The relevant evidence also includes some aspects of education systems in other countries, the ineffectiveness of reforms that do not harness competition, and, especially, the unacceptable recurring effects of the status quo—a monopoly.

Widespread linkage of "choice," "competition," and "experiment" creates the perception that choice and competition are untested. While freedom of choice in competitive settings is an American tradition, choice advocates seldom challenge the implicit assumption that competitive education systems are novel concepts. An exception, choice advocate Quentin Quade pointed out, that "it is not parental freedom that needs to justify itself, but any policy that limits it."[2] Absence of choice is the aberration, but choice advocates assume the burden of proof, and then support so-called experiments that cannot deliver it. Choice advocates should point out that "there is *no* historical experience indicating that government has a comparative advantage in the *production* [italics in the original] of goods and services."[3]

COMPETITION: TRIED AND TRUE

Competitive markets have an outstanding track record.[4] Industries struggle when competition is weak, and flourish when it is strong. Countries that increase the domain of market forces prosper, while countries that expand the government's economic planning role suffer, often to the point of stagnation and collapse.

Education markets will have relatively few of the well-known—though quite rare—potential limitations of markets, such as poorly informed buyers, fraud, and harmful side effects. Consumers are typically well informed when it comes to recurrent, big-ticket purchases like tuition. Schools will struggle to establish and maintain the good reputations that many education shoppers already rely on, especially in higher education.

The specific track record of competitive education industries, though small and historically scattered, is outstanding. Samuel Blumenfeld,[5] Andrew Coulson,[6] and E. G. West[7] studied the United States' pre-"public" school, competitive education industry era (before 1840). Curricula were challenging, and literacy rates were high, even though many low-income families had to rely on charity for their children's education. Coulson also examined history's other competitive education industries, not expecting the history of civilization to speak so unequivocally in favor of competitive education systems. His finding that "free educational markets have consistently done a better job of serving the public's needs than state-run school systems have" was contrary to his self-described centrist political beliefs.

"PUBLIC" SCHOOL AUTOPSY

What happens without competition is also significant evidence. The effects include the unacceptable results of the status quo and the apparent futility of reforms that do not harness market forces.[8] Evidence that the certainties associated with the status quo are much more dangerous than the uncertain effects of a competitive education industry is an important complement to the general track record of competition and the historical evidence of competition in K–12 education.

The children who started school when *A Nation at Risk*[9] appeared in 1983 have graduated already, or dropped out of schools that even prominent Democrats say are "a disaster."[10] Reforms have left the governance and funding systems intact, and the nation is still at risk. Failure to implement a major transformation guarantees major losses. Taking the time to design, implement, and run experiments means another generation of poorly educated children.

Because "stories of academic mediocrity have become so common that they have lost power to shock,"[11] only a few horror stories follow. More exist elsewhere.[12] "By the fifth grade the *best* [emphasis in the original] American schools had lower scores than the worst schools from China, Taiwan, and Japan."[13] *Education Week* reported 1994 and 1996 data for fourth and eighth grade mathematics, science, and reading skills from the National Assessment of Educational Progress. Twenty-three percent of U.S. eighth grade children were proficient in math, and 39 percent had below basic skills. Forty-one percent of fourth graders were below basic readers, an omen of years of underachievement to follow. No state had more than 41 percent of children with proficiency in any subject at either grade level.[14]

For decades, taxpayers have spent thousands of dollars per student per year, yet a "literacy study flunks nearly half of adults."[15] "Sixty-six percent of 17-year-olds cannot read at a proficient level."[16] Businesses must teach new employees basic skills. Forty-three percent of companies provided remedial academic instruction in 1995.[17] Employability is a bigger concern than unemployment,[18] and businesses and universities must import skilled talent, especially in mathematics- and science-related fields.

Some states have celebrated modest gains in still-dismal test scores, but other indicators suggest causes other than school improvements. For example, the two college admission tests do not tell the same tale. ACT gains did not accompany SAT score gains. The SAT gains occurred after a revision of the test that some analysts said would make it easier, especially for top students.[19] Use of college remedial courses continues to increase. In Texas, the increased importance of the Texas Assessment of Academic Skills (TAAS) test—the tenth grade test is a high school graduation requirement—led to more lesson targeting (teaching the test) and greater use of prep firms.[20] That apparently raised TAAS scores, but not academic skills. Businesses did not report improved skills in their entry-level applicants, and universities spend more than ever on remedial courses.

There are more subtle indicators of failure. Recall from chapter 3 the allegations that "competition" forced Milwaukee Public Schools (MPS) to improve. The first claim accompanied the 1990 enactment of Milwaukee's voucher program. Pete DuPont (former governor and presidential candidate) claimed that MPS's fear of the voucher program had already led to major reforms.[21] MPS Superintendent Robert Peterkin denounced the claim, insisting that the reforms cited by DuPont began in 1987, well before the voucher issue arose. Note that despite the 1987 reforms and others, MPS barely averted a June 2000 state takeover. The story is typical. Academic outcomes did not improve significantly anywhere in the United States despite the enormous pressure that came from "public" schools' status as the nation's number one political issue.[22] Prominent education author/analyst Eric Hanushek pointed out that "we have been in the midst of reform for decades,"[23] and longtime author/analyst Seymour Sarason found that "whatever remedial measures were taken, . . . the system seemed intractable to change."[24]

Important evidence, and a key reason for persistent disappointment, is "public" school leaders' discomfort with—even hostility toward—success stories. When a school stands out, the public asks why every school is not that good. That embarrasses the system's leaders. Success stories create demands for duplication, which means change and more work for the same paycheck. Major changes, especially those involving funding and governance, arouse hostility by disturbing the existing power structure.[25] Recognition means endangerment, not duplication. "Short-lived success stories help breed cynicism about public institutions."[26] In one especially telling example, an incoming district superintendent eliminated an innovative elementary school with an undisputed record of success with an at-risk population. The new superintendent dismissed the school's teacher-director and merged it with a more traditional school because "the school was too autonomous, that its efforts to maintain a racial balance and its insistence on being different made it elitist, too much like a private school."[27]

Energetic reformers are endangered, too. Significant changes in operating procedures produce an *Empire Strikes Back* reaction. Former superintendents Anthony Trujillo (Ysleta District of El Paso, Texas) and Diana Lam (San Antonio District, Texas) made major changes and achieved improved test scores. The Ysleta improvements were especially spectacular.[28] Trujillo was practically lionized by school reform observers across the political spectrum. When Trujillo and Lam were fired, at considerable cost to taxpayers, both blamed the political power of teachers unions and union opposition to teacher accountability. Despite his ability to achieve noteworthy results within the current system, Trujillo said "the system is rotten"; that productive reforms will not spread and persist without [unspecified] governance system change. Along with a number of teachers and school administrators, Trujillo signed a *Statement of Principles* that included: "A market-based education system will expand educational options for families, employment opportunities for teachers, and will reward entrepreneurship. American education should use a system in which the best new approaches to teaching and learning can emerge from the marketplace of ideas."[29]

The disappointing results of past reform efforts are strong evidence that the current funding and governance system will not only continue to resist repair, but deteriorate further: "The striking thing is the opposite directions of the spending and achievement results: less spending, more student achievement. Of course, this has powerful implications for productivity."[30] Those outcomes are consistent with National Urban League president Hugh Price's belief, "That politicians and school administrators are going about the business of improving things exactly backwards."[31] Rexford Brown assailed a widespread, underachievement-assuring definition of success: "Success in urban school districts is often defined as the avoidance of large-scale violence. Think what it would be like to work in a company whose managers define success as the absence of an angry mob of customers sacking the store and assaulting the employees."[32] Teachers frequently define success within those limitations: "We're doing a good job. You can go to any other district and see they are having the same type of problems."[33]

Milwaukee, like virtually everyplace else that has acknowledged its unacceptable academic outcomes, describes its reform efforts in terms such as "decades of frustration."[34] Desperation over persistent academic deficiencies has led to state takeovers in many cities.[35] The public still tolerates seemingly futile attempts to reform a reform-resistant system because we are "socialized to regard the system as if it had been given to us on an educational Mount Sinai."[36] The means—taxpayer support of "public" schools—are widely confused with the goal of educating children. That persistent futility even has a catchy name that captures its futility: "More-of-the-Same-Harder—the MOTS-H approach"[37] Richard Sherlock's assessment attaches some optimism to the perceived futility of most current reform efforts: "This [reform effort] is a no win game that will continue its divisive spiral until the exhausted parties recognize the solution that lies before them: true [universal, full] school choice."[38]

Seymour Sarason[39] conducted countless interviews with educators, foundation executives, and U.S. Department of Education officials and couldn't find anyone who believed that the current governance system closely resembled their ideal system. Despite such feelings, and harsh criticism, the current governance system has immense staying power. Choice opponents claim that experience with choice justifies abandonment of choice-based reforms, even though the track record of current governance and funding practices is much worse.[40]

Many families are fed up with every choice offered by the status quo. They are incurring enormous expenses and inconvenience to abandon the system through home schooling. There is incredible growth in home schooling,[41] including by parents who can afford most private schools.

According to some choice opponents, a "market-based system of schooling would destroy the few democratic gains made in public education in recent decades."[42] Though that harsh backhanded condemnation of political control is inconsistent with choice opponents' glowing praise of "democracy,"[43] it is consistent with achievement data and the opponents' fear of parental choice. Choice opponents equate vouchers with "public" school abandonment,[44] so they apparently don't believe that "democratic gains" through the political process include choiceworthiness. "The education standards movement is gaining momentum"[45] means that one has to set up semipermanent political organizations to lobby for high standards, and that there is considerable resistance to these high standards.

Parental involvement is low, despite the high cost of removing children from "public" schools and pressure to exercise "responsibility to get involved in public schools."[46] Lack of support from educators, not lack of interest by parents is to blame for parents' apathy.[47] Parental choice, not assignment to a school, fosters involvement, because the choice-making process empowers parents and matches school characteristics and family preferences.

Perhaps "democratic control" is a contradiction? Political accountability can only create indirect accountability of educators to children and their parents, and in our current system, "accountability is so diffused that no one is accountable."[48] That diverts enormous resources from classrooms to political/administrative processes. Recall the Organization for Economic Cooperation and Development (OECD) study[49] that found that our "public" schools employ four nonteaching staff per three classroom teachers, the highest ratio in the survey of OECD members, and, despite those numbers, or because of the system, good administrators are scarce.[50] Among OECD members, the average was two nonteaching staff per five teachers. Though no OECD member has a competitive education industry, most OECD members allow more parental choice and school-based decision making than the United States. In addition, many of the countries that outperform U.S. students consistently are also quite unhappy with their academic outcomes. Major reform of their school systems is one of their top priorities.[51]

Choice opponent Alex Molnar bemoans unequal funding, which he blames on conservative politics;[52] an incredible claim for three reasons. Molnar's claim was in a book that included an interview with Jonathan Kozol, who documented *Savage Inequalities*[53] in the 1980s. The Reagan administration didn't create the "inequalities"; they evolved over decades of political control, including especially the post-Depression decades of confidence in "big government" and mistrust of the market.[54] Second, Molnar's condemnation of political outcomes is inconsistent with his claim that the political process reflects the will of the people much better than a market can. Third, as chapter 6 argues more extensively, very well-funded schools often do very poorly,[55] and most of the better schools are still not very good.

CURRENT EXPERIENCE AND EVIDENCE

What can we learn from the current limited parental choice programs, including the parental choice that exists in other countries? There is some rivalry in Cleveland and Milwaukee, and some competitive behavior abroad, but there is no competitive education industry anywhere. Chile has a universal voucher program. Nongovernment schools receive considerable taxpayer support in countries like Australia and the Netherlands. The exercise of some degree of choice, and the resulting absence of a common, politically chosen education experience, has not destroyed the social and political fabric of those countries.

In most states, parents don't have the data to compare their "public" school to other schools or to an objective achievement standard. Still, many families are unhappy with their assigned school. They want genuine choices. The condescending claims[56] of choice opponents that parents can't make good choices are false and disingenuous. Even without parent information centers, many parents think they can use choice to improve the welfare of their children, even with the limited options available in the current system. The information deficiencies that exist in most states are no accident. A handful of states have already shown that existing raw data can be converted into the critical school-level data that parents want.

The limited data indicate that even small vouchers will induce the formation of new private schools.[57] In Cleveland, a $2,350 voucher was enough to attract private school entrepreneurs. This book advocates equal public support of all equally situated children, so market entry for $2,350 per student is noteworthy because it

is strong evidence that the current system is inefficient. It means that there are entrepreneurs who believe they can produce a competitive product for much less
than what the "public" school system spends per child. Market entry for much less
than the current public expenditure per child hints that an entrepreneurial explosion will result from universal parental choice funded with the tax money currently earmarked for K–12 education.

The effects of Chile's voucher program, Australia's experience, and a model developed by Dennis Epple and Richard Romano[58] illustrate why taxpayers should
fund a high minimum level[59] of support for every equally situated child. Since key
features of Chile's program and the Epple and Romano model are similar, the discussion below focuses on the Chilean policy. Chile funds a system of municipal
("public") schools directly, and a small voucher is available to every child. Middle-
and upper-class families typically use the vouchers to help pay private school tuition.[60] Lower-income families have to choose between the municipal schools
abandoned by everyone else and the least expensive private schools.

Municipal schools' guaranteed funding reduces their incentive to perform at a
high level, and neglect by the affluent who can escape them further reduces the
schools' ability to perform at a high level. That the gap between the educational
haves and have-nots is widening is an unfortunate situation, but it is not necessarily due to the voucher program. After all, no system can eliminate the direct
(ability to pay tuition) and indirect (home environment) advantages of wealth.
Also, the wider gap doesn't mean that low-income children are learning less than
they would otherwise.

As the United States illustrates—school improvement is a top political issue,
yet improvements are scant—political activity does not ensure improvement.
However, political inactivity probably ensures that improvement will not occur.
Chile's voucher option may have made Chile's municipal schools worse by reduc-
ing political activism among the upper- and middle-income families' who are able
to supplement the vouchers with their own money. Because it allowed many families to escape, the voucher option reduced the cost of political indifference to
Chile's municipal schools. Eliminating the vouchers isn't the solution. The answer
is higher minimum public support per child: spend school taxes only through the
vouchers, and fund children rather separate school systems. Stop the direct funding of the government-owned municipal schools, and use that money, and perhaps more, to increase the value of the vouchers.

Means testing the value of vouchers isn't the answer either. There is a fairness
issue (chapter 10 has more details). Parents deserve a direct return on their school
taxes, especially those who pay the most. Even regressive tax systems usually extract much more money from wealthier families. Also, varying benefits by income
makes the policy an income redistribution program, not an education program,
and it raises a compelling practical issue. The political process typically ensures

that programs for the poor (when low-income families contribute relatively little and receive relatively more) become poor programs.[61]

Similar issues arise in parts of Maine and Vermont where local authorities pay tuition at schools parents choose, instead of building neighborhood schools. Some fine private schools serve those students. Frank Murray[62] says that "public" schools' failure to respond to assumed competitive pressures indicates that "choice" is not such a great idea. Murray's conclusion is flawed for at least two reasons. First, it's an unwarranted generalization because the Maine-Vermont version of parental choice doesn't create much competitive pressure. Since the choices don't greatly affect the financial well-being of the Maine and Vermont "public" schools, they have little to gain or lose from pursuing competitiveness, or failing to do so. Second, the reaction and fate of "public" schools is not the critical outcome. The "public" school response matters in the long run only if families are penalized for going elsewhere—that is, if some children are stuck there. If every family can exercise choice without financial penalty, "public" school failure to improve just means that more choiceworthy private schools gradually will replace them. Howard Fuller supports parental choice, including vouchers, even though (and, perhaps, also because) his experience as MPS superintendent convinced him that "public" school systems won't muster significant competitive behavior.[63] Fuller said "public" school systems can't overcome their restrictions, even if their survival is in jeopardy, and no such jeopardy exists in Maine or Vermont. Fuller believes that vouchers are the best way to help children, even if they cause parents to gradually abandon "public" schools.

Michael Fine's observation supports Fuller's conclusion that "public" schools won't muster competitive behavior, but Fine matched Murray's faulty analysis. According to Fine, the failure of Philadelphia's "public" schools to improve, even though 36 percent of Philadelphia schools are private, is evidence that competition won't "breed quality education."[64] As in Maine and Vermont, the problem in Philadelphia is that "public" schools are still certain they will have many students, and a large amount of funding per student. Philadelphia private schools' ability to compete—strong as it already is—is still diminished significantly by the "public" schools' access to equal or better funding per student without having to charge tuition. Some rivalry and a few footloose buyers aren't enough to establish market conditions.

Interpretation of evidence depends on political ideology. The role of political ideology in the school choice wars is the subject of the next chapter.

NOTES

1. Samuel Blumenfeld, *Is Public Education Necessary?* (Boise, Idaho: The Paradigm Company, 1981); Andrew Coulson, *Market Education* (New Brunswick, N.J.: Transaction Publishers, 1999).

2. Quentin Quade, *Financing Education* (New Brunswick, N.J.: Transaction Publishers, 1996): p. 131.

3. Herbert Gintis, "The Political Economy of School Choice," *Teachers College Record* 96, no. 3 (Spring 1995): 503.

4. The countries with the greatest reliance on markets, are the wealthiest and have the most rapid growth rates. See the data and discussion in Kim R. Holmes, "In Search of Free Markets," *Wall Street Journal* (December 12, 1994); *Wall Street Journal* editorial board, "Free to Grow," *Wall Street Journal* (September 3, 1996); Andrei Shleifer, "State versus Private Ownership," *Journal of Economic Perspectives* 12, no. 4 (Fall 1998): 133–50. Most of the information is general, coming primarily from outside of education service industries. However, many countries have moderately competitive education industries—for example, Australia and Chile.

5. Blumenfeld, 1981.

6. Coulson, 1999.

7. E. G. West, *Education and the State*, 3rd edition (Indianapolis: Liberty Fund, 1994).

8. That futility needs much more systematic documentation, which would be a significant choice advocacy weapon. Still, there is much published evidence of reform futility. Some of it is discussed later in this chapter. Also see Frederick Hess, *Spinning Wheels: The Politics of Urban School Reform* (Washington: Brookings Institution, 1999).

9. National Commission on Excellence in Education, *A Nation at Risk: The Imperative for Educational Reform* (Washington: U.S. Department of Education, 1983).

10. California Governor Gray Davis quoted in David Broder, "Reforming Education a Tough Assignment," *San Antonio Express-News* (March 2, 1999): 7B; U.S. Senator Joseph Lieberman (D-CT) quoted by Nina H. Shokraii, "What People Are Saying about School Choice," *The Heritage Foundation Backgrounder* 1188 (June 2, 1998); David Kirkpatrick, *School Choice: The Idea That Will Not Die* (Mesa, Ariz.: Bluebird Publishing, 1997).

11. Dan Coats, "The Bell Is Sounding for School Choice: DC Example Shows Why Support for It Is Growing inside Congress," *Roll Call* (June 2, 1997): 10.

12. See pp. 139–48 of Joseph Murphy, *The Privatization of Schooling* (Thousand Oaks, Calif.: Corwin Press, 1996), for many more examples.

13. Harold W. Stevenson, "Learning from Asian Schools," *Scientific American* 267, no. 6 (December 1992): 70–76.

14. January, 2000 "Quality Counts," special issue of *Education Week*.

15. A front-page headline of the September 9, 1993, *San Antonio Express-News*.

16. Cal Thomas, "No Brainer to See Education Is Failing," *San Antonio Express-News* (July 15, 1996).

17. George Clowes, "Interview with Andrew Coulson on Computers in K–12 Classrooms," *School Reform News* (April 2000): 10–11.

18. Bernard Avishai, "Companies Can't Make Up for Failing Schools," *Wall Street Journal* (July 29, 1996).

19. Bruno V. Manno, "The Real Score on the SATs," *Wall Street Journal* (September 13, 1995).

20. Michael Totty and Anne Reifenberg, "Fear of TAAS Scores Has Prep Firms Booming," *Wall Street Journal* (April 29, 1998): T1, T3.

21. Robert Peterkin, "Choice and Public School Reform" in: Robert Lowe and Barbara Miner (eds.), *Selling Out Our Schools* (Milwaukee, Wisc.: Rethinking Schools, 1996), p. 29.

22. The latest poll to confirm that fact is the Kaiser Family Foundation and Harvard University Survey cited on p. 30 of the October 21, 1998, issue of *Education Week*. According to the

Public Agenda Foundation ("Given the Circumstances: Teachers Talk about Public Education Today, 1996"), "recent polls show that education has jumped to the top of the list of public concerns."

23. Eric A. Hanushek, "Why True Reform of Schools Is So Unlikely," *Jobs and Capital* (Winter 1997): 23–27.

24. Seymour B. Sarason, *How Schools Might be Governed and Why* (New York: Teachers College Press, 1997), p. xii.

25. Seymour B. Sarason, *The Predictable Failure of Educational Reform* (San Francisco: Jossey-Bass Publishers, 1990).

26. Deborah W. Meier, "The Little Schools That Could," *The Nation* (September 23, 1991): 1, 338.

27. Ibid.

28. Anthony Trujillo interview, "Wall-to-Wall, for All Children," *School Reform News* (February 1999): 20, 16.

29. Maintained on the Children's Scholarship Fund Web site, *www.teachersvoice.org/principles.asp*.

30. Caroline Hoxby quoted in Robert J. Barro, "Can Public Schools Take Competition?" *Wall Street Journal* (March 10, 1997).

31. Hugh B. Price, "Establish an Academic Bill of Rights," *Education Week* (March 17, 1999): 54–55, 76.

32. Rexford G. Brown, *Schools of Thought* (San Francisco: Jossey-Bass, 1993), p. 137.

33. Mark Walsh, "Ground Zero for Vouchers," *Education Week* (March 17, 1999): 46–51.

34. Kerry A. White, "Ahead of the Curve," *Education Week* (January 13, 1999): 34.

35. There have been 19 such takeovers since 1988, including Baltimore, Boston, Chicago, Cleveland, Hartford, Newark, and Washington, D.C. (*School Reform News* [May, 1999]: 5).

36. Sarason, 1997, p. 39.

37. Wayne B. Jennings, "Let's Ride the Wave of Change," *Enterprising Educators* 6, no. 2 (Spring 1998): 1.

38. Richard Sherlock, "Choice v. Conflict in Education," *A Sutherland Institute Policy Perspective* (August 27, 1996).

39. Sarason, 1997, p. x.

40. TSTA/NEA, *Our Public Schools: The Best Choice for Texas*, Mimeographed (1994): 29. The report alleges that since parental choice (only very limited versions were examined) didn't increase voucher students' test scores, choice-based reform is unproductive, and should be abandoned. See also, note 11 in chapter 3.

41. Mark Brandly, "Home Schooling Leaps into the Spotlight," *Wall Street Journal* (June 9, 1997); "Explosion in Home Schooling," *U.S. News & World Report* (February 12, 1996): 57–58.

42. Robert Lowe and Barbara Miner in Robert Lowe and Barbara Miner (eds.), *Selling Out Our Schools* (Milwaukee, Wisc.: Rethinking Schools, 1996), p. 3.

43. There is much discussion of the importance of "democracy," which is virtually nonexistent and quite different from our form of government, a representative republic.

44. According to National Education Association President Bob Chase, "Vouchers would be the final, brutal act of abandonment." ("An Idea Conservatives Could Dislike," *The Beacon Journal* [September 19, 1997]: A15).

45. Price, 1999.

46. Lowe and Miner, 1996, p. 14.

47. A. P. Dixon, " Parents: Full Partners in the Decision Making Process." *NASSP Bulletin* (April 1992): 15–18; R. K. Pierce, *What Are We Trying to Teach Them Anyway?* (San Francisco: Institute for Contemporary Studies, 1993).

48. Sarason, 1997, p. 36.

49. OECD. *Education at a Glance: OECD Indicators* (Paris: Author, 1995): pp. 176–77.

50. Lynn Olson, "Policy Focus Converges on Leadership," *Education Week* (January 12, 2000): 1, 16–17.

51. H. Beare and W. L. Boyd (eds.), *Restructuring Schools* (Washington and London: The Falmer Press, 1993).

52. Alex Molnar, "School Reform: Will Markets or Democracy Prevail?" in Lowe and Barbara Miner, 1996, 16–17.

53. Jonathan Kozol, *Savage Inequalities: Children in America's Schools* (New York: Harper Perennial, 1992).

54. Daniel Yergin and Joseph Stanislaw, *The Commanding Heights* (New York: Simon and Schuster, 1998).

55. American Legislative Council, *You Can't Buy Higher Grades: 50-State Report Card on American Education Funds* (April, 2000).

56. For example, State Senator Greg Luna's (D-San Antonio) comment that his low-income constituents were incapable of making informed school choices (*San Antonio Express-News* editorial, "Legislators: Don't Hold Consolidation Hostage" [April 18, 1997]).

57. Bob Davis. "Dueling Professors Have Milwaukee Dazed over School Vouchers," *Wall Street Journal* (October 11, 1996): A1.

58. Dennis Epple and Richard E. Romano, "Competition between Private and Public Schools, Vouchers, and Peer-Group Effects," *American Economic Review* 88 (March 1998): 33–62.

59. Defined previously as enough to induce—because of competition—many schools to accept the public funding as full, or nearly full, payment.

60. Martin Carnoy, "Lessons of Chile's Voucher Reform Movement" in Lowe and Miner, 1996, pp. 26–27.

61. This insightful phrase surfaces frequently. Milton Friedman said he heard it in a 1972 debate on Social Security from Wilbur Cohen, Secretary of Health, Education, and Welfare during the Johnson administration ("Polemics and Exchanges," *Chronicles* [December 1998]).

62. Frank B. Murray, "What's So Good About Choice?" *Education Week* (January 27, 1999): 52.

63. Ronald Wolk, "What Is Best for the Children?" *Education Week* (November 4, 1998): 47.

64. Michael Fine, "Democratizing Choice," in Edith Rasell and Richard Rothstein (eds.), *School Choice: Examining the Evidence* (Washington: Economic Policy Institute, 1993), p. 270.

2 Issues in the Debate over Parental Choice

CHAPTER 5

Liberal/Conservative Role Reversal

Senate Minority Leader Tom Daschle (D-SD) described two definitions of freedom at the 1996 Democrat National Convention—definitions crystallized by political theorists some time ago. Daschle said Democrats define freedom as empowerment, not just legal rights, but the ability to do things. Liberals see legal rights as meaningless without the financial means to exercise them. To conservatives (an umbrella term for parties that advocate lower taxes and less government), freedom means an absence of government restrictions. Those two versions of freedom are often in direct conflict. Financial empowerment through the political process means the freedom to take and spend other people's earnings. Increased freedom from taxation means less financial empowerment through transfer payments.

The liberal and conservative sides in the school choice wars seem to contradict their positions on other issues. Conservatives want to use tax dollars to subsidize access to private schools through vouchers and tax credits. Liberals want to deny the financial empowerment that vouchers and tax credits would provide.

CONTRADICTION OF THE LIBERAL POSITION

Liberals seek more equal access to goods and services through taxation, including education programs offered by businesses. In his 1998 State of the Union speech, President Clinton said—all in the same breath—that parental choice should be limited to "public" schools, but that taxpayers should help finance adults' freedom to seek job training or go to the public or private college of their choice.

Taxes pay for job training—education supplied by businesses—and liberals supported the GI Bill that helped millions attend virtually any college. Food stamps increase low-income families' access to food. Medicare and Medicaid broaden access to private medical services. Social Security increases senior citizens' access to goods and services.[1] Low-income families have access to legal aid. Tax dollars empower low-income women to exercise their freedom to have an abortion. Taxpayers subsidize child-care expenses. Those programs create freedom, defined as the power to do things. In contrast, the liberal defense of the government-owned schools' monopoly on public support strictly upholds the definition of freedom as the absence of government restraint. The government does not keep you from home schooling your children or sending them to private schools. If you can't afford private school tuition in addition to school taxes, that is regrettable, but your inability does not infringe on your freedoms.

Daschle's discussion of freedom put him in a precarious position on parental choice, but choice advocates didn't take advantage of it. Deroy Murdock did note a similar inconsistency by Vice President Al Gore.[2] Neither Vice President Gore nor Senator Daschle can support parents' freedom to select education services for their children, because such a stand would alienate the teacher unions—a major Democratic constituency. Teacher unions fiercely oppose parental choice; even partial deregulation of some "public" schools (i.e., charter schools), or a minimal tax credit for private schooling. Richard Riley, the Clinton administration's Secretary of Education, said some "public" schools are so badly broken that they "should never be called schools at all,"[3] yet many prominent liberals won't even allow transfers to other "public" schools. Arthur Levine said "no parent should be forced to send a child to such a school [deplorable "schools" that had resisted 15 years of intense improvement efforts],"[4] but liberals require someone's children to attend every "public" school.

Children from low-income families typically attend the least effective "public" schools. They need freedom to attend a private school more than anyone, but they have a better chance of attending Stanford University, where financial aid is available, including aid funded by taxpayers. For example, when 1,300 privately funded, low-income partial tuition vouchers became available in New York City for the 1997–98 school year, parents filed applications for more than 17,000 children.[5] The odds against getting one of the vouchers were literally "greater than the odds of getting into Stanford."[6] Applicants for the Children's Scholarship Fund (CSF) private voucher initiative faced even longer odds. When the CSF offered 40,000 partial tuition vouchers to low-income families, it received 1.25 million requests.[7]

Nearly monolithic Democratic Party opposition to parental choice programs, even weak versions that don't create any competition, contradicts liberal rhetoric on individual liberty, diversity, and experimentation. Jonathan Rauch said: "I've always found it a little odd that liberals hand the voucher idea to Republicans. For poor children trapped in execrable schools, the case [for vouchers] is moral rather than merely educational."[8] Charles Wheelan said, "It's illogical for Democrats to be against vouchers."[9] According to Cal Thomas, "Normally, this [parental choice] would be an ideal issue for liberals, who regularly wail against the 'unfair advantages' enjoyed by 'the rich.'"[10] Daniel Akst made an increasingly common assertion that the financial penalty for choosing a private school undermines the traditional liberal assault on segregation. That penalty increases migration to the suburbs, so "lack of choice in schooling has helped segregate our cities and keeps them segregated."[11] Bruce Goldberg offered *A Liberal Argument for School Choice,* including this brutal critique: "America's schools are failures because they systematically suppress children's interests, values, and idiosyncratic potentials. The denial of individuality—the idea that everyone must follow the same general plan—lies at the core of the ["public"] schools' failure. Today's public school system, despite its lip service to diversity, is fundamentally at war with individuality. And that is why it is failing."[12] The case for a competitive education industry doesn't require agreement with Goldberg, but his widely shared opinion illustrates the contradiction of other liberal policy positions.

The public critics include some liberals. Ira Cutler said, "I would favor it [parental choice] as a matter of individual rights, even if most public schools were excellent."[13] Senator Daniel Moynihan (D-NY) noted that: "In the late 1960s, educational vouchers were generally regarded as a progressive proposal. All liberal faculty members would wish to be associated with it. If it [educational vouchers] prevails only as a conservative cause, it will have been a great failure of American liberalism."[14]

The liberal contradiction does not exist in countries that are arguably much more liberal than the United States. The European republics pursue financial empowerment through transfer payments much more than we do, and many comfortably fund education in whatever kind of institution their parents choose. "Ours is the only advanced democracy that does not provide public funds for children to attend private schools."[15] In virtually every industrial democracy, children can even receive public support to attend church-run schools.

Liberals are willing to test controversial, underinvestigated curricula and pedagogical theories on millions of children,[16] but they vehemently oppose much smaller tests of theoretically sound governance and funding methods. One large town is enough of a "laboratory" to test a competitive education industry, as defined by the characteristics discussed in chapter 2. Freedom and competition are time-tested ingredients of success and vitality, and there are regions where the "public" schools are so bad that only certain school employees have anything to lose from even ill-conceived experiments.[17]

The decision to create a government-run school system did not begin with a careful study of alternate means of delivering education services. The "public" school system started with wishful thinking, not sound research. The current system evolved from a mid-1800s Protestant bias against Catholic Schools (chapter 11 has more details).[18] The Protestant-dominated political leadership wanted to deny Catholic schools access to the public support Protestant schools received. They accomplished this by creating "public" schools infused with Protestant beliefs. Private schools became less popular because very few could compete with a free service.

The current system survives politically, even though it lacks an intellectually sound justification, and despite economic and demographic trends that make government-run systems less appropriate. Teachers' unions, the largest element of the Democratic Party, are the current system's key defenders.[19] The public funding monopoly of "public" schools is a contradiction of other liberal policy positions. It survives because most politically active teachers believe the union leadership's assertion that the current funding and governance system is better for teachers than the well-known alternatives. Chapter 14 challenges that assertion and explains how prominent choice advocates unwittingly help teachers' union leaders galvanize teacher opposition to parental choice.

CONTRADICTION OF THE CONSERVATIVE POSITION

A few staunch conservatives avoid the contradiction that exists for most conservatives. They oppose public support for parental choice because they argue that increased government funding of private schools moves policy in the wrong direction. Those conservatives, especially the libertarians, want a complete separation of politics from K–12 education. They fear that even indirect government funding will deprivatize private schools (chapter 7 has more details).

However, many conservatives want taxpayers to support parental choice, an apparent contradiction of many of their other policy positions. After all, they oppose transfer payments for higher education, housing, health care, food stamps, and other social services. While this inconsistency is troublesome to conservatives, they defend it as a way to reduce government management of schools, a step toward the conservative ideal of more limited government. Indeed, the conditions that underlie the case for housing vouchers are nearly identical to the "public" school conditions that underlie the interest in K–12 reform, including parental choice. Rising costs and widespread dissatisfaction with typical outcomes characterize both.

THE CONTRADICTIONS ARE COSTLY

The status quo is contrary to the ideals of liberals and conservatives, and it's not because of compromise. Conservatives oppose the K–12 status quo, but prominent parental choice proposals assume its key elements. So few conservatives remember that genuine competition for the benefit of all children is a key argument for parental choice, or the majority of them dismissed universal choice as an unrealistic goal, that nearly all choice proposals are extremely limited. Virtually every discussion assumes that parental choice means a limited number of transfers within a largely unchanged governance and funding status quo.[20] As a result, a frequently cited argument against parental choice is that it only affects a few students![21]

Incredibly, and tragically, choice opponents talk about all the children more than most choice advocates do. The opponents of the 2000 Michigan voucher ballot initiative named their campaign "All Kids First!" to highlight that the "Kids First! Yes!" proposal would directly affect only the worst school districts.[22] National Education Association general counsel Robert Chanin said the "problems of urban school districts cannot be solved by schemes [the expanded Milwaukee program] that skim off 5,000–15,000, but leave 85,000–95,000 behind."[23] New York City Schools chancellor Rudy Crew "criticized the parental choice program for serving only a tenth of the students in Milwaukee."[24] Top Clinton administration officials, including Education Secretary Richard Riley,[25] Assistant Education Secretary Gerald Tirozzi,[26] and Riley aide Terry Peterson[27] made similar statements. During a debate with William Bennett (a Reagan administration Secretary of Education and prominent choice advocate), Riley conceded that a proposed Washington, D.C., voucher program would leave the vast majority of children in inadequate schools.[28] Bennett was appropriately outraged ("there is no moral defense for keeping students in these lousy, rotten schools"), but part of Bennett's reply was very disappointing. He didn't note that the solution was choice for all children. Instead, Bennett reacted with: "It's a very odd argument that unless we can help everybody, then we will help no one."[29] Such weak replies to choice opponents' objection to limited parental choice are so commonplace that the objection was named after a well-known disaster. It is called the "if the *Titanic* doesn't have enough lifeboats for everybody, nobody should use one" argument.[30] The perception of choice as a lifeboat, rather than a reform catalyst, is an especially unfortunate aspect of the school choice wars. Existing "public" school spending is enough to publicly fund universal choice at a very high level.

Political control of the "public" school system means that politics resolves building design, curriculum, textbook content, class size, teacher salaries and qualifications, and virtually everything else for about 88 percent of the student population, and it discourages private spending on formal schooling. The political decision-making burden, and the burden of high and rising school taxes, are major reasons why the contradiction is costly.[31] High tax rates reduce the incentive to work. That, and an undereducated workforce, lowers economic efficiency.[32] Mobile families also pay a hidden tax; housing costs rise when they compete for property in the attendance zones of better "public" schools.

The total burden is much larger than the impact on taxpaying households' purchasing power and the pressure to participate in policy making. In sharp contrast to the promises of the current system's founders that it would bring a diverse population closer together, it creates enormous social tensions that damage the collective decision-making process at all levels of government. It does so by forcing society to resolve contentious, divisive issues through politics that individuals could resolve for themselves.

Supposedly, middle- and upper-income families have choices because they can relocate or enroll their children in a private school. However, the current system distorts and reduces the quality of their choices, another major source of inefficiency. Most families assume that the better suburban "public" schools are good, when they usually are just not quite as bad (chapter 6 has more details). Because private schools[33] have to starve themselves to stay price competitive with "free" public schools, private schools are often not much more effective.

Liberals cannot celebrate the preservation of governance and funding methods that conservatives oppose. After all, liberals genuinely abhor the inequities—*Savage Inequalities*[34] in the words of Jonathan Kozol. Disadvantaged children need a good school the most, but the lowest-income families are the least mobile. Therefore, they end up in inner city schools that have the most problems, and that enroll a much higher percentage of low-income and minority children.[35] The process is self-reinforcing. The concentration of more affluent families around the better schools shifts the tax base and the most advantaged students to those schools. The more experienced teachers soon follow. Funding equalization lawsuits only address the tax base shift and, often, not very well, and only with significant negative side effects.[36]

Much is spent on "public" schools,[37] but the disadvantaged see the fewest benefits. "Public" schools' failure to specialize to any extent is especially regrettable in the inner city, where education challenges resulting from problems like drug abuse, crime, underage parents, and broken families are especially common. Instead of receiving the specialized services they need, disadvantaged children often end up in large inner city schools supposedly capable of serving a broad spectrum of needs and wants, schools widely seen as the nation's worst. It is impossible for any institution to be everything to everybody, and pursuit of the impossible can do more harm than good. The local property taxes and state taxes that support "public" schools are generally regressive,[38] so even the better inner city schools can cost nearby families more than the value of their children's minimal education.

Education services end up much less diverse than the interests and learning styles of the student population. "Public" schools can't specialize because specialization is not compatible with the assignment of children to schools through attendance zones. An open enrollment policy for "public" schools wouldn't increase specialization as much as a competitive education industry (CEI). CEI schools can specialize in controversial subjects like religion and offer controversial courses like sex education. In addition, some specializations entail additional work, a major barrier when there is no profit motive, merit pay, or competitive pressure to overcome resistance to it.

RESOLVING THE CONTRADICTION

Conservatives will begin resolving the contradiction when they act like a competitive education industry is their top priority. Their restrictive proposals contradict their claims that they desire competition. Once the competitive education industry is in place, the liberal-conservative debate should focus on regulation and tax-payers' share of education expenses. Liberals will seek more taxpayer funding and regulation than conservatives. The public funding issues are inequitable economic opportunity; inefficiency effects of taxation; the inefficiency of underconsumption of education services, especially by low-income families; and use of taxation to transfer purchasing power from some people to other people.

Buyers make better choices when they personally bear a larger share of the costs, so some conservatives want parents to bear a large share of the cost of educating their children. Many conservatives believe that transfers to low-income families should occur through charity rather than taxation. However, most conservatives don't have the libertarian faith that charity can supplement private spending on education adequately. Donor funding has many theoretical advantages over government funding,[39] but even if the advantages became compelling, there would still be compelling reasons to eliminate government participation slowly. The repeal of school taxes would provide much tax relief, but a large share of the benefits would go to households with no school-age children. All of the new tuition expense would fall on families with school-age children, an unbearable burden for many.

For most conservatives, the issue is the best mix of philanthropic and taxpayer support for low-income families and how best to target that support. Nondiscriminatory public support for mainstream[40] children will ensure broad-based political support for the program. Recall from chapter 4 that programs just for the poor become poor programs.[41]

Liberals and conservatives have different subject matter inclusion and exclusion agendas. For example, conservatives want time for prayer and greater discussion of values. Many conservatives argue that they are seeking less regulation of prayer, not more. They argue that misinterpretation of the Constitution is the reason for regulations that took prayer out of "public" school classrooms. Liberals want more open discussion of alternative lifestyles and environmental issues. Some conservatives strongly oppose the former, and they want more "balanced" discussion of the latter.

Liberals believe that children will develop a core of shared values (the common school concern—Chapter 11 has more details) only if the government chooses some of the content. Therefore, liberals typically prefer more mandated content. Conservatives argue that regulation can easily become excessive, and that it is unnecessary because the content that parents will demand will have the critical items.

Such was the debate and the education system of the United States, at least through the first half of the 19th century. There were few government-run schools, but private schools received some government assistance.

Milton Friedman's initial voucher proposals[42] launched a similar, but short-lived debate. Liberals were the first[43] to support the use of vouchers to remedy such problems as bureaucracy, inefficiency, stratification (segregation), and uneven distribution of resources. The current perception of problems and the impact of common misperceptions are the subjects of chapter 6.

NOTES

1. Social Security is a transfer payment between generations and income levels. Nearly all future retirees will get less from Social Security than if the payroll deductions had gone to a private pension fund. However, "some" low-income retirees will receive more, and the workers who neglect to save for retirement voluntarily get more from Social Security than they would have from a private pension.
2. Deroy Murdock, "Will Reinvented Gore Embrace Vouchers?" *Wall Street Journal* (June 21, 1999).
3. Secretary of Education Richard Riley quoted in Diane Ravitch, "Somebody's Children," *The Brookings Review* (1994).
4. Arthur Levine, "Why I'm Reluctantly Backing Vouchers," *Wall Street Journal* (June 15, 1998).
5. William J. Bennett, "School Reform: What Remains to Be Done," *Wall Street Journal* (September 2, 1997).
6. Susan Jacobsen, "School Choice: It's a Seller's Market," *Education Week* (October 1, 1997).
7. Jeff Archer, "Huge Demand for Private Vouchers Raises Questions," *Education Week* (April 28, 1999): 1, 12.
8. Jonathan Rauch in Nina H. Shokraii, "What People are Saying about School Choice," *The Heritage Foundation Backgrounder* 1188 (June 2, 1998): 4.
9. Charles Wheelan, "Turning the Tables on School Choice," *New York Times* (May 25, 1999): A31.
10. Cal Thomas, "School Choice Saves Children," *San Antonio Express-News* (June 15, 1998): 11A.
11. Daniel Akst, "Why Liberals Should Love School Choice," *Wall Street Journal* (April 6, 1998).
12. Bruce Goldberg, "A Liberal Argument for School Choice," *The American Enterprise* (September/October 1996): 26, 29.
13. Ira M. Cutler, "This Card-Carrying Liberal Endorses School Choice," *Education Week* (October 30, 1996).
14. David Kirkpatrick, School Choice Choir Has a Broad Range of Voices," *School Reform News* (July, 1999): 9.
15. Denis Doyle, "Vouchers in Religious Schools," *The Public Interest* (Spring 1997): 89.
16. Charles J. Sykes, *Dumbing Down Our Kids* (New York: St. Martins Press, 1995); E. D. Hirsch, Jr., *The Schools We Need* (New York: Doubleday, 1996). Additional examples are discussed in Andrew J. Coulson, *Market Education* (New Brunswick, N.J.: Transaction Publishers, 1999).
17. For example, Newark or Hartford, where the state education agency seized control of the schools, or Chicago, where the "public" schools were turned over to the mayor. In each case, per pupil funding was (and is) well above the national average. Regions where entrepreneurs were hired to manage some of the schools (see chapter 3) are also good candidates. The nation's capitol may be the best place of all. The District of Columbia's chief academic officer said (*School Reform News* [March 1998]: 3) her own system was responsible for "educational genocide." Eighty percent of students cannot read even at the basic level, and the children fall behind further the longer they are "educated."

18. Derek Neal, "Religion in the Schools: Measuring Catholic School Performance," *The Public Interest* (Spring 1997): 81–93.

19. Myron Lieberman, *The Teacher Unions* (New York: The Free Press, 1997).

20. The question and answer segment of Robert Lowe and Barbara Miner (eds.) "Selling Out Our Schools," special report of *Rethinking Schools*, an Urban Educational Journal: (*www. rethinkingschools.org*) in December 1998 is typical in that regard.

21. The latest prominent example: Carol Ascher and Richard Gray, "Substituting the Privilege of Choice for the Right to Equality," *Education Week* (June 2, 1999): 33, 44.

22. June Kronholz, "In Michigan, Amway Chief and Wife Give School Vouchers a Higher Profile," *Wall Street Journal* (October 25, 2000).

23. Mark Walsh, "Vouchers Face Key Legal Test in Wisconsin," *Education Week* (March 11, 1998).

24. "Two School Chiefs Talk about Vouchers," *School Reform News* (January 2000): 10.

25. Dorman E. Cordell, "Answering Objections to School Vouchers in D.C.," *National Center for Policy Analysis Brief Analysis* 266 (May 22, 1998): 1–2.

26. Gerald Tirozzi, "Vouchers: A Questionable Answer to an Unasked Question," *Education Week* (April 23, 1997): 64–65.

27. Tiffany Danitz, "Private Vouchers are Going Public," *Insight* (September 8, 1997): 15.

28. Cordell, May 22, 1998, p 2.

29. Ibid.

30. Ibid.

31. Based on average daily attendance, government-run schools cost $6,084 per pupil in 1994–95, an inflation-adjusted increase of 23 percent in 10 years, and those data are incomplete (see Myron Lieberman, *Public Education: An Autopsy* [Cambridge, Mass.: Harvard University Press, 1993] for details). The property taxes levied by the San Antonio Independent School District (where the author lives), which comprise less than one half of the district's budget, are more than twice all the other local property tax levies combined.

32. A National Association of Manufacturers study (*School Reform News* [March 1998]: 1) reported that 40 percent of 17-year-olds can't compute well enough, and more than 60 percent can't read well enough, to perform a production job in a modern auto plant. Employers must hire college graduates to get the skills that should have been learned in high school.

33. See the National Center for Education Statistics comparison of private and government schools ("How Do Private and Public Schools Differ?" 1997). Also see Albert Shanker and Bella Rosenberg in Simon Hakim, Paul Seidenstat, and Gary Bowman (eds.), *Privatizing Education and Educational Choice* (Westport, Conn.: Praeger Publishers, 1994). Both demonstrate that private schools achieve comparable to slightly better results for much less money per pupil. Shanker and Rosenberg say results are comparable and equally unacceptable. Ron Wolk ("What Is Best for the Children," *Education Week* [November 4, 1998]: 47) states the same conclusion.

34. Excellent examples include Jonathan Kozol, *Savage Inequalities* (New York: Harper Perennial, 1992); Lowe and Miner (eds.), December 1998; Carol Ascher and Richard Gray, "Substituting the Privilege of Choice for the Right to Equality," *Education Week* (June 2, 1999): 44, 33.

35. According to the latest data (1993–94) from the National Center for Education Statistics, African American and Hispanic children account for 53.8 percent of inner city school enrollment. Former Democratic Congressman Floyd Flake said (*School Reform News* [March 1998]: 3) black "children are being educationally killed every day in public schools."

36. The personal story of the Akst family ("Why Liberals Should Love School Choice," _Wall Street Journal_ [April 6, 1998]) is a good illustration of those side effects. Like millions of others, Mr. Akst is moving his family to the suburbs to get his children into a better school. It means more commuting time, natural resource consumption (car parts, energy), air pollution, and a diminished lifestyle. It also means economic segregation of neighborhoods and racial re-segregation of schools.

37. The total was 5.6% of GDP in 1995.

38. See the discussion of state and local tax regressivity in John Merrifield and Robert Collinge, "Efficient Water Pricing Policies as a Municipal Revenue Source," _Public Works Management and Policy_ (October 1999): 119–30.

39. Andrew J. Coulson, _Market Education_ (New Brunswick, N.J.: Transaction Publishers, 1999).

40. See note 11 of chapter 2 for a discussion of the term _mainstream student_.

41. This insightful phrase surfaces frequently. Milton Friedman said he heard it in a 1972 debate on Social Security from Wilbur Cohen, Secretary of Health, Education, and Welfare during the Johnson administration in "Polemics and Exchanges," _Chronicles_ (December 1998).

42. Milton Friedman, _Capitalism and Freedom_ (Chicago: University of Chicago Press, 1962); Milton Friedman, "The Role of Government in Education," in R. A. Solo (ed.), _Economics and the Public Interest_ (New Brunswick, N.J.: Rutgers University Press, 1955).

43. Douglas J. Lamdin and Michael Mintrom, "School Choice in Theory and Practice: Taking Stock and Looking Ahead," _Education Economics_ 5, no. 3 (1997): 211–42. See, for example: C. Jencks, "Is the Public School Obsolete?" _The Public Interest_ 2 (1966): 18–27; Laura H. Salganik, "The Rise and Fall of Education Vouchers," _Teachers College Record_ 83 (1981): 263; Frederick M. Hess, "Courting Backlash: The Risks of Emphasizing Input Equity over School Performance," _The Virginia Journal of Social Policy & the Law_ 6 (Fall 1998): 13.

CHAPTER 6

Fallacies about School Choice

"Whatever the dire circumstances, there are always those
who would rather risk peril than leave familiar surroundings."

— cartoon character Nacho Guarache (Leo Garza),
San Antonio Express-News (August 30, 1998)

This chapter is about serious intellectual deficiencies of the school reform debate. Each fallacy produces major policy-making errors, and they are also a major reason why arguments for parental choice are often counterproductive in the long run. Choice advocates created some of the fallacies, and they are partly responsible for the persistence of all of them. Each subtitle below states a fallacy.

ONLY A FEW SCHOOLS ARE BAD

A major fallacy is the assumption that the better schools are good schools. The most recent international comparison of students' math and science skills is the latest evidence that our best students are not very competitive.[1] Recall from chapter 4 that no state had more than 41 percent proficiency in any subject at either grade level tested.[2] A comparison of state math scores (North Dakota was number one), prompted former Assistant Secretary of Education Chester Finn to observe with general validity, "We are on various positions on the cellar stairs. Even the best students did miserably. At the top scoring schools, the average was well below grade level."[3] In Texas, schools escape the low-performing label if only 40 percent of their students pass a statewide, tenth grade minimum competency exam.[4] Until recently, the "standard" was 40 percent. School board members brag when two-thirds of the students at the district's top high school pass an easy math test.[5]

Chester Finn and Theodor Rebarber[6] cited the results of an especially informative National Assessment of Education Progress (NAEP) test question. It asked eleventh graders how much a borrower would owe after a year on a one-year, $850 loan with a 12 percent interest rate. Only 6 percent of the 11th graders knew to multiply $850 by 1.12, or to find 12 percent of $850 and add it to $850. There aren't very many good schools if 94 percent of the nation's high school juniors can't do that calculation.[7] In a 1992 survey of adult literacy, just 11 percent of U.S. high school graduates could restate in writing the main point of a newspaper article.[8]

Major deficiencies in suburban public schools are commonplace and well documented,[9] but they are often hidden[10] from a school's students and their parents. Opinion polls reflect the false sense of security. The polls indicate that a majority believes that most "public" schools are inadequate, but that the well-publicized deficiencies of the government-run system don't exist in their own schools.[11] According to the Manhattan Institute's John Miller, that's a major reason for the lopsided electoral defeats of voucher proposals: "Most suburbanites are happy with their kids' school systems. They admit the country's deep education crisis, but they just don't believe the problem affects them personally."[12] Perception and reality must differ. Most suburbanites cannot be in good schools when the country is in a deep education crisis.

The natural, but incorrect, assumption that top schools are good underlies the misperception of school quality. Rankings—often unpublished, informal, and impressionistic—strongly influence (usually the top factor) where people want to live.[13] In a *Wall Street Journal* editorial,[14] Daniel Akst said he'd move to the attendance area of a better suburban school when his children reached school age. Mr. Akst prefers his inner city home, so he must expect significant school improvement. A Denis Doyle and Douglas Munro[15] study demonstrates that the Akst story is common. Doyle and Munro found that expected change in school quality was a major reason for Baltimore's population decline, largely through relocation to suburbs.

The fallacy that top schools are necessarily good schools is dangerous for at least two reasons. First, it favors modest changes in the status quo and suggests that we should copy the better schools. Transfers to better schools are seen as "rescues," even though transferees are usually helped only slightly. This fallacy also produces parental choice programs like the recent Texas voucher proposals and the just-enacted Florida program[16] that focus on children enrolled in "low-performing" schools. In that kind of program, parental choice means that you can use some of the money earmarked for the education of your child if the government thinks your assigned "public" school is not good enough. In Florida, children become eligible for a voucher when two to four years of education negligence and malpractice are bad enough to make the government confess inadequacy.[17]

Second, parents able to relocate or who can afford private school tuition acquire a false sense of security. They put their children in a top school and assume that best at least means good. A better suburban school is not necessarily a good school. More often than not it is still inadequate. Former Assistant Secretary of Education Chester Finn said, "Millions of middle class children [are] emerging half-ignorant from suburban schools."[18]

Most of the private school sector is also inadequate. The "public" and private sectors have similar standardized test scores. An available and affordable but relatively resource-poor private school may be better than a family's assigned "public" school, but that doesn't make it a good school. The private school certainly would be better if it had similar per-student resources. Families like Mr. Akst's that have the financial means to choose from the existing school menu quite often still end up using bad schools.

The fallacy also reduces the political pressure for systemic reform. The most quality-conscious consumers are usually the most politically influential citizens.[19] If a reasonable substitute is within their means, they leave, and their departure weakens the political pressure for reform. The next fallacy is quite similar.

ONLY LOW-INCOME KIDS NEED HELP

This fallacy is seen in the discussion of vouchers, and in the interpretation of research findings that "the most significant determinants of educational success are the student's socioeconomic background and familial context."[20] Some studies conclude that school characteristics are not the cause of academic deficiencies. "Social measures that target the home and neighborhood environments of disadvantaged children might prove more effective than educational remedies."[21] Since statistical analyses explain differences in the data, the proper interpretation of such findings is that schools' impact on intellectual growth is consistent— consistently bad since academic outcomes are appalling where socioeconomic conditions are the worst, rising to dismal where socioeconomic conditions are good.

Greg Vanourek offered this generalization about vouchers: "Vouchers allow low-income families to send their children to the school of their choice."[22] "Why Vouchers are Needed for Poor Children"[23] is the title of a Denis Doyle report to the U.S. House Appropriations Committee. In addition, according to Joseph Viteritti, "The long-term goal must be to enhance the educational options available to disadvantaged populations so that their opportunities more closely resemble the opportunities that pertain to the middle class."[24] Jonathan Kozol said choice is "an escape hatch for a few students, instead of a way to improve the school system."[25] The prevailing view is that "tuition stipends [vouchers] would give poor families trapped in bad public schools more choice."[26] Similar statements are very common. Even Milton Friedman thinks that vouchers would improve the schooling available to the middle class only "moderately."[27]

A key assumption underlying proposals to means test vouchers is that the only deficient schools are inner city schools with high concentrations of low-income families.[28] Paul Hill said we need to "Empower educators who want to create new options for poor children."[29] Middle- and upper-income families can move to supposedly good suburban schools or afford private school tuition. Inner cities in large urban areas do have the worst schools, but that doesn't mean the others are good or even adequate. The mistaken assumption that "better" at least means "good" inappropriately distorts reform efforts of every kind. That assumption is a major impediment to the policy changes that would establish a competitive education industry.

Like other caps on participation, limiting choice to low-income families undermines the potential for a competitive education industry.[30] Quentin Quade's eloquent attack on the propensity to cap participation in parental choice programs deserves much more attention.

> There is no logic which says school choice should stop at any particular income level or any municipal boundary line. One thinks in such incomplete categories only if still an intellectual captive of the status quo, perhaps seeing the virtues of choice just as a corrective of today's worst educational results, rather than as the natural, parent-serving social policy it is when seen in its own right. That, no doubt, is why some of today's most-heralded advocates of school choice continue to speak of it as "good for the poor but not for all." There is no true line between rich and poor as regards the merit of school choice.[31]

FULL-TUITION VOUCHERS ELIMINATE FINANCIAL PENALTIES

"Comprehensive" choice includes private schools, and all children can participate. The rare prominent "comprehensive" proposals[32] still hinder competition. Their key defect is discrimination; private school users would receive less public support, usually much less.[33] Even Quade's eloquent plea for parental choice without financial penalty overlooks the discrimination issue.[34] Quade's definition of no financial penalty permits less support for private school users (discrimination)—say $3,000 per voucher versus $7,000 per "public" school student—if the voucher covers the tuition fully. Private school students still suffer a financial penalty because discrimination reduces private schools' access to resources. Discrimination against private school users also reduces the incentive to compete, which declines further if the tax dollars that follow transferees don't come from their school district's budget.

"'Comprehensive" proposals that limit private school eligibility to schools that accept tax dollars as full payment (they prohibit private add-ons) further reduce parents' choices and stifle competition. They limit choice because it costs parents a lot to buy slightly more education than public funds will allow. For example, suppose a voucher is worth $3,000, and private schools can cash them only if they accept them as full payment. A $3,000/year private school is then "free" in the same sense that a "public" school costs families only their school taxes, but slightly higher quality private schooling would cost families thousands of dollars. Without the option to add on, a $3,001 per year private school would cost families $3,001 more than a $3,000 per year private school. A $3,001 jump in buyers' education outlays to buy another dollar's worth of services has nearly the same effect as an explicit price (tuition) ceiling at the tax dollar amount.

Choice advocates should demand the right to use public support to buy more education than the taxpayer-funded amount will buy. Unfortunately, they often oppose the right to privately add on or they are silent on this critical issue. For example, Daniel McGroarty said prohibiting add-ons is "a sensible move to prevent the ratcheting up of tuition costs,"[35] a common view among choice advocates that reflects much confusion about economics and reform. Higher tuition costs are likely only in the short run, especially if the level of public support is—as recommended throughout this book—large. The increased profitability of a private school that would result from a large voucher would attract many entrepreneurs. The long-term net effect of the increased demand for private schooling on tuition, and the subsequent supply increase, is uncertain. Competition may force many schools to accept the voucher as full payment, a much different effect from the effect of a ban on private add-ons. With public support of each child the same, no matter which school the child attends, add-ons are parents' only out-of-pocket cost, and certainly less than private school users' costs without public support.

Choice advocates' stated interest in keeping private school tuition from rising is contrary to their desire to effect reform—that is, to change the system. Restricted-access voucher programs will raise the out-of-pocket costs of non-voucher private school users, and such programs cannot reform the system. Success in keeping tuition from rising means little or no expansion of the private sector, which surely is contrary to the aims of choice-based reform strategies. Tuition revenues don't cover the costs of many current private schools. Their ability to extend current subsidies to a larger student population is very limited, often to just the unused capacity of existing facilities. Increased resources per student are necessary for private schools to expand facilities and to become more competitive in teacher labor markets.

There are four major reasons to allow add-ons.

1. Equity: Everyone pays school taxes, so everyone should enjoy the benefits, even if they want to buy more than the tax dollars will let them.
2. Freedom: It maximizes the range of choices, and the decision to add on does not harm anyone else. Add-ons allow some children to learn more without other children learning less, and society benefits when anyone learns more.
3. Parental involvement: Parents choose more carefully when there is an out-of-pocket cost.
4. Efficiency: *Price movement is a primary market mechanism.* Without add-ons, price (tuition) changes can only reflect political forces. When parents cannot add on, prices cannot move to reflect market forces. *Price movement is how markets signal relative scarcity, motivate producers and consumers, and allocate resources. A price control—the effect of prohibiting add-ons—is an extremely debilitating, anticompetitive factor.*

Financial penalties accompany parental choice unless each child gets the same amount of public money, no matter which school the child attends. Public funds cannot cover the cost of every education option, so the freedom to add on enlarges the menu and increases total spending on education. It also allows the introduction of new practices that are expensive at first, but eventually become widely affordable; increases consumer vigilance; and establishes the critical market mechanism of price flexibility. Phasing in equal support is acceptable if the final outcome is certain at the outset.

CHOICE WILL OCCUR FROM THE EXISTING SCHOOL MENU

School reform discussions suffer greatly from the static world fallacy. The status quo is deeply ingrained even among its critics, and many analysts cannot imagine a system much different from what we have now. They speak as if the excess capacity of existing schools defines the upper limit on participation in parental choice programs. Such intellectual captives of the status quo assume that the overwhelming majority of children will always have to attend "public" schools organized into school districts, so that anything bad for the "public" school system is ultimately bad for children. They assume that the private sector will remain largely nonprofit and church-run, with a few extremely select, expensive schools.

The February 1998 *Mobilization for Equity* newsletter plainly reflected the fallacy. Private schools don't have "enough [empty] seats. The majority of students will be forced to remain in the public system *regardless of how voucher programs are implemented* [emphasis added]."[36] That's dangerous nonsense. A program with the high level of universal public funding recommended by this book—mainstream children receive the same level of public funding, no matter which school the child attends—would cause new schools to form quickly, perhaps in former "public" school buildings. Quite soon, children would stay in the public system only if their parents wanted them there.

There are many other less blunt examples of the static world fallacy. Based on empty seats in Catholic schools, Peter Cookson has said, "You could get some competition quicker if you included private schools in a choice plan, but it wouldn't be much more competition."[37] Stan Karp said, "this [the free market] meant [turn the education system over to] the local Roman Catholic Archdiocese,"[38] which Karp guessed had about 1,000 vacant slots. Linda Darling-Hammond said, "Vouchers are a smokescreen,"[39] a distraction from critical equity issues because there are only a "limited number of slots worth choosing." Robert Lowe and Barbara Miner said a voucher system would force parents "to compete for a few select schools."[40] Joseph Newman portrayed current private schools as the alternative to "public" schools.[41]

The assumption of restricted access also underlies Ann Lewis's certainty that "vouchers might help some students and some schools," but won't change the system.[42] Restricted access to vouchers is an underlying assumption of antivoucher campaign literature.[43] Particularly telling excerpts include:

- "Vouchers reward those who have not elected to attend public schools" (p. 2).
- "Vouchers abandon the many for the few" (p. 3).
- "The vast bulk of the voucher money would subsidize those who are already in private schools" (p. 3).
- The American Civil Liberties Union believes that "for most students, vouchers offer a choice between a religious school and a failing public school." [Vouchers] "single out a few for special privileges."[44]

David Berliner and Bruce Biddle believe a voucher system "sets up a two-class educational system."[45] They apparently believe that the voucher system will cause only a slight expansion of the private school sector, while most children remain in "public" schools that are harmed by losing students, even though per pupil funding of the "public" schools stays the same or goes up. Many others repeatedly imply the same conviction.

The potential magnitude of reform through parental choice is completely lost on the victims of the static world fallacy. They don't realize that parental choice can remake the entire school system. A competitive education industry will contain only choiceworthy schools. If choice opponents are right about "public school abandonment," a competitive education industry will not contain government-operated schools for very long. Nonreligion-based and for-profit schools will comprise a much larger share of a competitive education industry's private school sector than they do now.[46] In a competitive education industry, private schools will no longer suffer the significant handicap of having zero-tuition competitors, and they won't have to charge more for a service produced at a lower cost. The existing array of schools is no basis on which to evaluate the components and effects of a competitive education industry. For that reason, it is worth repeating an important point of chapter 3. The attractiveness of policies that use school choice to change the existing school system does not depend on whether existing private schools produce better academic outcomes than existing "public" schools.

Choice advocates like Denis Doyle and Douglas Munro recognize the power of choice to remake the system, but their actions frequently overlook that objective, and thereby make that outcome less likely. For example, Doyle and Munro administered a questionnaire to people leaving Baltimore to see if choice would have prevented their departure.[47] In the questionnaire, "choice" meant a restriction-laden program that would keep the school menu the same.

VOUCHERS ONLY HELP THE RICH

This is a typical assertion of antivoucher literature: "Poor parents cannot afford to pay the difference between a voucher and a private school's full tuition."[48] However, even when public support is worth much less than the per pupil funds of "public" schools (a mistake), the claim is only partially true. Many private schools are inexpensive enough that the demand for low-income vouchers usually exceeds voucher availability or private school capacity, whichever is less. That is true even for partial tuition vouchers. Many low-income families are making the major sacrifices necessary to transfer a child to a private school, and many more want to.[49]

With the high level of nondiscriminatory universal public support advocated throughout this book, the claim that vouchers would help only the rich is utterly false. Universal choice funded with current K–12 public funding would put all but the elite prep academies within the reach of every family with little or no add-on required. Most private schools would have much more money per student. That, and the competitive pressures, would greatly improve private schools. "Public" schools may also respond to the competitive pressures. Since low-income families are often in below-average "public" schools, they have the most to gain from the certain improvement and increased availability of private schools and the possible improvement of "public" schools. Rich people already have access to elite prep academies, so low-income families will gain the most from a competitive education industry. The lowest-income families would receive public support worth much more than their school taxes, so the truly rich would continue to pay more in school taxes than they'd get back.

EVERY SCHOOL SHOULD ACCEPT ANY CHILD

Choice opponents assert that vouchers give choice to private schools, not parents,[50] because private schools can practice selective admissions. Supposedly, private schools will take only the easiest to educate, and "dump" the rest in "public" schools. This is an utterly false and disingenuous claim, but it is often politically effective because choice opponents depict specialization as discrimination. It is a disingenuous claim because many "public" school systems[51] use private schools as a "dumping ground for dummies"[52] by paying private school tuition with public funds, another violation of choice opponents' demands.

The only discrimination in a competitive education industry is by parents who become discriminating consumers after they study the education marketplace and then choose a school that best suits their child's unique abilities and preferences. Except for elite schools, sellers only rarely exercise their right to refuse service to someone. The shortages that are possible in the early stages of a competitive education industry will disappear quickly, just as they do in any market in which demand increases and prices are flexible.

What is important is that every child have access to a high-quality education. Competing schools of choice as a group, but not individually, are better suited to that objective, precisely because market forces compel them to specialize. Market pressures push schools into particular niches. Neighborhood "public" schools try in vain to address a broad spectrum of education interests and abilities. Individual "public" schools need the right to exclude[53]—that is, to direct students to more appropriate services. Specialization opportunities need to be extended to "public" schools, not taken from private schools.

Choice opponents' ability to turn neighborhood "public" schools' inability to specialize—a major shortcoming—into a political asset does not change the fact that it is a major handicap. Requiring every school to accept any child is a big mistake. Specialization, which by definition makes the services of each school more suitable to some families but less suitable to others, is a cornerstone of high productivity. Because private schools can specialize, and neighborhood "public" schools can't—the latter must strive to serve every child in their attendance area—the private schools that accept "public" school cast-offs often serve them better for less than is spent on mainstream "public" school students. Private schools' ability to specialize in particular subjects or teaching styles significantly increases the total productivity of the private sector.

Limited, restriction-laden choice programs maximize the danger that private schools will acquire some of the handicaps of "public" schools (such as inability to specialize). A competitive education industry will produce the opposite effect. Private and "public" schools will acquire some of each other's advantages. Private schools will have more resources per student, and the government-owned schools will acquire some of the flexibility and freedom of a private school.

Two more false premises underlie choice opponents' claim that private schools, not parents, will exercise choice. The first is another result of the static world fallacy, and both are harsh, backhanded criticisms of "public" schools. Many choice opponents assert that the existing excess capacity of private schools limits parents' ability to exercise choice (the static world fallacy). Choice opponents misinform their listeners because they imply that space shortages are permanent. Private schools supposedly would have to discriminate because they could accept only a small fraction of the likely flood of applicants.

The second false premise is choice opponents' claim that typical restriction-laden choice programs will allow private schools to "dump" hard-to-educate children on "public" schools. In other words, parents who prefer more cheaply produced private school services will be forced to settle for more costly "public" school services. By making that claim, choice opponents are saying that the most costly services (supplied by "public" schools) are the least desirable. When the least desired service costs the most, the reason is inefficiency. Once again, choice opponents' defense of the "public" school system is thinly disguised condemnation. It is much more devastating criticism than choice advocates' arguments for parental choice.

Not only is the "dumping" claim contrary to the existing "public" school practice of dumping children in private schools, but it also is theoretically unsound. The claim contradicts two fundamental traits of competitive settings: specialization and the profit motive. With significant specialization, the easiest to educate are much harder to differentiate. When schools specialize, the easiest to educate student varies from school to school, and high achievers are easier to educate only when expectations are low. Specialization addresses the reality that children excel in some subject areas more than in others. Specialized schools facilitate ability grouping—different from controversial tracking, which falsely assumes that children are uniformly high or low achievers.

In a competitive education industry, high achievers definitely will not be among the cheapest to educate. The parents of high achievers and their children demand challenging instruction, no matter how far above average they are. In addition, parents of high achievers demand much more customized attention to their children and to themselves. That's a major reason why their children are high achievers.

The profit motive means that it will not matter if some children cost more to educate than others, as long as costs remain below revenues. That is another reason to start a competitive education industry by allocating virtually 100 percent of current school spending through parental choice. The resulting high minimum level of per pupil funding will allow entrepreneurs to serve virtually every mainstream child profitably with little or no private add-on. With specialized schools, mainstream children will include many now labeled "special ed."

COURT OPINIONS ON CHURCH-STATE ISSUES ARE KEY FACTORS

The public focus on restriction-laden versions of parental choice greatly exaggerates the functional importance of church-state litigation. Mistaken claims like these appear quite often.

> In the end, the fate of school choice will turn on the willingness of the Supreme Court to impose its own constitutional guidelines upon the States in order to protect the free exercise rights of individuals.[54]

> Perhaps the biggest question for state policy makers is whether appropriating public funds that can be used for tuition at religious schools will ultimately pass constitutional muster.[55]

> The [U.S.] Supreme Court could decide, once and for all, the constitutionality of school choice in the near future.[56]

While nondiscriminatory, universal choice proposals may not be politically feasible without a church stake in them,[57] a competitive education industry can function just fine, no matter what the U.S. Supreme Court, or any State Supreme Court, ultimately says about parents allocating public funds to church-run schools. If, as advocated here, parents allocate the public money earmarked for K–12 schooling to individual schools, a competitive education industry will evolve even if parents can't use public funds at church-run schools. Church-state legal issues are potential "show-stoppers" only if choice is too limited to allow a competitive education industry to evolve.

Exclusion of church-run schools does not prevent compliance with the necessary conditions of a competitive education industry described in chapter 2. That's important because, even though there is widespread confidence that the U.S. Supreme Court will uphold properly structured programs, many State Supreme Courts are less likely to do so. In addition, a parental choice program may have to contain major restrictions before judges will allow participation of church-run schools.[58] The Wisconsin Supreme Court demanded random admissions of voucher students, and opt-out provisions so that children could skip disagreeable religious instruction.[59] Since religion themes exist throughout their curriculum, the opt-out option may compel major changes.

The court may not have demanded those restrictions, nor would they matter much, for parental choice in a competitive education industry. Then every child would receive a high level of public support, and it wouldn't take random assignment to avoid bias in rationing the oversubscribed private school space that results from limited choice programs. With the large number of choices in a competitive education industry, parents will not have to accept unappreciated religious instruction to enroll their children in a better academic environment. Such trade-offs are common in limited voucher programs. For example, a poll of New York City parents seeking privately funded scholarships to attend Catholic schools revealed that the first concern of 85 percent of the parents was academic quality.[60] Only 38 percent cited religious instruction as a significant attraction. Such data indicate that church-run schools will comprise a much smaller share of a competitive education industry than their current lion's share of the tiny private sector. When parents no longer have to trade off academics and religious values, they will not need the right to opt out of particular classes. The key point, though, is that a competitive education industry can exist no matter how the courts settle the church-state issue.

Parents' right to use public funds at church-run schools is still a significant freedom issue. Since "extremist" schools are easily discouraged,[61] parents' should have the right to use public support at church-run schools. Such freedom is morally correct, and it will allow a competitive education industry to evolve more quickly once new policies establish the conditions described in chapter 2.

This fallacy exists because the participation of church-run schools is critical for the restriction-laden programs that dominate voucher discussions. Such programs favor established private schools, the vast majority of which are church-run. Restriction-laden programs allocate public funds to only a few private school users, and the vouchers are too small and scarce to allow many new schools to form. Through the high level of public support advocated throughout this book, and decisions to add on, competitive education industries will have a much larger private sector than we have now, even if church-run schools cannot receive public funds, even indirectly through parental choices. The possible inability of church-run schools to receive public funds is another important reason to use 100 percent of the current K–12 spending to provide the same high level of public support to every equally situated (grade level, special need, etc.) child. With just the tiny, secular component of the private school sector as the starting point, rapid private sector growth is much more important.

CONTRACTING OUT IS REAL PRIVATIZATION

The latest privatization wave going around the world is making a splash in K–12 policy-making circles. One hopes it eventually will help sweep K–12 education services into the mainstream of competitive markets. However, so far the wave is claiming mostly drowning victims and leaving many others all wet.

The public's well-founded belief that businesses outperform bureaucracies underlies the political support for privatization. Supporters are driven by images of businesses cutting costs or improving their product to compete for market share. Unfortunately, like the terms, *parental choice* and *school choice*, the term, *privatization*, covers a lot of possibilities, and the effects expected by supporters will not result from some of the policies labeled "privatization."

Contracting out services, selling public assets to businesses, and load shedding (the government sheds responsibility for a service) fall under the privatization label. Contracting out was the dominant mode because it offended the fewest special interests.[62] Since the places that implemented "privatization" didn't privatize school ownership, "privatization" was a means, not an end, or, as Emanuel Savas put it, contracting-out is not "*real* [emphasis in the original] privatization."[63] Marketing mistakes by reform advocates and resistance from incumbent school personnel compounded the disappointment with "privatization."

Even contracting out management services (for example, Hartford; Dade County, Florida; Baltimore; Minneapolis; Wilkinsburg, Pennsylvania) will not contribute to the evolution of competitive behavior. Increased competition in the management service market—where the "public" school authorities are consumers—does not reduce the dominance of "public" schools in the delivery of instructional services. A minor exception occurs if attendance areas disappear, and several independent contractors manage an area's "public" schools. Otherwise, the increase in the number of producers of education services is insignificant, and the "public" school leaders and the contractors they hire are, at most, semi-independent. Differences may provide parents with some choice, but it is hard to imagine ferociously competitive behavior between "public" school authorities and the firms they hired. Furthermore, the barriers to entry remain and the market is not more contestable. Contracting out the delivery of instructional services usually changes a government-owned, government-run monopoly into a regulated, privately run government monopoly. Poorly conceived contract language creates other problems by misdirecting contractors' efforts or by causing an overly narrow focus on specific evaluation criteria such as standardized test scores.

The source of marketing mistakes is the fallacy that parental choice is an effective reform only if existing private schools are academically superior to "public" schools. Chapter 3 discusses that mistake, and chapter 8 addresses the cost dimension, so the discussion here focuses on the difference between establishing private ownership and contracting out.

It is probably fortunate that management contracts did not include cost reduction in their performance criterion.[64] Contracted managers lack many of the cost-cutting options of owners, so they probably can't approach the per-pupil costs of most private schools.

Charter school growth, calls for *real* privatization, and contracting out management are dramatic statements of pessimism and an admission of frustration with administrative and political processes. However, there are major differences between the conditions and incentives of contracted managers and competing school owner-operators. Contracted managers are paid by the authorities that hired them, not by the children and parents they serve. Carol Ascher's statement about performance contracting in the 1960s and early 1970s is still correct: "Performance contracting was never meant to increase parents' voice in schooling. Indeed, families remain noticeably absent from the stories of these experiments. They described accountability in terms of companies and school districts."[65] Contracted managers narrow the curriculum and focus their efforts on the politically relevant factors. Other suboptimal, even counterproductive, practices are common, including focusing teaching on particular standardized exams or whatever measuring devices officially determine the contractor's performance and compensation.

Competing owner-entrepreneurs face relentless pressure to cut costs and improve their services. Those dynamic factors are at the core of differences "between competitive market and political 'command-and-control' mechanisms of service delivery."[66] Contracted managers have no comparable pressures to motivate them. Their stockholders may demand cost-cutting measures, but the additional, much more important pressure from price-cutting competitors is lacking. Competitors also provide the critical cost and quality basis for comparison.

A contracted manager's most important initial competition is their predecessor's track record. The frustration that precedes the drastic step of contracting out management leads to contracts with short-term, static goals. Peter Hutchinson, president of Public Strategies Group Inc., defined success as "turning the district's performance around,"[67] ending decline and bringing the district closer to "normal." Catching up is easier to define in a performance contract, and it is much less ambitious than continuous pursuit of a rising standard of excellence. The Illinois State Legislature sort of contracted out management of Chicago's "public" schools to Mayor Richard M. Daley and his designated schools' chief, Paul Vallas. Despite significant gains, the situation is still so bad that their goal is for the Chicago "public" schools to reach the national norms of a nation at risk. Jonathan Alter said that if Vallas's reforms fail, they might have to [gasp!] try vouchers.[68] Sadder than the attitude toward vouchers—something that at worst transfers some children to schools better for them and saves tax dollars—is that Alter assumed unequal funding of voucher students and "public" school students. Because he assumed that voucher funding would be in addition to direct funding of "public" schools, rather than in place of the direct funding, he concluded that vouchers for everyone were impractical.

If contracted managers succeed initially and turn some schools around, rise to national norms widely seen as dismal, or just outperform the district employees who preceded them, the better nearby "public" schools become the new standard. There are no other education entrepreneurs to compete with, and direct rivalry with "public" schools can occur only if there are no attendance areas. Once contract objectives are met, there is little incentive to modify practices already deemed successful. Tampering with successful practices is risky, and, without real competition, the potential return to improvements is much lower. Education entrepreneurs from other regions are only potential competitors, and then only in a very limited way. Potential competitors cannot contest customers continuously. They are limited to periodically contesting the renewal of the incumbent manager's contract with the school authorities.

The politics that created the problem and convinced the authorities that they could not fix it themselves will infect the contract's terms. The contracted manager often has little discretion in politically sensitive areas such as personnel, curriculum, student distribution, and potential areas of specialization. Putting those policies off limits greatly reduces the potential for improvement. Such restrictions were a major factor in the nonrenewal of Education Alternatives, Inc.'s (EAI) contracts for Baltimore and Hartford. EAI had to keep the existing curriculum and teachers who were openly hostile to the new policies. Teacher unions are openly hostile to privatization, even when it involves far less than contracting out management.

The Wilkinsburg, Pennsylvania school authorities hired Alternative Public Schools (APS) of Nashville to manage a single elementary school that serves a largely minority population. APS believed it had the authority to choose its own staff. The Pennsylvania affiliate of the NEA filed a lawsuit that reversed APS's decision to terminate the union contract and dismiss the incumbent teachers.

Uncertainty about contract longevity can create other problems. Political support is fragile, and the range of politically acceptable behavior changes with current events and elections. Early termination clauses like the Hartford/EAI contract—termination with only 90 day's notice—necessitate constant attention to political correctness.[69] Even if contracted managers have the authority to make politically sensitive decisions, they may not exercise it. Politically sensitive criteria like test scores receive too much attention to the detriment of other important, but less measurable or interpretable education outcomes.

Politics is not the only uncertainty problem. For capital improvements, the issue is uncertainty about enough time for payback. The payback time for many capital investments is longer than the contract period. The approach of the renewal date and the contracted manager's estimated probability of nonrenewal directly affect investment decisions. Nonrenewal produces major losses, so the risk premium is very high. The higher the probability of nonrenewal, the stronger the incentive to cut corners. Despite the nonrenewal, early-termination risks, EAI made some major investments. When the contract expired, EAI unsuccessfully sought a $3 million reimbursement.

Privatizing management has fewer potential benefits than private ownership, and the political risks for choice advocates are significant. Glitches and resentments accompany transitions to new managerial regimes, so it is not at all surprising when contracted managers cannot quickly produce the significantly better test scores that are the political process's primary contract renewal criterion. Contracting out management services is a time-consuming, deceptive detour off the road to genuine system reform.

Confusion about privatization and well-publicized, but poorly explained disappointments reduce the political feasibility of a competitive education industry. Attempts to duplicate them in different settings can tarnish success stories, and problems that should be interpreted narrowly give all forms of privatization costly image problems. Disappointment with something called "privatization" will make the public less receptive to the concept of market reforms, including choice-based reforms that incorporate the productive versions of privatization.

When frustration with the political process prompts the authorities to give private enterprise a try, choice advocates should demand private ownership. To privatize education services, the authorities should sell school facilities to several independent education entrepreneurs, a step that does not preclude taxpayer subsidies for education spending.

SCHOOL CHOICE IS A GAMBLE

A symptom of the confusion about parental choice, and an underlying premise of parental choice "experiments" and pilot programs, is the implicit assumption that we risk making things worse. The only apparent basis for that assumption is that parental choice will produce change. A key finding of a November 14, 1997, conference at the Federal Reserve Bank of New York is a typical example: "participants *cautioned* [emphasis added] that the existing evidence [from restriction-laden parental choice programs] is insufficient to justify expanding choice proposals to the student population as a whole."[70]

Caution is appropriate only if something of value is in jeopardy, and if competition is a mysterious, untested force. In addition, as this book points out repeatedly, "existing evidence" is of little relevance to universal parental choice. Indeed, some conference participants noted the poor design of the "experiments." However, they did not note that the evidence includes disappointment and frustration with the current system, a strong theoretical case for a competitive education industry, and the spectacular track record of competitive forces in hundreds of industries, including education.[71] Certainties associated with the status quo are much worse than the uncertainties associated with implementing competition. Failure to implement a competitive education industry guarantees major losses. It will take a generation to design, implement, run, and evaluate a valid experiment.

The funding and governance policies that preclude competition have resisted change, but other kinds of change are part of the problem. "Public" school policy makers constantly try new rules, curricula, and teaching procedures in a desperate search for the magic set of commands that will make teachers successful. Policy makers are conducting unplanned, uncontrolled experiments; their hopeless, desperate search just produces constant upheaval. The unending parade of ostensible solutions is a major source of the low achievement problem. Denis Udall said it perfectly: "Teachers are in a virtual state of panic, caught between crushing district mandates and the need to raise standardized test scores."[72]

A gamble!? What actual—as opposed to theoretical or potential—education outcome of the status quo would the general public miss? The actual outcomes of "public" schools are the number one political concern of Americans. Literally hundreds of studies[73] show that "public" schools almost never achieve academic improvement with extra resources. Choice advocates cite that evidence to contest calls for more "public" school funding, but they do not exploit a legitimate interpretation of greater significance: the system's failure to respond favorably to additional resources is solid evidence of a totally dysfunctional system.[74] Citizens have to establish semipermanent political organizations to demand accountability and high standards. Colleges[75] and businesses[76] spend increasing millions on remediation. Polls show that a majority of families would use private schools if they could afford the tuition. Despair by desperate low-income families and generous philanthropists is such that "privately funded voucher programs are booming,"[77] even though the privately funded vouchers are worth a fraction of taxpayer support of "public" school students and cover only part of the cost of producing cheaper education services. Increasing numbers of parents are rejecting an expensive "public" school education they have already paid for, and relatively inexpensive private schools most of them could afford, in favor of the difficult task of home schooling.

Supposed relative virtues of a "public" school-dominated education system are only theoretical; unrealized to any great extent in "public" schools, and not systematically absent from private schools.[78] Recent research indicates that even limited parental choice actually produces the social benefits that only government-run "common schools" are supposed to generate.[79] The current system ostensibly exists largely to increase the economic opportunities of children from low-income families, but the least advantaged children attend the worst schools. Wide disparities in funding and other measures of resource allocation (e.g., teacher experience) exist in "public" school systems even where court rulings demand equal funding. Despite the expense and agony of busing, neighborhood schools are still relatively homogenous by race and socioeconomic status. The only common outcomes instilled by the experience intended from "public" schools are high rates of nonproficiency, much of which is below the basic skills level. The extremism that receives so much attention, including in parental choice debates, was learned in "public" schools or despite the schools' best efforts to instill common values.

The existing debate is whether "public" schools are "a disaster"[80] or a gold-plated disaster,[81] whether existing private schools are any better, and—in either case—exactly what reforms are appropriate. Most parental choice opponents admit that "public" schools are not choiceworthy. Probable abandonment is one of their key objections to parental choice proposals. Even ardent defenders of the current governance and funding mechanisms like David Berliner admit the K–12 system is not capable of being effective: "It is clear that our system is not designed to produce masses of high-achieving students before the college years."[82]

DANGEROUS MISTAKES

Restriction-laden choice proposals are a gamble; they jeopardize the political feasibility of a competitive education industry. The statements that many parental choice advocates make about experiments and other indicators also threaten the parental choice cause, however narrowly or broadly it is defined. Two especially egregious examples reinforce this point.

Recall from chapter 3 a prominent choice advocate's assertion[83] that the parental choice cause would be discredited unless current programs produced significant academic and equity gains. Since the existing programs are restriction-laden, small programs, such gains could not occur apart from the few voucher students. There was a good chance that statistical analyses would not reveal gains to voucher students, and several studies claimed just that. In addition, when other studies found gains, choice opponents said that gains for a few come at the expense of students left behind in schools with less money and fewer active parents.

In a *Wall Street Journal* editorial, John Chubb and Terry Moe, authors of one of the most widely read books advocating parental choice, asserted that choice is pointless unless current private schools are much better than "public" schools (chapter 12 has details). The stakes are too high—our nation is at risk[84]—to keep making such blunders. We can't afford to assign immense relevance to irrelevant comparisons, pretend to assess competition when it does not exist, and confuse potential reforms—agents of school system improvement—with programs that only shuffle a few students among existing schools.

Choice advocates choose their battles poorly and frequently ignore or abandon high-caliber ammunition. In the two examples cited above, parental choice advocates transferred ammunition to the enemy. Language like the strong words of the 1983 *Nation at Risk* report seems to apply to a great many prominent advocates of real reform through parental choice. If a foreign power was doing it [compromising their cause] to them, they would see it as an act of war, but they are doing it to themselves and placing the nation's future in greater jeopardy.

OVERVIEW

This chapter has discussed several troublesome fallacies, and the facts contradict much of the conventional wisdom. Fallacies are also a significant part of the next five chapters, but there is more room for informed disagreement. Chapters 7–11 criticize inappropriate perspectives rather than ignorance, misunderstanding, and denial of reality. The next chapter is an especially good example of inappropriate perspective. It discusses the fear of increased regulation of private schools, an issue that parental choice advocates need to thoroughly re-examine.

NOTES

1. Third International Mathematics and Science Study (TIMSS), *School Reform News* (April 1998): 1.
2. NAEP data from 1994 and 1996 as reported in *Education Week*, January 11, 1999.
3. Barbara Kantrowitz and Pat Wingert, "A Dismal Report Card," *Newsweek* (June 17, 1991): 65.
4. The pass percent threshold is scheduled to rise five percentage points each year, to a maximum of 70 percent in 2004.
5. Julian H. Trevino, "Education Goal Is to Provide Choices," *San Antonio Express-News* (June 15, 1998): 11A.
6. "The Changing Politics of Education Reform," in Chester E. Finn and Theodor Rebarber, *Education Reform in the '90s* (New York: MacMillan Press, 1992), p. 189.
7. Because of its consistency with other indicators of educational achievement (remedial edu-

cation spending by colleges and businesses, other standardized tests), the inference derived from this terrible result survives the criticism of the NAEP test that scores are low because students have no incentive to try hard. See Joseph Murphy, *The Privatization of Schooling* (Thousand Oaks, Calif.: Corwin Press, 1996), pp. 139–48 for more examples illustrating that student achievement is utterly unacceptable nearly everywhere.

8. Chester E. Finn, Jr., "The Schools," in N. Kozodny (ed.), *What to Do About . . .* (New York: HarperCollins, 1995).

9. The evidence is direct and indirect. The appalling tests scores, including the embarrassing international comparisons, are based on the entire student population. Growing expenditures on remediation by businesses and colleges are not limited to inner city high school graduates. Direct evidence of troubled suburban schools includes Daniel J. Singal, "The Other Crisis in American Education," *The Atlantic Monthly* (November 1991): 59–74; "Dollars Don't Mean Success in California District *Education Week* (December 3, 1997) on the troubles of a California school district that spends $12,100 per student. In San Antonio, Texas, community college-bound high school graduates must take the TASP test to determine if they can begin college courses without remediation. Thirty students from San Antonio's wealthiest district, the suburban Alamo Heights District, took the TASP test in September 1992. Of those 30 students, 22, 15, and 16 required math, english, and reading remedial courses, respectively. See also Jay P. Greene, Paul Peterson, and Jiangtao Du. *The Effectiveness of School Choice: The Milwaukee Experiment* (Program in Education Policy and Governance, Harvard University, 1997) for a description of Milwaukee's dismal secular private schools; Kamrhan Farwell, "Money Doesn't Always Equal High Test Scores," *The Press Enterprise* (August 10, 1998) is about several California school districts; exploding remedial education spending by businesses, community colleges, and universities; George Clowes, "The Dark Side of Suburban School Achievement," *School Reform News* (January 2000): 7.

10. See chapter 4 of Myron Lieberman, *Public Education: An Autopsy* (Cambridge, Mass.: Harvard University Press, 1993) for an explanation of how parents are deceived.

11. In "Up from Mediocrity," *Policy Review* (Summer 1992): 80–83, Finn calls it the "complacency problem." The phenomenon is also discussed in G. Carl Ball, and Steven Goldman, "Improving Education's Productivity," *Phi Delta Kappan* (November 1997): 231. It's similar to the public's attitude toward another major political institution, the U.S. Congress. People think little of the U.S. Congress, but congressional incumbents rarely lose an election.

12. John Miller, "Why School Choice Lost," *Wall Street Journal* (November 4, 1993).

13. Gallup Poll cited in Paul G. Wyckoff, "A New Case for Vouchers," *Journal of Policy Analysis and Management* 10 (Winter 1991): 112 –16.

14. Daniel Akst, "Why Liberals Should Love School Choice," *Wall Street Journal* (April 6, 1998): A14.

15. Denis Doyle and Douglas Munro, *Reforming the Schools to Save the City* (Baltimore: The Calvert Institute, 1997).

16. Jessica L. Sandham, "Florida OKs 1st Statewide Voucher Plan," *Education Week* (May 5, 1999): 1, 21. A similar proposal was rejected by the 1999 Texas legislature.

17. A metaphor may help to illustrate the incredible absurdity of such policies. Imagine having to pay a restaurant until the owner (not you) decides, only after at least two years, that the food isn't good enough. Then, even if the owner admits the establishment is low-performing, you can only take some of your money elsewhere.

18. Finn, in Kozodoy, 1995.

19. Albert O. Hirschman, *Exit, Voice, and Loyalty* (Cambridge, Mass.: Harvard University Press, 1970).

20. Frederick M. Hess, "Courting Backlash: The Risks of Emphasizing Input Equity Over School Performance," *The Virginia Journal of Social Policy & the Law* 6 (Fall 1998): 13.

21. Ibid.

22. Greg Vanourek, "The Choice Crusade," *Network News and Views* (December 1996).

23. Denis P. Doyle, "Why Vouchers Are Needed for Poor Children," *Heritage Foundation Committee Brief* (May 10, 1996).

24. Joseph Viteritti, *Choosing Equality* (Washington: Brookings Institution Press, 1999), p. 14.

25. Troy Segal, "Saving Our Schools," *Business Week* (September 14, 1992): 70–78.

26. Rene Sanchez, "Riley Launches Attack on School Vouchers," *Washington Post* (September 24, 1997): A6.

27. Friedman quoted in Edwin G. West, *Education Vouchers in Practice and Principle: A World Survey* (Washington: Human Capital Development Working Paper #64, February 1996), p. 7.

28. The mistaken idea that the major problems of the system exist primarily in inner city schools is deeply ingrained. Consider for example, the title of *Education Week's* (January 8, 1998) special issue: "The Urban Challenge." The same assumption was asserted constantly in the January, 22, 1997, "Quality Counts" special issue; many if not most *Education Week* articles on K–12 reform; and by Carol Ascher, Norm Fruchter, and Robert Berne, *Hard Lessons* (New York: Twentieth Century Fund, 1996). Titles like *An Imperiled Generation: Saving Urban Schools* (Carnegie Foundation for the Advancement of Teaching, 1988) are common. Robert Lowe and Barbara Miner (eds.), *Selling Out Our Schools* (Milwaukee: Rethinking Our Schools, 1996) contains repeated references to "problems in urban public schools" and "hundreds of fine suburban school systems" (Jonathan Kozol, p. 13). Ann Bastian (p. 18) talks about the "crisis in urban education" and says the "real places in crisis [are] 25 or so major urban systems, plus some hundreds of decaying industrial suburbs and dying rural districts."

29. Paul T. Hill, "The Innovator's Dilemma," *Education Week* (June 14, 2000): 33.

30. For vouchers as a general tool of government policy, that principle is well established; see C. Eugene Steurle, "Common Issues for Voucher Programs," in *Vouchers and Related Delivery Mechanisms: Consumer Choice in the Provision of Public Services*. Conference (October 2–3, 1998) Papers (Washington: Brookings Institution, 1998): 15.

31. Quentin L. Quade, "Watch Your Step! If School Choice Is So Great, Why Don't We Have It?" *Network News and Views* (January/February 1996).

32. For example, California's 1993 and 2000 parental choice ballot initiatives.

33. CEO America is lobbying for a Tax Credit Program (Linda Morrison, *The Tax Credits Program for School Choice* [National Center for Policy Analysis, March 1998]), that has the explicit aim "to discourage non-government schools from raising their tuition and fees"—that is, limiting private schools' access to resources.

34. Quentin Quade, *Financing Education* (New Brunswick, N.J.: Transaction Publishers, 1996), p. 35.

35. Daniel McGroarty, *Break These Chains* (Rocklin, Calif.: ICS Press, Prima Publishing, 1996), p. 98.

36. "School Vouchers on Trial in Milwaukee and Cleveland," *Mobilization for Equity* (February 1998): 1, 3.

37. Peter Cookson in Edith Rasell and Richard Rothstein (eds.), *School Choice: Examining the Evidence* (Washington: Economic Policy Institute, 1993), p. 252.

38. Stan Karp in Lowe and Miner, 1996, p. 32.

39. Linda Darling-Hammond interview in Lowe and Miner, 1996, p. 12.

40. Editors are interviewed in Lowe and Miner, 1996, pp. 14–15.

41. Joseph W. Newman, "Bribing Students out of Public Schools," *Education Week* (January 27, 1999): 76, 53.

42. Ann C. Lewis, "A Modest Proposal for Urban Schools," *Phi Delta Kappan* 78, no. 1 (September 1996): 5.

43. Albert Fondy, *School Vouchers in Pennsylvania: Bad Education Policy, Worse Public Policy* (Philadelphia: Pennsylvania Federation of Teachers, 1998).

44. Statement by Nadine Strossen, president of the ACLU, posted on the Freedom Channel Web site (*www.freedomchannel.com*), August 8, 2000.

45. David C. Berliner and Bruce J. Biddle, *The Manufactured Crisis* (Reading, Mass.: Addison-Wesley, 1995), p. 178.

46. This assertion is supported and discussed in greater detail in the context of the "Court Opinions on Church-State Issues are Key Factors" fallacy below.

47. Doyle and Munro, 1997.

48. Fondy, 1998.

49. The Goldwater Institute, "The Top Ten Myths about School Choice" (Phoenix, Ariz.: Author, 1994). The findings are based on data from Atlanta, Indianapolis, Milwaukee, Phoenix, and San Antonio. In each city there are long waiting lists for half-tuition grants available only to low-income families. The latest privately funded partial low-income voucher program attracted 1.25 million requests for 40,000 vouchers.

50. For example, that assertion is a centerpiece of virtually every piece of "No on Prop 174" literature. For example, consider this line from an anti-174 handout entitled, "It hurts kids, it hurts taxpayers": "voucher schools would choose which kids get in." According to Wendy Wagenheim ("Why Public Money Shouldn't Go to Private Schools," *Michigan Education Report* [Fall, 1998]: 12): "Under a voucher plan, it is schools that will do the choosing, not parents or students." Also see the letter written by the National Coalition for Public Education (July 29, 1997), and the comments of Elliot Mincberg with People for the American Way posted on the Freedom Channel Web site.

51. Janet R. Beales, "Educating the Uneducatable," *Wall Street Journal* (August 21, 1996).

52. McGroarty, 1996, p. 102.

53. Barry McGhan, "Choice and Compulsion," *Phi Delta Kappan* 79, no. 8 (April 1998): 610–15.

54. Joseph Viteritti, "Blaine's Wake: School Choice, the First Amendment, and State Constitutional Law," *Harvard Journal of Law and Public Policy* 21, no. 3 (Summer 1998).

55. Darcia H. Bowman, "States Giving Choice Bills Closer Look," *Education Week* (March 1, 2000): 1, 24.

56. Nina Shokraii Rees, "School Choice 2000 Annual Report," *The Heritage Backgrounder*, no. 1354 (March 30, 2000).

57. The political importance of church-state litigation is uncertain. Some church groups like the Catholic Church support publicly funded vouchers (as they understand them), while other church groups oppose them. For examples of the latter, see Steve Kloehn, "Protestants Take Aim at School Voucher Programs," *Chicago Tribune* (November 11, 1998).

58. Llewellyn Rockwell, "School Vouchers: An Enemy of Religion," *The Wanderer* (September 1998).

59. Ibid.

60. Ed Feulner, "Is School Choice a Bad Idea?" *Heritage Member News* (Autumn 1998).

61. Lieberman, 1993, 290–92.

62. Carol Ascher, "Performance Contracting: A Forgotten Experiment in School Privatization,"

Phi Delta Kappan 77, no. 9 (May 1996): 615; Polly Carpenter and George Hall, *Case Studies in Educational Performance Contracting: Conclusions and Implications*, Report #R-900/1-HEW (Santa Monica, Calif.: Rand Corporation, 1971).

63. Emanuel S. Savas, *Privatization: The Key to Better Government* (Chatham, N.J.: Chatham House, 1987), p. 278.

64. Education Alternatives, Inc. (EAI) is motivated to seek cost savings because it gets to keep half of each dollar saved, but the primary performance criteria are test scores; Elizabeth Gleick, "Privatizing Lives," *Time* (November 13, 1995): 88.

65. Ascher, May, 1996: 622.

66. David F. Bradford and Daniel Shapiro, "The Politics of Vouchers," in *Vouchers and Related Delivery Mechanisms: Consumer Choice in the Provision of Public Services.* Conference [October 2–3, 1998] Papers (Washington: Brookings Institution, 1998): 52.

67. Peter Hutchinson, "The Five C's," *Education Week* (September 17, 1997): 37, 39.

68. Jonathan Alter, "Chicago's Last Hope," *Newsweek* (June 22, 1998): 30.

69. Nancy Gibbs, "Schools for Profit," *Time* (October 17, 1994): 48.

70. FRBNY *Economic Policy Review* 4 (March 1998).

71. Andrew Coulson, *Market Education* (New Brunswick, N.J.: Transaction Publishers, 1999).

72. *Education Week* (July 8, 1998): 41, 43; several articles in a special "Schoolhouse Blues," Insight section (June 1, 1997) of the *San Antonio Express-News* said the same thing. Constantly changing programs are taking teachers out of their classrooms and creating low morale and panic.

73. Eric Hanushek, "School Resources and Student Performance," in Gary Burtless (ed.), *Does Money Matter?* (Washington: Brookings Institute, 1996); the latest evidence: American Legislative Council, *You Can't Buy Higher Grades: 50-State Report Card on American Education Funds* (April 2000).

74. For more detail, see Lieberman, 1993.

75. In a 1997 survey, three-quarters of the college deans reported an increase within the last decade in the proportion of students requiring remedial or developmental education. Arthur Levine and Jeannete S. Curetin, "Collegiate Life: An Obituary," *Change* (May/June 1998): 14–17, 51. In Texas, spending for remedial education rose dramatically, from $38.6 million in the 1988–89 biennium to $172 million by the 1998–99 biennium; a 346 percent increase; Jeff Judson, *The True State of Texas Education* (San Antonio: Texas Public Policy Foundation, 1998); Nationwide, "30 percent of first-time college students take remedial courses because they can't read, write, or do math adequately. At community colleges, the percentage is often much higher—and it's rising," David Wessel, "The Outlook," *Wall Street Journal* (November 19, 1998): A1.

76. *School Reform News* (April 1998): 7: "According to *Training* magazine, 20 percent of the companies it recently surveyed taught their new hires reading, writing, arithmetic, or English—even though two-thirds of them already sported high school diplomas."

77. Chester E. Finn, Jr., and Michael J. Petrilli, "Washington versus School Reform," *The Public Interest* (Fall 1998): 63.

78. Henry Levin, "The Economics of Educational Choice," *Economics of Education Review* 10 (1991): 137–58; Carol Ascher, Norm Fruchter, and Robert Berne, *Hard Lessons: The Promises of Privatization* (New York: The Twentieth Century Press, 1996).

79. Mark Schneider, Paul Teske, Melissa Marschall, and Christine Roch, "School Choice Builds Community," *The Public Interest* (Fall 1997): 86–90.

80. California Governor Gray Davis quoted in David Broder, "Reforming Education a Tough Assignment," *San Antonio Express-News* (March 2, 1999): 7B.

81. See the findings of the U.S. Congress cited in David Kirkpatrick, *School Choice: The Idea That Will Not Die* (Mesa, Ariz.: Bluebird Publishing, 1997).

82. David C. Berliner, "Mythology and the American System of Education." *Phi Delta Kappan* 74 (1993): 638.

83. Jeanne Allen, president of the Center for School Reform, said, "if these things [charges that the minimal choice, nearly zero competition, tried in Milwaukee since 1993 hadn't helped students academically or created more equity for racial minorities] were true, two of the key arguments of choice proponents would be refuted."

84. George Clowes, "After 15 Years, Nation Is Still at Risk," *Intellectual Ammunition* (September/ October 1998): 5; William J. Bennett, Willard Fair, Chester E. Finn Jr., Rev. Floyd Flake, E. D. Hirsch, Will Marshall, Diane Ravitch et al., "A Nation Still at Risk," *Policy Review* 90 (July/August 1998).

CHAPTER 7

Government Regulation Issues

A significant number of conservatives and libertarians prefer the status quo to the anticipated effect of mainstream parental choice proposals. They have opposed the prominent proposals because they are afraid that the regulatory maze that hobbles "public" schools[1] would engulf private schools. The maze is so stifling that state and local school authorities sometimes refuse federal dollars because of the new rules they would bring.[2]

The fear of increased regulation of private schools is self-reinforcing. It drives away the most conservative supporters of parental choice, which leads to weaker proposals. In one instance, the strong fear of regulation caused a set of conservative groups to offer a modest tax credit proposal[3] that *specifically aimed* to change the status quo as little as possible! The tax credit plan's two primary objectives are to prevent private school tuition from going up, and to minimize the impact on "public" school funding. The stated goals amount to helping existing private school users, transferring a few more children to private schools, and keeping the school system the way it is. Restriction-laden programs are more vulnerable to regulatory encroachment because they leave most of the status quo in place as a natural constituency for regulation.

The key premise of conservative opponents of parental choice is "the crucial principle that control follows subsidy."[4] Llewellyn Rockwell said that proposals like California's Prop 174's $2,600 voucher are an enemy of religion,[5] and they would hurt private schools because the government would attach debilitating conditions to the money.[6] The theory underlying such views is that the debilitating conditions would emerge gradually as the private schools became addicted to the money.[7] Charley Reese said that "the long-term result [of vouchers] will be that private schools will become as bad as government schools."[8] According to Quentin Quade, a sharp critic of that attitude, people who hold that view "believe that any tax dollars, no matter the distribution method, will ultimately and inevitably become a vehicle for state dominance and loss of independent identity."[9] In the Reese scenario, private and "public" schools become more similar as private schools acquire the handicaps of "public" schools. If private schools become more like "public" schools, longtime private school users suffer losses, and the benefits to choice program participants gradually disappear.

The limited choice proposals that receive the most attention now may do just what conservative critics like Rockwell and Reese fear. However, a competitive education industry is much less likely to have such effects. It would force all schools to be choiceworthy, and private schools would benefit greatly from no longer having to charge more for services that are produced more cheaply, their biggest handicap. A competitive education industry would make "public" and private schools more similar by spreading some advantages of private schools to "public" schools.

KEY ISSUES

When public funds generally enhance purchasing power or subsidize the purchase of specific goods or services, does that lead to restrictions on the behavior of the subsidized buyers or their suppliers? How burdensome are the resulting restrictions? How does the likelihood of negative effects compare to likely long-term improvements in K–12 education? Is the devil in the details? Will some versions of choice foster burdensome restrictions much more than others? Are trade-offs involved in the resolution of the key issues?

Choice programs that would establish a competitive education industry entail some risks. When tax dollars follow children to private schools, some private school users may regret declines in the autonomy of their school. In contrast, failure to adopt a competitive education industry entails intolerable certainties. Failure to take that risk—minimized by the competitive education industry version of choice—means that the effects of the status quo continue, including the significant peril of many private schools. Many private schools, including some that are quite popular, are in serious financial trouble.[10] Private schools suffer considerable ill effects from having to compete with relatively lavishly funded, zero tuition "public" schools. Catholic school officials explained that they have to keep tuition low to avoid becoming exclusive schools for the financially elite, and "the practical impossibility of maintaining the present system with only the present formula (low tuition—a $500 [elementary] to $700 [high school] per student subsidy) for support."[11] "Some school closings may be necessary."[12] According to Peter Cookson, "The parochial system is in a rapid state of decline and facing bankruptcy in the inner cities."[13] Quentin Quade pointed out that private schools "are damaged, often unto death, because they are deprived of the resources that would come their way if parents were free to choose without financial penalty."[14] Recent examples include a popular private school that had to use an emergency loan to meet its payroll.[15] Failure to implement a competitive education industry will endanger many private schools. According to Quade, the conservative critics of vouchers and tax credits "display a fundamental lack of proportion in assessing degrees of risk and immediate vs. remote dangers."[16] Quade goes on to point out that vouchers and tax credits reduce the probability of federal interventions. "By diminishing the role of central state authorities, it [choice through vouchers or tax credits] would lessen federal capacity to intrude via such state agencies."[17]

EVIDENCE

Vouchers and tax credits directly subsidize education buyers, not education producers, a crucial point for two reasons. That policy maintains the separation of church and state, and control follows money much more often when the government buys something directly.

There is very little empirical basis for serious concern about increased regulation of private schools resulting from tax credit or voucher subsidies for education buyers. Australia provides public support to government-owned and non-government schools, and the private sector "is remarkably free of regulation."[18] Here in the United States, experience with other major purchase subsidy programs doesn't support the fear of government control. There is no basis to predict damage to private schools large enough to justify denial of even modest, widespread benefits to the other K–12 students. Nearly every example[19] of purchase assistance, including voucher programs, produced no new regulation of the subsidized buyers or their suppliers.[19] Such examples include Social Security, food stamps, Aid to Families with Dependent Children (AFDC = "welfare"), housing vouchers, training vouchers, and especially the GI Bill support that was spent at private universities, including church-affiliated colleges. Some control followed a buyer subsidy for only a few *federal* programs. However, *state* governments have the larger role in K–12 policy, and they regulate private schools, even those that don't accept state money. States derive their authority to regulate from compulsory attendance laws.[20] In any event, the government has a much better overall track record[21] as a regulator than as a producer.

The regulation of colleges and universities is the most often alleged example of control accompanying tax dollars. Colleges and universities that admit students subsidized by federal grants or loans must comply with antidiscrimination requirements. Though Joseph Bast and David Harmer[22] and David Kirkpatrick[23] argue that compliance is not burdensome—course offerings and content are not affected—Hillsdale and Grove City colleges felt they had to exclude federally subsidized students. Home loan subsidies for veterans and first-time homebuyers are another example. Builders that cater to these homebuyers must comply with certain building requirements. Though it may annoy builders, and the net benefits are doubtful, an undue burden isn't readily obvious.

The greatest threats to private schools are: 1) "competitors" that don't have to charge tuition (i.e., "public" schools, especially charter schools); 2) highly restrictive choice programs that force schools to accept every applicant, or reject applicants at random if the demand exceeds the space available; and 3) programs that prohibit add-ons (private schools must accept the public funds as full payment). A universal choice program that prohibits add-ons would eliminate services that cost little more than the publicly funded amount. No one would pay thousands more for a few hundred dollars worth of additional service.

The Private School Plan approved by the Houston School District[24] is a good example of the second threat. To receive money from the district, a school must accept the district payment of $3,575 as full payment, and "schools would have to meet state accreditation standards, *abide by state laws governing public schools* [emphasis added], and accept all students, regardless of conduct and academic performance"; basically they would become "public" schools. Students can attend eligible pseudoprivate schools only if they are failing in a low-performing school. Houston's school superintendent insists that the Private School Plan is not a voucher program, just an expansion of the district's existing policy of contracting with private schools for special education, alternative education, and relief from overcrowding. The same requirements apply to the "private" schools that are willing to help Houston cope with overcrowding. Students can attend a participating pseudoprivate school only if the district says there is no space to accommodate them in their neighborhood "public" school.[25]

Houston superintendent Rod Paige is right that his policy is not a voucher program. It's not even much of a parental choice program. You can pick from a government-defined menu if the Houston School District decides the school it assigned you to is not good enough, or is too full. Incredibly, *School Reform News*[26] described the Houston program in the 'Parents in Control' (of what?) section, and the Center for Education Reform gave the Houston program its *unqualified* strong support.[27]

The just-enacted Florida program is another example of the second threat and, along with Milwaukee, an example of the third (it prohibits add-ons). The much-celebrated Florida voucher program has a highly compromised definition of parental choice.[28] Florida families can use some of the tax dollars earmarked for the education of their children if the government decides that their assigned "public" school was not good enough during at least two of the previous four years. The government, not parents, decides if it keeps all of the tax money earmarked for each child, or just part of it. Only 23 percent of Florida's fourth graders are proficient readers (50 percent are below basic).[29] Eighth grade science proficiency is about the same, and math proficiency is even worse. Still, the state thinks only four Florida "public" schools are so bad that parents should be allowed to spend some of their school taxes elsewhere. The standards are set to increase, though. In the 2000–2001 school year, the state could designate 170 failing schools; just 6.1 percent of Florida's 2,790 "public" schools, even though 50 percent of its fourth graders are below basic.[30] The extremely low upper limit on participation is one of the major reasons why the Florida program will not create a competitive education industry. The program also contains another major competition killer. It created price controls by prohibiting private tuition add-ons.

COMPETITION AND ETERNAL VIGILANCE

Parental choice policies that maximize competition minimize the risk of new regulations. Maximizing competition does not compromise other important school reform goals. As upcoming chapters argue, the opposite is more likely true. Competition is the key regulatory mechanism of most of the economy. Choice proposals that create the conditions described in chapter 2 will benefit private school students enormously, including, especially, the many children who will transfer to private schools that do not exist yet.

The likelihood of burdensome regulation is very small with any large-scale parental choice program. Choice proposals typically contain language that discourages new restrictions on private schools. In addition, a coalition large enough to enact significant parental choice can defend it against all but the most covert, marginal assaults. Examples like the Houston plan are important exceptions, but even the weak versions of parental choice that produce little competition are usually no threat to the autonomy of most existing private schools. A key reason is that most current private schools are church-affiliated. Regulations targeted at them would violate the constitutional separation of church and state. Secular private schools get no protection from the first amendment, but they are scarce. Restriction-laden parental choice will keep their numbers small, and the small constituencies of secular private schools places them in the greatest jeopardy of increased regulation. However, in a competitive education industry, secular private schools will have much larger constituencies, and proregulation forces will be much weaker.

Fear of debilitating regulation of private schools is a serious problem. The current funding and governance mechanisms will survive anything but a well-conceived assault by united parental choice advocates. Choice advocates must minimize the risk of increased regulation, resolve to maintain eternal vigilance against it, and convince disaffected conservatives and libertarians that alternate risks to private schools and the nation are a much greater threat. Support for a competitive education industry version of parental choice is the best way to do that.

A move toward a competitive education industry is self-reinforcing. By minimizing the risk of debilitating regulation, such a move would bring back some dissident conservatives. Their return would help to reorient the parental choice movement to the critical objective of reforming the entire system. Only genuine competition can accomplish that.

While the fear of increased regulation receives too much attention, cost issues—the subject of the next chapter—do not receive enough.

NOTES

1. Joe LeConte, "Schools Learn that Vouchers Can Have a Hidden Cost," *Wall Street Journal* (January 26, 1999).

2. Gregory Fossedal, "Help for Schools? Try Deregulation," *Wall Street Journal* (March 27, 1996).

3. Linda Morrison, *The Tax Credits Program for School Choice* (Mackinaw, Mich.: National Center for Policy Analysis Policy Report #213 (1998).

4. Murray Rothbard, *Free Market* (January 1994): 1.

5. Llewellyn Rockwell, "School Vouchers: An Enemy of Religion," *The Wanderer* (September, 1998).

6. Llewellyn Rockwell, "Costly Initiative Will Hurt Private Schools," *Human Events* (August 28, 1993): 10.

7. John Miller, "Opting Out," *The New Republic* (November 30, 1992): 12–13.

8. Charley Reese, "Vouchers Are a Bad Idea," *The Orlando Sentinel* (November 19, 1998).

9. Quentin Quade, "Must Tax Dollars Kill School Independence?" Blum Center Web site, *www.marquette.edu/blum/taxkill.html* (August 8, 2000).

10. Quentin Quade, "Strap on the Armor and Go: Never Give In!" *School Reform News* (June 1998): 16, 20.

11. Jeff Archer, "Chicago Catholics to Reform Their School Funding," *Education Week* (January 13, 1999): 1, 14.

12. Ibid.

13. Peter Cookson, "Response to Bruce Cooper's Review of the Choice Controversy," *Journal of Education Finance* 19 (Fall 1993): 223–25.

14. Quentin Quade, *Financing Education* (New Brunswick, N.J.: Transaction Publishers, 1996): p. 2.

15. Joe Klein, "Parochial Concerns," *Newsweek* (September 22, 1996): 27.

16. Quade, August 8, 2000.

17. Ibid.

18. William L. Boyd, "Balancing Public and Private Schools: The Australian Experience and American Implications," *Educational Evaluation and Policy Analysis* 9, no. 3 (Fall 1987): 183–97.

19. Joseph L. Bast and David Harmer, "Vouchers and Educational Freedom: A Debate," *Policy Analysis Monograph* no. 269, The Cato Institute (1997); Quade, August 8, 2000.

20. Since attendance at a "school" is mandatory; the government must establish and enforce a definition of a "school." Milton Friedman, "The Only Solution Is Competition" (interview with George Clowes), *School Reform News* (December 1998): 20, 16–17.

21. Herbert Gintis, "The Political Economy of School Choice," *Teachers College Record* 96 (Spring 1995): 492–511.

22. Bast and Harmer, 1997, p. 6, endnote 15.

23. David Kirkpatrick, *School Choice: The Idea that Will Not Die* (Mesa, Ariz.: Bluebird Publishing, 1997), p. 97. The Supreme Court upheld the federal intervention because Congress had specifically stated that its intent was to aid particular *institutions* (emphasis in Kirkpatrick).

24. "Houston School District OKs Private School Plan," *School Reform News* (June 1998): 11.

25. "Houston May Contract with Private Schools," *School Reform News* (January 1997): 15.

26. Ibid., note 24.

27. *Monthly Newsletter* 45 (June 1998).

28. "Victory in Florida!" was the conservative Heartland Institute's headline and cover story for *School Reform News*, June, 1999.

29. National Assessment of Education Progress (NAEP) published in *Education Week* (January 11, 1999): 110, 137. Reading data are for 1994; math and science data are for 1996.

30. *School Reform News* (June 1999): 4.

CHAPTER 8

The Neglect of Costs

The status quo is unacceptable at any price, but that doesn't make cost irrelevant, either as a reform outcome or as a defect of the current system. The cost issue is especially important to households with no school-age children, and to families that assume their suburban school is good.[1] Inflation-adjusted outlays of "public" schools rose rapidly even when the decline in achievement was most rapid, and official public sector costs understate the full cost.[2] Real increases in per pupil outlays (172 percent between 1960 and 1990),[3] as well as nonmonetary indicators like teacher-student ratio (50 percent rise from 1960–1990) and administrative "support,"[4] did not produce noteworthy, much less proportional, achievement gains. Indeed, only recently have *some* achievement measures, like test scores, stopped falling. Having perhaps hit bottom, some test scores actually rose. Proficiency rates are still quite low, and the scores are still well below previous levels.[5] In addition, there is considerable suspicion that test-specific coaching and changes in the tests are responsible for the rebound.[6] Indicators such as rapidly rising cost of remedial courses for college freshmen suggest continued deterioration in "public" school effectiveness.[7]

Though expenditure statistics cannot include the information collection, communication, decision making, contract enforcement, and access costs that parents incur, those transaction costs recently joined the parental choice debate. Again, effects vary from typical restriction-laden programs that shuffle a few children among little-changed existing schools to the competitive education industry version that changes the system. The latter has lower transaction costs, probably much lower than the current system's transaction costs.

MORE MONEY!?

Incomplete official data[8] indicate that per pupil expenditures average at least $7,000 per year. There are many examples (urban systems in New Jersey, New York, Washington, D.C.) of school systems with annual per pupil outlays well over $10,000. Nearly all private schools spend less per pupil, still true after adjustments account for differences in public and private school obligations.[9] Literally hundreds of studies fail to associate higher expenditures with better performance.[10] That does not mean that schools cannot use increased resources to improve, only that they usually do not.

A total of $100,000 to $200,000 in taxes supports a classroom of 20 children, and an average teacher costs less than half of the lower figure.[11] Still, some analysts believe that more money is the answer to the achievement crisis. Choice opponents like Kevin Smith and Kenneth Meier find it "hard to fathom how educational policymakers can realistically hope to improve student performance given the limited resources at their disposal."[12]

"PUBLIC"-PRIVATE COMPARISONS

Achievement

Unqualified private school-"public" school achievement comparisons are a major concession to opponents of competition like Albert Shanker and Bella Rosenberg,[13] Kevin Smith and Kenneth Meier,[14] and skeptics like Donald Frey[15] and Dan Goldhaber.[16] Standardized "test scores are a pretty crude measure of success."[17] They do not reflect many of the advantages that private schools must have to achieve the high levels of parental satisfaction they enjoy. Criteria like discipline, safety, moral climate, and individual attention are especially important in the vast majority of relatively inexpensive private schools that have no snob appeal. Parents who choose private schools for nonreligious reasons, quite often including sectarian schools, would not keep paying the tuition without large net benefits. Of course, choice opponents make comparisons that are least favorable to private schools. For example, Shanker and Rosenberg used 1990 National Assessment of Educational Progress (NAEP) data to point out that "students in all schools ["public" *and* private; emphasis is in the original] are achieving at disastrously low levels."[18] Frey made a similar comparison.

The key qualification of the test score comparisons is private schools' financial handicap; they must compete against much better-funded, zero tuition "public" schools. The private schools that are most often compared to "public" schools are the secular ones that don't benefit from church subsidies, and are therefore more vulnerable to financial problems. Comparisons under-utilize and understate private schools' cost-effectiveness advantages.

Cost

Choice advocates should make much greater use of cost comparisons.[19] That is true even though cost data understate private schools' cost advantages. Public sector cost data are incomplete,[20] and efforts to control for differences favor "public" schools. Analysts like Robert Genetski overadjust for "public" schools' obligations to accept all children.[21] Cost comparisons do not account for all of the efficiency differences imposed by the political process and the use of attendance zones. Every attempt is made to factor out completely the special needs expenses of "public" schools, with the result that comparisons do not favor private schools as much as they should. For example, comparisons adjust the private school cost estimates to reflect that every "public" school campus accepts nearly every child. The adjustments don't take into account that failure to specialize inflates costs. It costs more per child to offer special education services on nearly every campus than on just a few. Spreading special services over many campuses also creates greater mismatches between the service requirements of children and the skills available on a particular campus. Mismatches reduce the quality of services special needs children receive. The same thing is true of many of the elective courses offered to mainstream students. Parental choice and specialization would cut costs and improve quality. The use of attendance zones rather than parental choice to determine each school's users raises the number of apparent special needs children by increasing the variability in student skills, interests, and learning styles present on each campus. Specialized private schools chosen by their users serve special needs much more efficiently. The cost comparisons also don't take into account the greater level of parental satisfaction with private schools.

Private schools already serve children that "public" schools don't pretend to serve adequately.[22] Taxpayers pay to enroll thousands of children in private schools, but school authorities, not parents, exercise choice.

THE COSTS OF CHOICE

Perception

Higher costs seem obvious to the many people who think only in terms of very limited choice. Henry Levin and Cyrus Driver said that parental choice—defined as a restriction-laden voucher program—would mean cost increases of up to 25 percent or more.[23] Edward Fiske made an even more puzzling generalization. Based on a study of Cambridge, Massachusett's "controlled" choice, Fiske said, "all parties must acknowledge that choice will cost more."[24] It is debatable whether "controlled" choice is even real parental choice. "Controlled" choice means that parents identify their three favorite "public" schools before district officials choose the school, not necessarily one of the three.[25] Though Fiske says that controlled choice is a great idea because "the laws of supply and demand must take their toll [p. 197]," the conditions of controlled choice do not remotely resemble the conditions of a competitive market.

Hold-harmless approaches to parental choice keep "public" schools from losing money when students leave. Since the public money that assists the transfer from the assigned "public" school does not come from the school district budget, hold-harmless approaches drive up costs by design. For example, Puerto Rico funds parental choice with money from the sale of some telecommunications assets. Families can use $1,500 vouchers for private school tuition or to move to a different "public" school. Puerto Rican "public" schools receive $1,500 when they accept a transfer, but do not lose $1,500 when someone leaves. If $1,500 exceeds the school's incremental student cost, there is a financial incentive to attract students. Note that "public" schools would gain from student turnover. Through programmatic or methodological specialization, a Puerto Rican "public" school could attract some choice transfers, while driving away some of its assigned students, for a net gain of $1,500 per replaced student. Hold-harmless plans are expensive; they reduce competitive pressures,[26] however slight; and, as the Puerto Rico example illustrates, they can create perverse incentives.

It is undeniably true that choice for a few, with its extra paperwork and the staff for a parent information center, will cost more, but parental choice need not increase public K–12 spending. In an era where politicians launch campaigns with promises like "read my lips, no new taxes,"[27] where they lose elections for breaking that promise, and the term *tax revolt* is heard and seen often, choice advocates must demonstrate how parental choice restrictions affect administrative expenses, and vigorously refute sweeping generalizations about parental choice costs. Unfortunately, rather than explain that administrative expenses depend on which version of parental choice is adopted, parental choice advocates make another mistake. To deflect the accusations that choice will cost more, parental choice advocates propose a lower level of government support for transferees (discrimination) than for "public" school students so that the difference will cover the additional expenses supposedly associated with parental choice.

Reality

Studies of parental choice costs, like the findings of Levin and Driver, have shown only that restricted versions of choice are at least as costly as the status quo. That's no surprise. Restriction-laden voucher programs and "public" school choice won't eliminate any administrative functions, and they do add some. For example, adoption of choice among "public" schools, with or without charter schools, adds administrative chores to track student movement and shift resources accordingly. In addition, limited flight from unpopular schools could raise capital costs by increasing excess capacity.

It would not require bureaucratic expansion to establish the critical elements of a competitive education industry. The authorities won't have to manage parents' choices. In fact, a competitive education industry will probably shed many of the administrative expenses that characterize the status quo. If district offices don't disappear entirely, they will look more like the much smaller administrative apparatus of the Catholic school system than the much larger administrative structure typical of large urban districts.[28] A competitive education industry will probably make schools smaller and more numerous, so parental choice may not even increase transportation costs permanently.

Less restrictive versions of parental choice that maximize competitive forces can operate with the current level of public funding of K–12 education services, or less. A competitive education industry would provide similar children with the same public support no matter which school they attend, so a competitive education industry would achieve funding equalization, a court-mandated outcome in an increasing number of states.

Through free entry and exit, a competitive education industry would tell officials when public funding is consistent with their goals. Changes in the number of sellers equalize the profit rates of markets with similar levels of risk, so education entrepreneurs will open more schools until typical schools earn normal rates of return. Families unable to add on with private funds get a good education as long as the public funding level is enough to cause numerous schools to accept the public funds as nearly full payment.[29] Overcapacity and low-value frills would signal that public support is excessive, just as they did in the preregulation airline industry. Most of the fares set by the Civil Aeronautics Board (CAB) were very attractive to the airlines. The CAB protected the regulated airlines from competition from new airlines, so rivalry for passengers occurred through more frequent flights (overcapacity) and low-value frills that cost the airlines more than they were worth to passengers. Evidence of the latter is that deregulation prompted the termination of such frills to cut costs and fares.

The Outlook

In a competitive education industry, current private school pupils will receive as much public support as "public" and new private school students. With current public K–12 spending, most private schools will have much more than they spend now,[30] even without add-ons. Therefore, significant excess capacity is a very likely early outcome of a competitive system publicly funded with as much money as "public" schools spend now. Because political opponents vilify advocates of education cuts, the authorities may not react to evidence of overcapacity with funding cuts. However, since excess capacity reduces the pressure to increase funding, spending should rise less rapidly than before. Funding growth at less than the rate of price inflation is the most likely cost-cutting scenario.

There are three reasons why such a cost-cutting scenario is likely to accompany major improvements:

1. Rule compliance will consume fewer resources. Since high rule compliance costs are inherent in government operations, "public" schools may have difficulty competing with private schools. Therefore, a competitive education industry probably will decrease the number of children attending schools burdened by the expense of district offices.

2. The pressure to remain choiceworthy will strengthen productivity incentives.

3. Each household's freedom to supplement its share of public funds with private money can cause education funding to rise while taxpayers' burden declines. Choice advocates must make that case.

OMITTED PUBLIC SECTOR COSTS

U.S. Department of Education estimates of "public" school expenditures per pupil suffer from several major omissions.[31] For example, the federal component does not include federal spending on education research and development, training, or remedial or compensatory programs like Head Start. Fees charged to parents and donations of time (parent volunteers, school board members, and meeting attendees) or money are not included.

The state component omits some pensions, employer contributions to Social Security, textbooks, administrative costs, school district labor relations, judicial costs, and noneducational agencies performing K–12 services. School district figures do not include capital outlay, interest, capital equipment, and the rental value of already paid for facilities.

TRANSACTION COSTS

Economists believe that rational pursuit of self-interest underlies virtually all personal choices and societal outcomes. In other words, policies such as government ownership of school systems result from pursuit of self-interest by individuals in the context of political institutions. Inertia and special interests underlie the rational explanation of "public" school dominance of the K–12 system. The current system began with the early 1800s' combination of taxpayer support for private schools, a growing number of Catholic Church-run schools, and anti-Catholic prejudice. The "public" school system arose to deny public funding to Catholic schools. "Public" schools spread and became deeply entrenched because they established powerful special interests, and because private schools have great difficulty surviving in an economic environment where they must charge hefty tuition for a less expensive product than "public" schools offer for "free." Inertia includes the enduring belief—despite mounting evidence to the contrary—that only government-run schools can produce the melting pot effect of the "common school" (discussed in chapter 11).

Some economists have sought out more contemporaneous explanations of why the key elements of a severely criticized status quo are so durable. John Lott said that governments run school systems to consolidate their power through indoctrination.[32] According to Byron Brown, governments run school systems to reduce uncertainty and minimize transaction costs.[33]

Brown notes that schools do not specialize and he offers an explanation consistent with individuals' pursuit of self-interest. Brown said parents want one-size-fits-all schools because "school choices are lumpy (lots of all-or-nothing choices) and fraught with uncertainty."[34] Parents demand "comprehensive uniformity" to eliminate the time costs and potential for error inherent in a diverse school menu. Brown said the political process created "an *implicit* [emphasis in the original] contract between schools and their clients (students, parents, and taxpayers)" to offer comprehensive programs that cater to a variety of interests and tastes. According to that rationale, it is in clients' self-interest for every school to be "remarkably similar in substance and in means of production." Brown cited private schools' failure to specialize much beyond religious instruction to support his assertion of clients' interest in comprehensive uniformity and clients' disdain for specialization.

In light of differences in parents, differences in the interests of students and the ways they learn, and the different comparative advantages of teachers, Brown's claim that one size does fit all best is truly incredible. It deserves immediate attention lest it become choice opponents' newest justification of the "public" school system's monopoly on public funds.

Brown is wrong about the nature of the implicit contract between the public and school decision makers. "Comprehensive uniformity" exists because it is the only politically viable alternative to universal parental choice. Parents would not tolerate assignment to specialized neighborhood schools. Significant specialization is feasible only with parental choice. Furthermore, high transaction costs characterize the "public" school system. A competitive education industry will not have many of the significant transaction costs of the current system, and restriction-laden choice programs create additional transaction costs.

The Transaction Costs of the Current System

Comprehensive uniformity produces some simplification, but the resulting benefits are small, and the system creates offsetting burdens. Influencing decision making is difficult, and parents still expend considerable effort to exercise choice. Most families must relocate to exercise "public" school choice, so they must evaluate neighborhoods to choose a school. The perceived differences in "public" schools are big enough to make them the top determinant of residential choice and home prices.[35] Some families provide a false address to escape the dilemma between undereducated, perhaps physically threatened children, and a costly move. Middle-class families are willing to cheat to become eligible for low-income vouchers.[36] Most people take the law quite seriously, so for most of the families that escape detection, "black market school choice"[37] is a significant psychological burden. Still, it is common enough that taxpayers must fund detection and enforcement efforts.[38] Those significant transaction costs offset at least some of the savings that result from the greater ease of comparing comprehensively uniform "public" schools.

The alleged "implicit contract" between school clients and school decision makers must adjust to change with virtually no communication on school policies. There isn't even much involvement in school elections. The provisions of the alleged implicit contract are certainly not clear to the authorities. Multiple, overlapping authorities keep changing their minds, adding new restrictions and mandates, including contradictory ones. "When federal, state, and local programs and things the general public wants the schools to do all arrive at the same time, it gets crazy."[39] Contrary to the alleged implicit contract, school officials pursue limited forms of specialization with growing numbers of magnet and charter schools, and other versions of "public" school choice. "Clients" collectively demand comprehensive uniformity because they can't choose from a menu of specialized schools.

The futility of participation in school policy making,[40] and all of the well-established reasons for low participation in political decision making, are better reasons for the minimal communication between clients and policy makers. The political process suffers from a lot of apathy because participants bear 100 percent of the high participation costs, but enjoy only a fraction of the benefits, and then only if their position(s) prevail. Long ballots and frequent elections dilute awareness of most ballot propositions and public offices. Since people naturally respond to the large number of issues and high participation costs by focusing their efforts where the stakes are highest for them, particular groups like teachers have especially high participation and awareness rates.

Teacher union clout greatly exceeds its share of the electorate. Typically low voter turnouts often make the unions powerful enough to choose the people that ostensibly represent the taxpaying public in collective bargaining. Union officials often sit across the collective bargaining table from public officials they elected, including recent union officials.

Issues that would arouse the masses to overthrow entrenched special interests define the real implicit contract, issues like "no big tax increases" and "don't assign my kids to a specialized school." Because of a poorly informed public, such hot button issues are few and general, and controlling special interests do not have to endure much scrutiny or accountability.

School system-specific factors reinforce the political process' natural predisposition toward low levels of political participation and issue awareness. Complicated budgetary, curriculum, and personnel issues resist conversion into catchy, compelling slogans. That, plus most families' lack of school-age children, directly reduces grassroots interest, and makes the issues and candidates all but invisible in the local media. Having school elections by themselves does not seem to help ease the cumulative burden of the large number of electoral decisions. More systematic study of factors, such as long ballots, separate polling places, and separate elections is in order, but there is already evidence that the widespread practice of having different polling places and times for school elections actually seems to cut turnout further. The propensity to hold minimally publicized meetings at inconvenient times further reduces exposure to school issues.

School board members are another source of concern. School board failure is common, and perhaps even the norm. According to Eugene Smoley, "In district after district, they [boards] repeat a handful of practical errors."[41] Another influential report, *Governing Public Schools,* urged a reassessment of school board governance,[42] and the Twentieth Century Fund authored a scathing assessment of school board governance.[43] The concerns cited in those reports frequently surface in the popular media and in the general public. For example, the editors of the November 15, 1995, *San Antonio Express-News* stated this common viewpoint. "Career school board members put petty politics ahead of children and education. Entrenched politicians tend to keep superintendents careers relatively short."[44] Eugene Smoley found that citizens are "suspicious of the board members they elect."[45] Donald Roberts was not as kind: "The weakest links in the American chain of poor public school performance may well be ill-prepared, poorly educated, shortsighted, parochial-minded, weak-willed local school board members."[46]

The combination of the system's resistance to change, disappointment with K–12 outcomes, and K–12 education's status as the nation's top political issue[47] do not support the assertion that participation is low because of complacency or satisfaction with the status quo. It suggests that large transaction costs may frustrate efforts to bring about substantive change.

Huge additional transaction costs lie elsewhere in the political/administrative process that governs school policies. There are no dollar figures, but the large number of nonclassroom personnel is a revealing indicator. According to OECD data cited previously, the U.S. system contains three classroom teachers per four nonteaching staff, the lowest ratio of teaching to nonteaching personnel in the OECD's survey of its multicountry membership.[48] The average was five teachers per two nonteaching staff. Most of the countries in the OECD study allow parents more school choice than does the United States, and they have more school-based decision making, though none of them has a competitive education industry. Choice and efficiency are correlated.

The lopsided OECD data are not surprising. The U.S. K–12 system contains many layers of control—federal, state, local, union contract—and overlapping constraints. Much of the administrative structure exists to regulate, monitor, or comply with the actions of administrators and legislators in another part of the system. Carl Ball and Steven Goldman noted that: "Education is composed of several separate systems that function without an overall plan. A great deal of resources and personnel are wasted as a result of unstable governance, lack of incentives to improve, structures that reinforce continuity, and the absence of quality controls."[49] There was some recent interest in abolishing the Texas Education Agency (TEA), but the debate ended when State Representative Christine Hernandez pointed out that most of the TEA was federally funded or necessary to comply with federal mandates.[50] There is no "overall plan" because the system is compliance driven, rather than performance driven.[51] Compliance issues require lots of paperwork, meetings, and enforcement effort. Lauro Cavazos, President Bush's first Secretary of Education, made this observation:[52] "This top-down hierarchical structure is ineffective and inefficient. State and district administrators have limited contact with individual schools and virtually no association with students and teachers."

Together, federal, state, and district mandates leave little autonomy in schools and classrooms. A major aim of each requirement is greater accountability to the public and its representatives, but their combined effect is the opposite. The maze of rules leads to frustrating contradictions, costly reporting requirements, and demoralizing micromanagement that denies professionals many opportunities to excel. It also shields them from blame for failure. Professional autonomy is especially important in K–12 schools that match clients and service providers through assignment, rather than by choice. If teachers had more control of the nature of the service (curriculum, methods, textbooks) they deliver, it would eliminate some of the tension that results from principals, teachers, and parents not choosing one another.[53] Reduced autonomy and less freedom of choice generate transaction costs in the form of uncooperative behavior, complaints, conflict resolution efforts, and lawsuits.

Union contracts are among the most significant restrictions. Taxpayers pick up the tab for whatever is agreed to, but the secrecy that shrouds the process means the general public has little opportunity to influence contract provisions before they attain the force of law. The collective bargaining process, and other aspects of establishing and maintaining worker organizations, is another significant source of transaction costs. Costly strikes, the ultimate in transaction costs, occasionally make big headlines.

Several studies assert that union contracts deter achievement,[54] and that they contribute significantly to hostility between teachers and school officials.[55] Compliance issues that union contracts establish often go beyond personnel policy, and union presence makes it extremely difficult to dismiss unproductive employees. Right now, incompetent teachers and low-performing schools are more durable than the Energizer" Bunny. They keep going and going, even though they're broken. Diane Ravitch put it more bluntly. Referring to "public" schools that had resisted at least 15 years of intense reform efforts, including many that contained genuinely dangerous conditions, Ravitch highlighted an incredible fact: "Somebody's children are assigned to those schools."[56]

The difficulty in dismissing unproductive employees imposes several significant transaction costs. The well-established practice of giving troublesome employees glowing performance evaluations to get other schools to hire them devalues such information. That makes it more difficult to make personnel decisions, and counterproductive people get a chance to mess up more schools. Skepticism about performance evaluations reduces the mobility of experienced people and tilts personnel decisions toward inexperienced applicants.

Another frequent ploy is to shift an unproductive employee into an administrative position, sometimes a new one created just for that person. In addition to the direct cost of that person's compensation, concealment of the practice usually requires that the new job sound important. At a minimum, the effect is another distraction for teachers, and it may mean more paperwork or another infringement on teacher autonomy.

Corruption is a final source of transaction costs. Public officials spend other people's money, which creates a temptation to channel some into their personal bank accounts. There is much evidence that costly safeguards are far from foolproof.[57] The cost of nepotism, cronyism, and patronage is even harder to quantify. Since it probably affects who is hired more than how many are hired, the effect on quality probably exceeds the impact on expenditures.

The Real Reason for "Comprehensive Uniformity"

As noted above, you can't assign all the children from a neighborhood to a specialized school. The diverse interests and aptitudes within each attendance area demand a similar diverse menu from each school. The very limited types of specialization that exist in some "public" school systems exist outside neighborhood schools.

A restaurant analogy may clarify this issue. It's not as "lumpy"[58] as school selection, and the commitment is shorter, but picking a place to eat is "fraught with uncertainty."[59] If we had a system of taxpayer-funded, neighborhood restaurants, the public would indeed demand "comprehensively uniform" restaurants, even though it's obvious from the status quo that the public wants a selection of specialized restaurants. They're not against specialization or afraid to make choices, but the public would demand comprehensive uniformity because each restaurant attendance area would contain diverse culinary tastes and preferences. You can't assign all those diverse people to any kind of genuinely specialized restaurant. For most of the same reasons that we have very few effective "public" schools, we'd then have a lot of lousy restaurants that most people would frequent only because taxpayer support would give the government restaurants a considerable price advantage. The quality of the food would suffer immediately from chefs' inability to specialize.[60] Every restaurant would have to try to prepare a similar diverse menu, and chefs would have to prepare many meals far outside their area of culinary expertise. No doubt one of the justifications of assignment to neighborhood restaurants, and the bland culinary fare, would be the importance of common eating experiences that would bring together people who otherwise would patronize different restaurants.

The restaurant analogy can demonstrate one other important point. You can address consumers' aversion to uncertainty without comprehensive uniformity. Restaurants and other businesses often exist as part of franchises that—like McDonald's, Subway, and Pizza Hut—are often global in scope. The combination of several franchises and numerous independent restaurants provides consumers with the mixture of genuine diversity of services a diverse population demands, and a degree of certainty that mobile, risk-averse people want. The same mixture of franchises—like "public" school systems—and independent businesses would characterize a competitive education industry. In fact, that mixture exists already, but on quite a small scale because the private sector is tiny and dominated by church-run schools.

The Apparent Uniformity of Private Schools

What about the observation that private schools don't specialize much beyond religious instruction? The answer has two parts:

1. Except for religion, there isn't much demand for subject-specific specialization at the lower grade levels, and the precarious competitive situation of private schools—having to demand a significantly larger payment for a less expensive service—precludes much subject-specific specialization at any grade level. To hold tuition levels down, private schools have to concentrate on the basics. They have to stick to subjects that a large number of parents will demand, and subject areas with enough qualified teachers that some will work for much less than "public" school salaries.[61] In fact, instruction in religion is probably the only subject specialty area that is cheap enough to produce, yet valuable enough to convince a significant number of families to incur thousands of additional dollars in school expenses. Church dominance of the private sector supports that belief. A competitive education industry with equal taxpayer support of private school and "public" school students will produce more subject area specialization, especially in the higher grades.

2. Subject-specific specialization is not the only kind of useful specialization. Private schools' propensity to be much smaller than "public" schools is a quite significant form of specialization. So is the greater level of parental involvement. Structure, flexibility, and focus on discipline are other existing forms of specialization. Student ability differences, special needs, and use of technology are growing areas of specialization.

Lower Transaction Costs with a Competitive Education Industry

A competitive education industry will reduce transaction costs in several ways—for example, it allows families to exercise choice without changing neighborhoods. When "public" schools must compete with private schools with equal public support, the "public" schools will have to trim some overhead to remain competitive. If government-owned institutions require significantly more administration, "public" schools will become increasingly rare as more efficient alternatives become more popular.

A competitive education industry will not eliminate corruption, anymore than it will fundamentally change human nature. Markets contain fraudulent behavior, but it cannot persist when buyers are free to abandon unscrupulous businesses. Chronic corruption requires a captive audience. Only large organized political movements and external legal assaults can overturn corrupt political regimes. Choice within a competitive education industry creates another check against chronic corruption. Corruption will sew the seeds of its own destruction because it will drive paying customers to competing schools. The nature of education services, and the infrastructure used to deliver them, is such that episodic corruption is likely to be less common in a competitive education industry than in most other markets. Both school owners and their parent/child clients will greatly prefer a continuous, long-term business relationship. Reputation will be a very large determinant of choiceworthiness. The difficulty of converting much of the physical capital required to deliver education services to other profitable uses encourages education entrepreneurs to adopt a long planning horizon and discourages hit-and-run episodes of fraud.

In a competitive education industry, many school employees will discover that they can achieve more for themselves by shopping the market than through collective bargaining.[62] The increasing payoff to individual professionalism will weaken or eliminate the rationale, even the possibility of collective bargaining, and with it the reason for teachers to tax themselves to maintain collective bargaining agents. That will eliminate a huge impediment to change and a significant source of transaction costs. However, even if collective bargaining ceases, teacher organizations will remain. Existing professional associations will grow, and teacher unions could revert to the professional associations they once were.

Another huge impediment to change is the widespread tendency to confuse the goal of education with the dominant delivery mechanism of "public" schools. For much of the public, taxing themselves to support "public" schools is synonymous with supporting the education of children. Chapter 9 discusses how the frequent failure to make the distinction between goals and processes influences political strategy—in particular, the key elements of school reform proposals, including the ones that include additional parental choice.

NOTES

1. John Miller, "Why School Choice Lost," *Wall Street Journal* (November 4, 1993).
2. Myron Lieberman and Charlene Haar, *The Real Cost of Public Education* (in press).
3. A calculation made by Douglas J. Lamdin and Michael Mintrom, "School Choice in Theory

and Practice: Taking Stock and Looking Ahead," *Education Economics* 5, no. 3 (1997) from raw data in the *Digest of Education Statistics* (National Center for Education Statistics, 1995): p. 82.

4. Ibid. Other types of staff "support" have also risen dramatically. According to an international comparison by the Organization for Economic Cooperation and Development (OECD), the United States is the only country with fewer teachers than nonteaching staff (a 3:4 ratio, compared to a 5:2 ratio for the other countries examined by the OECD). See *Education at a Glance: OECD Indicators* (Paris: OECD, 1995).

5. For example, the 1996 National Assessment of Educational Progress math exam for eighth graders showed that 23 percent were proficient, unchanged from 1992 (*School Reform News* p. 13 [March, 1998]: 13), and the Third International Mathematics and Science Study that ranked U.S. 12th graders 19th and 16th, respectively, among 21 countries in math and science (*The Center for Education Reform Monthly Letter*, #43 [March/April, 1998]: 8).

6. Steve Stecklow, "SAT Scores Rise Strongly after Test Is Overhauled," *Wall Street Journal* (August 24, 1995): B1, B12.

7. David Wessel, "The Outlook." *Wall Street Journal* (November 9, 1998): A1.

8. Many costs are not included in the official estimates. For the lengthy list of excluded items, see Myron Lieberman, *Public Education: An Autopsy* (Cambridge, Mass.: Harvard University Press, 1993), p. 119. For more detail, see Lieberman and Haar, in press.

9. Robert Genetski, "Private Schools, Public Savings," *Wall Street Journal* (July 8, 1992); at least a third cheaper in the Chicago area.

10. Eric A. Hanushek, "Why True Reform of Schools Is So Unlikely," *Jobs and Capital* (Winter 1997): 23–27.

11. For a more detailed example, see Jami Lund, "How Much Bureaucracy Is Carried by Classroom Teachers?" *Policy Highlighter* 9 no. 5 (Evergreen Freedom Foundation, March 31, 1999).

12. Kevin B. Smith and Kenneth J. Meier, *The Case against School Choice* (New York: M. E. Sharpe, 1995), p. 21.

13. Chapter in Simon Hakim, Paul Seidenstat, and Gary Bowman (eds.), *Privatizing Education and Educational Choice* (Westport, Conn.: Praeger Publishers, 1994).

14. Smith and Meier, 1995: "If regulation is ceded from democratic institutions to the market, public schools will mimic private schools" (p. 64).

15. Donald E. Frey, "Can Privatizing Education Really Improve Achievement? An Essay Review," *Economics of Education Review* 11, no. 4 (1992): 427–38.

16. Dan D. Goldhaber, "Public and Private High Schools: Is School Choice an Answer to the Productivity Problem?" *Economics of Education Review* 15, no. 2 (1996): 93–109.

17. Terry Moe in "Responses to a Harvard Study on School Choice: Is It a Study at All?" Pioneer Institute for Public Policy Research *Dialogue* (1995): 6.

18. Chapter in Hakim, Seidenstat, and Bowman, 1994, p. 60.

19. Emanuel S. Savas, *Privatizing the Public Sector* (Chatham, N.J.: Chatham House, 1982), p. 102.

20. Lieberman, 1993.

21. Genetski, July 8, 1992.

22. Janet R. Beales, "Educating the Uneducable," *Wall Street Journal* (August 21, 1996).

23. Henry M. Levin and Cyrus E. Driver. "Costs of an Education Voucher System," *Education Economics* 5, no. 3 (December 1997): 265–83.

24. Edward B. Fiske, *Smart Schools, Smart Kids* (New York: Simon and Schuster, 1991), p. 196.

25. Most are "granted" their first choice, but 15 percent aren't allowed any of their three choices.

26. Caroline Hoxby, "What Do America's Traditional Forms of School Choice Teach Us about School Choice Reforms?" FRBNY *Economic Policy Review* 4 (March 1998): 47–59. Hoxby found that "when competition has little fiscal implication, a public school is less likely to react."

27. Vice President and Republican Presidential Nominee George Bush at the 1988 Republican National Convention.

28. Recall the OECD data cited in chapter 2—OECD. *Education at a Glance: OECD Indicators* (Paris: Author, 1995): 176–77.

29. Some scholars have concluded that public funds should never cover 100 percent of education expenses, even for low-income families. Having some out-of-pocket expense makes parents more demanding consumers. For example see the discussions in E. G. West *Education and the State*, 3rd Edition (Indianapolis: Liberty Fund, 1994); Lieberman, 1993; and Milton Friedman's views quoted in Amity Shlaes "The Next Big Free-Market Thing," *Wall Street Journal* (July 9, 1998).

30. David Boaz and R. Morris Barrett, "What Would a School Voucher Buy? The Real Cost of Private Schools," *Cato Institute Briefing Papers* #25 (March 26, 1996).

31. Lieberman, 1993, 118–22: Omissions vary by state and even by district within some states.

32. John R. Lott, Jr., "Why Is Education Publicly Provided? A Critical Survey," *Cato Journal* (Fall 1987): 475–501.

33. Byron W. Brown, "Why Governments Run Schools," *Economics of Education Review* 11, no. 4 (1992): 287–300.

34. Brown, 1992: 294.

35. See survey results cited in Paul G. Wyckoff, "A New Case for Vouchers," *Journal of Policy Analysis and Management* 10, no. 1 (1991): 112–16; Kathy J. Hayes and Lori L. Taylor, "Neighborhood Characteristics: What Signals Quality to Homebuyers?" *Federal Reserve Bank of Dallas Economic Review* (4th Quarter, 1996).

36. Mark Walsh, "Audit Criticizes Cleveland Voucher Program," *Education Week* (April 15, 1998); Steve Esack, "Seeking a School, Finding Jail," *Philadelphia Enquirer* (September 21, 2000).

37. Angie Garcia, "Vouchers Not Edgewood's Real Problem," *San Antonio Express-News* (December 6, 1998).

38. "Suburban districts are setting up elaborate programs to apprehend and expel the urban students who are sneaking into suburban schools in order to get a better education," David Boaz, "Five Myths about School Choice," *Education Week* (January 27, 1993): 36.

39. Leo Freiwald, "Recognizing the Horses," *Phi Delta Kappan* 78, no. 2 (October 1996): 180.

40. Individuals experience futility because organizations carry more political weight, and because authority is spread over several administrative levels. A. P. Dixon, "Parents: Full Partners in the Decision-making Process," *NASSP Bulletin* (April 1992): 15–18, has documented that a feeling of powerlessness (futility) is the primary reason for the low level of parental involvement. Parental involvement is low now because of a lack of support from educators, not lack of parental interest; R. K. Pierce, *What Are We Trying to Teach Them Anyway?* (San Francisco: Institute for Contemporary Studies, 1993) reported similar findings.

41. Eugene R. Smoley, Jr., *Effective School Boards* (San Francisco: Jossey-Bass Publishers, 1999), p. 1.

42. J. P. Danzberger, M. W. Kirst, and M. D. Usdan, *Governing Public Schools* (Washington: Institute for Educational Leadership, 1992).

43. Twentieth Century Fund, *Facing the Challenge: The Report of the Twentieth Century Fund Task Force on School Governance* (New York: Twentieth Century Fund, 1992).

44. *San Antonio Express-News* editors, November 15, 1995.

45. Smoley, 1999: 2.

46. Donald J. Roberts, *Policy Review* (Fall 1990): 58.

47. The latest poll to confirm that long-standing fact is the Kaiser Family Foundation and Harvard University Survey cited in *Education Week* (October 21, 1998): 30. According to the Public Agenda Foundation, *Given the Circumstances: Teachers Talk About Public Education Today*, 1996, "recent polls show that education has jumped to the top of the list of public concerns."

48. OECD, 1995: 176–77.

49. G. Carl Ball and Steven Goldman, "Improving Education's Productivity," *Phi Delta Kappan* 79, no. 3 (November 1997): 228–32. Similar sentiments are expressed elsewhere, including in considerable detail by Stanley Pogrow, "Reforming the Wannabe Reformers," *Phi Delta Kappan* 77, no. 10 (June 1996): 656–67.

50. Kemper Diehl, "Setting Out to Slay the TEA Dragon," *San Antonio Express-News* (December 12, 1993).

51. Ball and Goldman, November 1997, 228–32.

52. Lauro F. Cavazos, "Achieving Our National Education Goals: Overarching Strategies," *Harvard Journal of Law and Public Policy* 14, no. 2 (1991): 357.

53. Seymour B. Sarason, *The Predictable Failure of Educational Reform* (San Francisco: Jossey-Bass Publishers, 1990).

54. Myron Lieberman, *The Teacher Unions* (New York: The Free Press, 1997), pp. 217–25, notes 14–20 on p. 288; more recently La Rue G. Munk, *Collective Bargaining: Bringing Education to the Table* (Midland, Mich.: Mackinac Center for Public Policy, 1998).

55. Ann Bradley, "Teachers' Pact Deters Achievement, Study Says," *Education Week* (October 1, 1997): 1, 13.

56. Diane Ravitch, "Somebody's Children," *Brookings Review* (Fall 1994).

57. Frederick Wirt and Michael Kirst, *The Political Dynamics of American Education* (Berkeley, Calif.: McCutchan Publishing Corporation, 1997).

58. Brown, like many other economists, uses the term *lumpy* to describe all-or-nothing choices, a situation where you cannot unpack and reassemble customized bundles of goods or services. For example, if you want to enroll your child in a program that is only available in one school, you have to accept all the other characteristics of that school, including many you do not like. The program you want might come bundled with other school attributes you don't want.

59. Brown, 1992, 287–300.

60. It can't be because of low-quality chefs, because they'd be the same chefs as before the government set up the "public" restuarants. Over time, quality declines further because of the absence of profits and competition to motivate attentiveness to customer wants and risk-taking innovation.

61. The average is 73.5 percent, according to Dale Ballou and Michael Podgursky, *Teacher Pay and Teacher Quality* (Kalamazoo, Mich.: The Upjohn Institute, 1997).

62. Even if a teacher realizes a lower salary (there may be none), he or she may value the changed working conditions more, including opportunities to specialize, smaller schools, better relationships with parents because parents have chosen the school, rather than been assigned to it, etc.

CHAPTER 9

Fund Children or Institutions?

"America's schools do not exist for teachers and
other employees. Schools exist for the children."
— Robert Chase, president of National Education Association,
Vital Speeches (May 1, 1998): 444–46

"Systems are not sacred; children are."
— Ted Forstmann, CEO of Children's Children's Scholarship Fund,
"School Choice by Popular Demand, *Wall Street Journal* (April 21, 1999)

"They [children], not the schools they attend, are our destiny."
— Hugh Price, president of Urban League, from an August 3, 1997, speech

The "public" school system has a long history. Among Americans, only education scholars and well-traveled citizens can describe other education systems. Most citizens equate schooling with tax-supported "public" schools staffed by government employees. They assume that any U.S. school system will enroll the vast majority of children in "public" schools. Education analyst and many-time New York City and State teacher of the year John Gatto noted: "Among even the best of my fellow teachers, and among even the best of my students' parents, only a small number can imagine a different way to do things."[1] Most citizens see not penalizing families for using private schools as public support for two school systems. Even conservative members of Congress like Marge Roukema (R-NJ) see education funding in terms of systems, not support for children: "No matter how proposals of relief for private school costs are designed, the ultimate effect is to burden the taxpaying public with support of two school systems."[2] Relief for private schools is not the rational for allocating school taxes through parental choice. Parental empowerment is a good idea because education outcomes take priority over preservation of systems and institutions.

Choice opponents assert that we should support the dominance of "public" schools—their education finance monopoly—because the "public" schools dominate now:

Voucher schemes will divert vital resources away from public schools. Nearly 46 million children attend public schools. America's tax dollars should be invested in public schools where 89 percent of school age children are enrolled.[3]

With 90% of our nation's children attending public schools, we must commit ourselves to providing the world's best public education system.[4]

Quentin Quade stated the problem eloquently: "When only one *means* is provided to achieve a good *end* [emphasis in the original], the means comes to be treated as an end-in-itself. When that happens, there is no effective way to evaluate and test the means, and criticism of it is portrayed as an attack on the end itself."[5] Perhaps the ends-means confusion is more than an intellectual prison. According to Charles Glenn, "Blind self-righteousness persists among the public education establishment today."[6] That combination of narrow-mindedness and self-righteousness is a major part of the school choice wars.

Even choice advocates often equate support for children with support for "public" schools. That, ends-means confusion, and antimarket bias, is also evident in the mainstream media. This passage from Walter Shapiro's article in *Time* is a good example: "This [Friedman's voucher plan] extreme free-market proposal would literally destroy the public schools in order to save them. Few advocates of choice are willing to go that far."[7]

Note that "them" refers to the "public" schools. Friedman didn't want to destroy "public" schools, or save "them." His focus was the children, but Shapiro's was the school system.

Choice opponents exploit the belief that support for children means supporting "public" schools by indirectly asserting "public" school ownership of school taxes. They insist on no public funds for private schools. "Public money should be spent on public schools. We should not spend public monies on private institutions."[8] They oppose "private education at public expense."[9] Even though private school users pay taxes, too, they want to limit public funding to the children enrolled in publicly owned, politically controlled schools. Choice opponents characterize parental choice proposals as attacks on "public" schools—"vouchers harm public schools"[10]—because many people equate alleged attacks on "public" schools with an attack on children. Unfortunately, choice proposals typically reinforce that perception with promises not to harm "public" schools.

A competitive education industry will not be politically feasible until choice advocates focus on the welfare of children. Such a focus requires political indifference to which institutions deliver education. That means the public support of a particular child must be the same, whether they use a publicly or privately owned school. Since uniformity of any kind will serve a large share of the population badly (one size cannot fit all), barriers to choice are inconsistent with a focus on the welfare of children.

Antichoice forces don't announce that preservation of the "public" school system's monopoly on public funds is a higher priority than the welfare of children. The ends-means confusion is such that some people may not even realize their priorities. However, their reform proposals would only slightly modify a system that contains major financial barriers to private services that are already better for some children, and competition would improve those services. Choice opponents are more worried about which schools receive tax money than what the money accomplishes. Public debate of competitive education industry proposals would expose the predominant focus on system preservation. Proposals to transfer a few children to better schools do the opposite. They implicitly sanctify the objective of system preservation.

THE SYMPTOMS

Choice opponents want us to believe that helping most children is synonymous with protecting and increasing funding of the current governance and funding system. However, disappointment with reform efforts makes it harder for choice opponents to reconcile their stake in a system in which they are powerful with the education needs of children. Gradually, more people will realize "that the education establishment is waging a war against children."[11] Howard Fuller included a similar statement in his resignation (as Milwaukee Public School Superintendent) announcement: "In this city and other cities around the country, we don't put children first; we put systems first."[12] Some prominent Democrats have publicly agreed. Senator Joseph Lieberman (D-CT) said the debate over parental choice is about whether we should do "what is necessary to put children first" or "preserve the status quo at all costs" ("sacrificing the hopes and aspirations of thousands of children for the sake of a process").[13] Education analyst Joseph Viteritti noted that: "Many charter laws have been written to put the demands of local school districts before the needs of children. To limit competition, the number of charter schools permitted to operate has been severely restricted."[14]

The system is so deeply ingrained that even critics worry that parental choice will undermine political support of "public" schools. For example, Dan Goldhaber believes that the effect of "enhanced choice" on "support for traditional public schools" is a critical issue.[15] He said that the authorities should consider linking voucher value to public school spending so that people "who opt out of the public system still have some incentive to support it."

Choice advocates like Florida's Governor Jeb Bush put the system first, even when they think they are putting children first.[16] Governor Bush's own words contradict his claim that the Florida voucher program is "child-centered." Limited parental choice exists only for children enrolled in chronically unacceptable schools. Governor Bush said, "The whole point of this [Florida's voucher program] is to achieve the exact opposite result [failing schools are left behind]."[17] Indeed, the thrust of the program is to keep Florida schools above a low minimum standard. The Florida program implicitly says that one school fits all as long as the state government says that the school is not "low-performing." Michigan's "Kids First! Yes!" November 2000 ballot initiative is another example.[18] Unless districts vote to support vouchers, only children in "public" schools with high dropout rates are eligible for them, and the voucher is worth much less than the per pupil funding of "public" schools. Both restrictions shortchange children to avoid harming "public" schools.

Choice Opponents' Priorities

Choice opponents' priorities surface regularly. Former National Education Association (NEA) President Keith Geiger said that choice advocates should "quit talking about letting kids escape."[19] The 1996–97 NEA Handbook says, "new approaches must not divert current funds from the regular public school programs."[20] The late Albert Shanker, longtime president of the American Federation of Teachers (AFT), said, "I'll start worrying about kids when they start paying union dues."[21]

NEA President Robert Chase recognizes the growing credibility problem of choice opponents. Like longtime AFT President Albert Shanker, he seeks credibility with lip service to key concerns and widely shared beliefs, such as the primacy of children's interests. Then he forgets the children and returns to the longtime NEA/AFT policy of support for the "public" school system. For example, there is widespread agreement that school infrastructure is in a sorry state, and that "public" school performance is intolerable, yet Chase repeatedly refers to "public" schools as "cathedrals."[22] His most telling comment was that we should accept "our responsibility to redeem our institutions."

Many policy initiatives are justified as "for the children," yet for the policy that matters the most to children—education policy—the same people who say "for the children" have the institution of "public" schools as their top priority.

D. A. Weber, the former president of NEA's California affiliate, was not as soft-spoken as Chase. Weber asserted that any threat to the "public" school system, even potential competition with only half the money per child (California's Proposition 174), is "evil."[23] Weber said Prop 174 should not appear on the ballot because voting on a proposition to eliminate "education finance monopoly"[24] is an immoral act of the highest order. He contended that such a ballot proposition is the same as "voting on legalizing child prostitution,"[25] or "empowering" the Ku Klux Klan in some unspecified manner.

Joan Buckley, American Federation of Teachers (AFT) associate director of education issues, says letting every child go to the school chosen by their parents is "abandonment."[26] Like AFT President Sandra Feldman, Buckley is worried about what will happen to the "public" school system if children leave, not what will happen to the children if they are forced to stay. Reacting to the September 1999 court ruling against the Cleveland low-income voucher program, Feldman said, "Now we can make sure the money will be in the public schools."[27] Comments like Feldman's, and titles like Robert Lowe's and Barbara Miner's *Selling Out Our Schools* typify the focus on the school system, rather than children.[28]

Similar statements were made about the just-enacted Florida voucher program, which is only barely parental choice, and certainly does not threaten the dominant position of the "public" school system. It will take two years before the children in 6 percent of Florida's schools are eligible for a voucher worth considerably less than the per pupil support of "public" school students. There's a big difference between reality and State Rep. James Bush's (D-Miami) summary of the vote to enact the program: ''It's like being at a funeral here today, a funeral for public education. . . . After two years, we will go to the cemetery and put public education in the ground, ashes to ashes, dust to dust."[29]

An incredible example of putting the system first comes from David Berliner and Bruce Biddle, who believe the alleged K–12 education problem is "a manufactured crisis."[30] Their discussion of about 15,000 children enrolled in 24 Philadelphia "public" elementary schools noted that 80 percent of fifth graders couldn't read. That's a real crisis! Instead of celebrating that some children can leave, they express regret that some parents school their children elsewhere. They regret one "Philadelphia effect"; that Philadelphia "has generated some remarkably fine private schools," and that more parents are using them. They fear that "high-status private schools would surely become more numerous, the position of public education would become threatened in more communities, and the "Philadelphia effect" would become the American educational norm." For the benefit of assumed, but unspecified future efforts to improve the government-run system, they regret escape from the other, truly alarming, "Philadelphia effect," thousands of fifth graders that cannot read.

Misled by the Limited Choice Definition

Though it does not fully explain complaining about children fleeing the unacceptable outcomes of a very reform-resistant system, a key premise of the Berliner and Biddle book is a conviction that parental choice will be very limited. Because of choice advocates' misguided or inadequate efforts, Berliner and Biddle, many other scholars, many journalists, and much of the general public believe that "public" schools will contain the vast majority of children no matter what form parental choice takes. That narrow definition of vouchers surfaced again in James Norton's article in the March 29, 2000, *Education Week*: "School vouchers provide opportunity for a selected group of students."[31] Norton was not describing a particular program; he thought he was restating a fact about parental choice through vouchers.

Joseph Viteritti pointed out that selective granting of choice "rests on an assumption that many poor people will remain left behind in failing public schools when others are allowed to choose. It is a gravely cynical assumption. It accepts the premise that under a system of choice, failing institutions would be allowed to persist much as they do now."[32]

In addition to assuming that parental choice is granted selectively, critics typically claim that the limited departures will cause "public" schools to decline further, despite constant or better per pupil funding, and despite choice advocates' expectations of competition. And even if a proposed program would allow everyone to leave with little or no financial penalty, critics still assume that many parents will keep their children in the declining "public" schools. It's counterintuitive parental behavior, but the expectation of such decision making is the only reason to equate the long-term welfare of children with the preservation, at all costs, of government-run school systems.

Against Free Enterprise

Despite the great track record of free enterprise,[33] and the dismal failures of socialism and government management of nationalized industries,[34] anticapitalist bias is alive and well in the ranks of choice opponents. Opponent Alex Molnar vilifies the market with Marxist-Leninist language: "For the market to produce winners, there always have to be losers. Market values have eroded and debased the human values of democratic civil society. Will America . . . be further ensnared in the logic of the market."[35] NEA President Bob Chase said, the "market god will stop at nothing in the name of money. The market is eager to grab hold of the public schools."[36] In the same NEA Convention keynote address, Chase said the "run-amok marketplace" was one of the "broader lessons of Littleton" (the Columbine, Colorado, "public" high school where two students killed several of their peers). Chase and many others characterize the market as a "thing" or a "being" capable of thinking or planning. It is not! The market is only a process of voluntary exchange guided by competition and property rights established and enforced by society. Competing entrepreneurs want to earn income by educating children, not "grab hold of public schools."

Market forces continuously improve goods and services all over the world, but Gerald Bracey said claims that market forces would improve schools significantly are "revolutionary ideas."[37] Andrew Coulson's *Market Education* demonstrated that the idea is not even revolutionary for education.[38] Educator Tony Wagner called such claims "free market fantasies."[39] The Weber and Chase comments cited above reflect a conviction that market forces—the results of voluntary exchange—are evil. Weber apparently believes that allowing private school entrepreneurs to profit by luring children to their schools with choiceworthy services is tantamount to child prostitution. I wonder what Weber thinks about his child's pediatrician, who does exactly what Weber is afraid school entrepreneurs would do—that is, capture business by delivering high-quality services to parents and children.

Arthur Levine's recent announcement of reluctant support for very limited parental choice programs reflects a similar, though more soft-spoken sentiment. Levine limited his support to "rescue operation[s] aimed at reclaiming the lives of America's most disadvantaged children,"[40] again implying that it is improper to profit by providing children the best education their parents can find for them, and that government-run schooling is too important to extend choice without financial penalty to all children. To Levine, "rescuing" especially disadvantaged children with vouchers is the lesser of two evils. Levine's willingness to support a small departure from education finance monopoly ("public" schools receive virtually all tax dollars) was "painful" for him, and "only in response to a desperate situation," a last resort to "save the most disadvantaged children." Many educators still have not come even that far. Levine made it clear that he was outside the mainstream of his education colleagues.

Unspecified Huge Losses

The introduction of *Education Week*'s 1997 "Quality Counts" issue said it would be "sad for America to have to give up its current system"[41]—that is, introduce competition. Why? The editors of *Education Week* did not say what the public supposedly would miss if the education finance monopoly ended, or what the public would miss if a much larger share of the K–12 population no longer attended schools operated by the government—that is, schools run by the political process. Likewise for Jonathan Alter, a prominent author and *Newsweek* writer. Alter revealed his antimarket bias when he "warned" that if the current reform efforts fail, they may have to try vouchers—allow consumers to choose, and thereby control production just like they do virtually everywhere else in the economy.[42] Parental choice advocates should ask their audiences what they think they would miss if the government (i.e., politics) no longer ran their schools. There aren't many possible responses, and each is easily rebutted.

Accepted Discrimination

Any major difference in taxpayer funding of private and "public" school students implies public institution ownership of school tax dollars, and that some students—the ones enrolled in privately owned schools—are less important than others. Daniel McGroarty's response to choice opponents' insistence on "No public funds for private schools" is typical. He does not point out that school taxes exist to support the education of children. Instead, McGroarty said taxpayers could support private school users because that precedent was already set.[43] Public funds already support some children in private schools.

Choice advocates go to great lengths to configure parental choice plans in ways that will allow them to claim that choice won't harm "public" schools, and to publicize that feature of their proposals. The right response to that political hot potato is to point out that funding a school system—any system—is not in the best interests of children. Instead, parental choice proposals typically address concerns about "public" school effects by providing families (usually low income) that prefer private schools only a fraction of the public funds earmarked for their children. The result, as described by Joseph Viteritti is that "the farther you get from an assigned public school, the more the funding goes down."[44]

Higher-income families bear more of the school tax burden, but only rarely do choice proposals earmark any public money for them. Choice advocates sometimes assert that higher-income families should get no direct benefit from the school taxes they pay unless their children attend "public" schools. They say that it is inequitable to help "rich" people pay for private schools.[45] Parental choice plans that ban private add-ons all but prohibit private funding of formal schooling, a restriction that is as unenforceable in spirit[46] as it is counterproductive. It means that families can use a voucher funded with the school taxes they pay only if they promise not to purchase more schooling than the publicly funded amount will buy.

CHANGING ATTITUDES

There is cause for optimism about this aspect of the school choice wars. An increasing, though still small number of choice advocates are publicly stating their indifference to school ownership and focusing on matching children to the best school environment, government-run or private. Children are increasingly the direct focus of their comments.

Public officials have begun to answer the typical demand of choice opponents ("Public money shouldn't go to private schools") with demands like Jersey City Mayor Brett Schundler's "Public money for the [entire] public."[47] Texas legislator Kent Grusendorf (R) said, "Publicly funded education was created for the benefit of our children and future generations—not for the benefit of any governmental institution."[48] Robert Aguirre, director of San Antonio's privately funded CEO programs, is unequivocally indifferent about education service providers. CEO voucher recipients can use them to enroll in another "public" school. When asked about the impact on "public" schools, Aguirre changes the subject to the children. Texas Justice Foundation President Alan Parker campaigns for choice with universal child-based funding.

The mainstream media contain efforts to disentangle the good *end* of public education from the deficient *means* of "public" school systems with a monopoly on public funds. In the *Wall Street Journal*, Robert Lutz and Clark Durant announced that "we need a fresh definition of public education, one defined by who is served rather than by who provides the service."[49] Andrew Coulson's *Market Education* demanded that we "stop asking how state schooling can be tweaked to minimize its faults, and start asking: What is the best we can do for our children?" Coulson pointed out that "for decades, government-owned schools in many nations have repeated a futile cycle of criticism, reform, failure to improve, criticism, and so on."[50] *Education Week* published an article by Coulson that made the same point,[51] and syndicated columnist William Raspberry cited Coulson: "In other words, the institution of public schooling is not the best mechanism for advancing the ideals of public education."[52]

INSTITUTIONAL INDIFFERENCE WITHOUT APOLOGY NEEDED

Choice advocates need to follow the lead of Quade, Lutz, Durant, and Coulson in even larger numbers. Education services and the ideal of public education are not the same thing as the "public" school delivery mechanism. Parental choice proposals are self-limiting, and ultimately self-defeating, as long as choice advocates worry about their impact on "public" schools or any other education provider. The only correct response to concerns about the fate of "public" school systems is to be assertively prochildren. Parental choice will be a limited escape hatch, not a reform catalyst, until choice advocates develop that attitude.

Taxpayer support of choiceworthy schools, owned by the government or privately owned, according to parental decisions, including the right to supplement public funds with private funds, raises equity issues that are a major part of the school choice wars. Those issues are the subject of the next chapter.

NOTES

1. John Gatto quoted in David Harmer, *School Choice* (Washington: Cato Institute, 1994), p. 61.
2. Representative Marge Roukema (R-NJ) quoted in Sharon G. Voliva, "Public Support for Nonpublic Schools," *PrairieNet.org* (accessed August 26, 1999).
3. A "Dear Senator" letter written by the National Coalition for Public Education, July 29, 1997.
4. Republican Main Street Partnership, *Defining the Federal Role in Education: A Republican Perspective* (Washington: Author, 2000).
5. Quentin Quade, *Financing Education* (New Brunswick, N.J.: Transaction Publishers, 1996).
6. Charles L. Glenn, "Where Public Education Went Wrong," *Family Policy* 11, no. 5 (September–October 1998).
7. Walter Shapiro, "Tough Choice," *Time* (September 16, 1991): 55.
8. Texas Federation of Teachers, "The Choice Issue," Undated (but certainly late 1990s).
9. Gerald Tirozzi, "Vouchers for Some Harm the Rest," *Education Week* (February 10, 1999): 37.
10. Rob Boston and Steve Benen, "Vouchers Harm Public Schools, Violate Church-State Separation, National Watchdog Group Charges," *Americans United for Separation of Church and State Letter* (July 29, 1997).

11. Michael Fox, "Remarks of Ohio State Representative Michael Fox," *State Legislator Guide to Teacher Empowerment* (Washington: American Legislative Exchange Council, February 1997): 17.

12. Statement cited in Quade, 1996, p. 35.

13. Nina H. Shokraii, "What People are Saying about School Choice," *The Heritage Foundation Backgrounder* 1188 (June 2, 1998): 3.

14. Joseph Viteritti, *Choosing Equality* (Washington: Brookings Institution, 1999), p. 78.

15. Dan D. Goldhaber, "School Choice: An Examination of the Empirical Evidence on Achievement, Parental Decisionmaking, and Equity," *Educational Researcher* (December 1999): 16–25.

16. Jeb Bush, "A Year's Worth of Knowledge in a Year's Time," *Heritage Lectures*, no. 648 (November 10, 1999): 3.

17. Ibid.

18. "School Choice Legislation in the States," *School Reform News* (April 2000): 20.

19. Larry King Show, November 10, 1992, cited in Peter Brimelow and Leslie Spencer, "The National Extortion Association?" *Forbes* (June 7, 1993): 72.

20. Quentin L. Quade, *The National Education Association vs America's Parents*, Marquette University, Wisconsin: Mimeographed (1997): 3.

21. "Overcoming Opposition to School Choice," *School Reform News* (December 1998): 11.

22. Robert Chase, *Vital Speeches* (May 1, 1998): 444–46.

23. In Myron Lieberman, "The School Choice Fiasco," *The Public Interest* (Winter 1994): 29.

24. Quentin Quade, *Financing Education* (New Brunswick, N.J.: Transaction Publishers, 1996).

25. Lieberman, Winter 1994: 29.

26. Tiffany Danitz, "Private Vouchers Are Going Public," *Insight* (September 8, 1997): 14–16.

27. Nina S. Rees, "Fighting for a Good Education," *A Heritage Foundation Op-Ed* (September 7, 1999).

28. Robert Lowe and Barbara Miner (eds.), *Selling Out Our Schools* (Milwaukee, Wisc.: Rethinking Schools, 1996).

29. Mark Silva, "House Approves Bush's Program for Public Schools," *Miami Herald* (April 29, 1999).

30. David C. Berliner and Bruce J. Biddle, *The Manufactured Crisis* (Reading, Mass.: Addison-Wesley, 1995). They say that everyone, up through and including the U.S. Congress, has been duped. The U.S. Congress's harshly worded indictment of government-run school systems is quoted and discussed in David Kirkpatrick's, *School Choice: The Idea That Will Not Die* (Mesa, Ariz.: Bluebird Publishing, 1997).

31. James H. K. Norton, "Solution or Problem?" *Education Week* (March 29, 2000): 47.

32. Joseph Viteritti, *Choosing Equality* (Washington: Brookings Institution, 1999), p. 114.

33. The countries with the greatest reliance on free markets are the wealthiest and have the most rapid growth rates. See the data and discussion in Kim R. Holmes, "In Search of Free Markets," *Wall Street Journal* (December 12, 1994); "Free to Grow," *Wall Street Journal* (September 3, 1996).

34. Ibid.; Andrei Shleifer, "State Versus Private Ownership," *Journal of Economic Perspectives* 12, no. 4 (Fall 1998): 133–50; Daniel Yergin and Joseph Stanislaw, *The Commanding Heights* (New York: Simon and Schuster, 1998).

35. Alex Molnar, "School Reform: Will Markets or Democracy Prevail?" in Lowe and Miner, 1996, pp. 16–17.

36. Bob Chase, *Keynote Address to the NEA National Convention*, The Education Intelligence Agency (July 3, 1999).

37. Fifth Annual Bracey Report quoted in *Educational Leadership* 55, no. 7 (1998): 66.

38. Andrew Coulson, *Market Education* (New Brunswick, N.J.: Transaction Publishers, 1999).

39. Tony Wagner, "School Choice: To What End?" *Phi Delta Kappan* 78 (September 1996): 70.

40. Arthur Levine, "Why I'm Reluctantly Backing Vouchers," *Wall Street Journal* (June 15, 1998).

41. January 22, 1997, special issue.

42. Jonathan Alter, "Chicago's Last Hope," *Newsweek* (June 22, 1998): 30.

43. Daniel McGroarty, "Voucher Wars: Strategy and Tactics as School Choice Advocates Battle the Labor Leviathan," *Issues in School Choice* 2, Milton and Rose Friedman Foundation, Indianapolis, Ind. (April 1998).

44. Education Policy Institute Update (January 14, 2000) summary of the January 12 Freedom and Equal Opportunity in Education Conference.

45. Private school tuition on top of school taxes is a trivial expense for only a tiny fraction of the population. According to 1996 Census Bureau data, it only takes an income of $75,316 to place a family in the top 20 percent of income earners, an amount that certainly does not make a family "rich," especially if they live in a major city. The *average* family income of the top 20 percent is $125,627.

46. "Rich" people can still purchase tutoring and after-school instruction.

47. Wendy Wagenheim, "Why Public Money Shouldn't Go to Private Schools," and Brett Schundler, "Public Money for the Public," *Michigan Education Report* (Fall 1998): 12.

48. Kent Grusendorf, "Test Vouchers before Flunking Them," *San Antonio Express-News* (April 29, 1995).

49. Robert Lutz and Clark Durant, "The Key to Better Schools," *Wall Street Journal* (September 20, 1996).

50. Coulson, 1999, p. 365.

51. Andrew Coulson, "Are Public Schools Hazardous to Public Education?" *Education Week* (April 7, 1999): 36.

52. Coulson cited in William Raspberry, "The Historical Case for School Choice," *Washington Post* (August 17, 1998): A19.

CHAPTER 10

Equity and Equality

There is "tremendous evidence that school
systems based on compulsion are neither fair nor equitable."

Paul Hill, "Responses to a Harvard Study
on School Choice: Is It a Study at All?" The Pioneer Institute
for Policy Research, *Dialogue* (1995): 1–11

Equal access is unfair, and it's unenforceable. Many families earn advantages, and the government cannot provide everyone with the education that some families can provide their children. Since the resources are not there to provide equal access at the high level some parents are willing to buy, pursuit of equal access means a less educated population.

The acquisition of knowledge by some doesn't hurt others. Quite the contrary; when families buy more education, other people usually benefit through increased innovation and better decision making by businesses and governments. Despite that, some parental choice proposals would discourage private spending on education. Implicit in such disincentives is the incorrect premise that disadvantaged children benefit when advantaged children learn less.

A high minimum level of opportunity for everyone is achievable and appropriate. That, and equality in the eyes of the government, define equity in this book. This book's stand for a nondiscriminatory, high level of public funding for every child achieves that outcome. The current system, existing parental choice programs, and most parental choice proposals do not.

EXISTING INEQUITIES

The current allocation of public K–12 dollars amounts to a caste system. The political process produces different levels of public funding for children, even though the "public" school system "is built upon the assumption that schools should educate all of the children and do so in approximately the same manner for each child."[1] Many states even mandate uniformity in their constitutions. A particular child's public funding level—that child's education consumer caste membership—depends on several characteristics, including family income, school ownership (government or private), and special needs on both ends of the academic potential spectrum. The status quo discourages private spending on formal schooling because families forgo their share of taxpayer support if they aren't satisfied with their assigned "public" school.

Savage Inequalities

The title of the book, *Savage Inequalities*,[2] describes school systems even in states under court order to equalize funding. Even within districts, budgeting and personnel policies favor affluent neighborhoods.[3] For example, experienced teachers seek transfers to affluent neighborhoods, and resignations occur more often in less affluent neighborhoods. The process reinforces itself because more teachers have to start their careers at the least desirable schools.

Some of the outrage about unequal funding of "public" school students takes the form of funding equalization lawsuits. The system demands a titanic struggle to achieve an equalization mandate that doesn't even include students enrolled in private schools. And reality continues to elude the mandated outcome.

Part of the reason for disappointment with the mandated outcomes is that children are not the real subject of efforts to equalize funding. Institutions like school districts, and schools, are the focus of equalization efforts.[4] Despite court decrees in several states, "public" school students still receive unequal support. The current system's key features guarantee that the education of children from lower-income families receive the least public funding.

Unequal public support by family income level is unintentional, but the other "castes" are intentional. The inequities are often large, and many are not rationalizable or defensible. Children enrolled in private schools are largely ignored. Their parents pay school taxes, but most of the children in private schools receive no public funds. Private school users have only slightly higher average incomes than "public" school users, so most private school users make major financial sacrifices to enroll their children in low-budget private schools. Their sacrifices include the taxes they pay to support the education of other children. Former Principal Marilyn Stewart made this key point: "Public schools currently use all their funding for a fraction of students—tax money that was collected for the education of all students."[5] People pay school taxes to educate children, not to support a specific set of institutions, but the families that prefer the services of private schools are treated like second-class citizens. Incredibly, the body politic sees some children as more deserving of public money than others.

To stay competitive with zero tuition "public" schools, most private schools must keep tuition levels well below "public" schools' per student spending. Therefore, even though the parents of private school students pay for education twice,[6] private school students receive less education than if they had the same financial support as their "public" school counterparts.

Virtually every parental choice program and proposal continues the tradition of treating private school users like second-class citizens. The proponents of those proposals often accept the opposition assertion that it is unfair to help so-called rich people[7] pay private school tuition. The proposals that adopt that definition of equity deny public money to families that want to purchase more formal education than the publicly funded amount will buy. Universal choice plans with such restrictions would all but eliminate private funding of schooling.

The most widely known parental choice proposals reinforce the Robin Hood effect of taxation—taking much more from richer families—by means testing expenditures. The resulting double Robin Hood effect is often more than deliberate. Benefits for low-income families funded by taxes collected from everyone are often the primary goal of parental choice proposals. Rules that prohibit private add-ons to publicly funded vouchers are another reflection of the Robin Hood philosophy. The implication of such school choice proposals is that "rich folks" can directly benefit from tax dollars that come disproportionately from their pockets only if they accept a service that many low-income families are competing to escape.

Special Needs

In principle, children with special needs—another "caste"—are an entirely appropriate focal point of special treatment. However, methods used to implement special treatment are controversial. Gifted children also have "special needs," yet they are largely ignored.[8] The status quo remains true to Admiral Hyman Rickover's words written over 40 years ago: "The system looks upon talented children primarily as a vexing administrative problem."[9] Thirty-four years later, Rexford Brown found that gifted and talented programs were seen as elitist by policy makers and hated by bureaucrats because "they hate making exceptions; exceptions always screw up the system."[10]

Greater per pupil funding of special needs children may underlie the rapid growth in the number of children alleged to have special needs.[11] For example, by the 1996–97 school year, Texas had 50 percent more special education children than gifted and talented children.[12]

"Public" schools' comprehensive uniformity is another major source of "special needs" problems. The inability to specialize significantly makes special needs seem more common, it increases the stigmatization of the children that seem to have special needs, and it reduces the quality of the services for the truly needy. In an editorial about his son, editor Bob Richter put the problem and the solution in the proper perspective when he said that his son had "dedicated, well-meaning, lovely teachers who truly cared about him, but couldn't teach him because for the most part, they had little experience with blind children . . . he's now in a place where every teacher is a specialist and every kid is like him."[13]

The "special ed" label arises—sometimes even for gifted children—for the same reason as such labels as *nerd* and *dweeb*. In one-size-fits-all neighborhood schools, more children stand out; there is just one mainstream and more variability.[14] Delivering the same curriculum at the same level to everyone serves the appearance of fairness imperative, but little else.

We label some gifted children special ed, and sometimes even medicate them, because they can't cope with boredom or certain teaching styles.[15] Children with as much potential as the so-called mainstream students are stigmatized as learning disabled if the means to realize their potential are not compatible with the official pedagogy.[16] Teacher micromanagement (details in chapter 14), including detailed, "teacher-proof" curricula and precise timetables, sometimes precludes minor adjustments that would address some of the learning style diversity present in most classrooms.

The system's demand for special services for some, but without the appearance of special treatment, further impairs the ability to serve the children who need special services.[17] In addition, many "inclusive" practices hinder the education of mainstream children. We don't have to help low achievers at the expense of the high achievers, but we do. There are also better ways to help the low achievers. "Public" schools are hurt by their inability to specialize or use ability grouping to any significant extent. That's why Barry McGhan argued that "public" schools (individual schools, not the entire system) need the right to exclude.[18]

We spend a lot to help low-achieving, nonmainstream children realize their potential. Federal Law 94-142 entitles children to an Individualized Education Plan. In contrast, we spend very little to help gifted children realize their potential. For example, in 1996–97, Texas spent $1.2 billion for special education and $174 million for gifted and talented, and many of the gifted and talented programs exist only in name. Officially, Texas has about 50 percent more special ed than gifted and talented children, so spending averages about 4.5 times more per special ed child. That is consistent with the Camilla Benbow and Julian Stanley finding that "public" school systems spend more per child on lower-achieving students: "Higher achieving students have been lost in the shuffle."[19] A 1993 *Newsweek* article contained the same conclusion: "They're the best and brightest, and they're bored. That's the conclusion of the federal government's first assessment in 20 years of education for the nation's smartest students. While other countries push their best students to do even better, Americans push them aside. Gifted programs are also viewed as elitist. Gifted programs are often seen as luxuries."[20] Ingrid Eisenstadter said it was "A Stupid Way to Treat Gifted Children."[21]

The Benbow and Stanley study found that: "Over the past three decades, the achievement of waves of American students with high intellectual potential has declined as a result of inequity in educational treatment."[22]

THE OUTLOOK WITH A COMPETITIVE EDUCATION INDUSTRY

In a competitive education industry, schools of choice must specialize to survive. Specialization creates several mainstreams, so children are closer to the mainstream of their school. That means fewer special needs issues will arise, and less stigmatization will result from those that do. Children will have peers with similar interests, aptitudes, and learning styles. The availability of specialized services will spare many parents and educators the often counterproductive formal process of findings, labeling, and Individualized Education Plans available through Federal Law 94-142.[23] Public support worth enough so that many schools will accept it as full or nearly full payment—recommended throughout this book—will reduce the use of Federal Law 94-142 further. Since specialization increases productivity, schools will provide better services at a lower cost. On a much smaller scale, for a very narrow range of special needs, specialized private schools already do. Special needs children typically cost more to educate, but the increased productivity that would result from specialization means that public support greater than the mainstream funding level would not be needed as often.

Private support through voucher add-ons will give some children access to more and better education services. Note, however, that unequal access to education services is already a big part of the status quo, and that public support of, say, $5,000 per child,[24] eventually would[25] give every child access to a private school education worth much more than the current average private school tuition of $3,116.[26]

That huge improvement over the status quo is not enough for some choice advocates, however. They believe symbolism should take precedence over substantive improvement. For example, John Coons and Stephen Sugarman strongly object to the freedom to add private funds to publicly funded vouchers because "conscious government finance of economic segregation exceeds our tolerance."[27] Their primary objection does not seem to be the economic segregation that no system can eliminate, and that exists now with public funds because of the larger property tax bases of more affluent districts. Their primary objection seems to be that the policy *consciously* allows "the rich" to use some of the school taxes collected from them to provide their children better schooling than everyone can afford: "What is today merely a personal choice of the wealthy, secured entirely with private funds, would become an invidious privilege assisted by the government."

DESTRUCTIVE PARANOIA

Some people believe that the size of the economic pie is fixed, so that low-income families can gain only at the expense of higher-income families. They advocate taxation to reduce disparities in access to education services, and they want add-ons banned.

Efforts to move closer to equality than a high minimum level of support[28]— possible with current public funding levels—would have several *very counterproductive* effects. Prohibiting the use of private funds ("add-ons") to supplement tax dollars—which many parental choice programs do—doesn't help children from low-income families. The children of low-income parents aren't better off when other children learn less. Permission to use privately funded voucher add-ons may give the children from higher-income families a slightly bigger edge in the future competition for leadership posts, but otherwise everyone suffers when some are held back. Extra education for anyone enlarges the economic pie for everyone. The extra productivity and the increased civic responsibility that result when any family invests more in their children is good for society.

There is also a freedom issue. Another name for most income is *earnings*. Still another is *compensation*. Higher-income families earn the right to make extraordinary investments in their children. The rest of us should cheer them on. There are few, if any, more socially beneficial ways for them to spend their earnings.

The most important reason (emphasized with italics in chapter 2) to allow add-ons is worth repeating: *Market-determined, flexible prices are a cornerstone of the market mechanism, and competitive forces.* Price controls have major debilitating side effects, such as shortages or surpluses, black markets, reduced quality, deceitful practices, and discrimination. A policy that bans add-ons amounts to price control. It passes the "duck test." If it looks like a price control, acts like a price control, and sounds like a price control, it's a price control. The example from chapter 2 is worth repeating, too. Say a taxpayer-funded voucher is worth $3,000. Three thousand dollars' worth of privately provided education services costs a family nothing beyond the school taxes they pay. If add-ons are banned, $3,001 worth of education services would cost a family $3,001 above and beyond their school taxes. That large jump in outlays to buy a little more education than taxpayers fund has nearly the same effect as an explicit price (tuition) ceiling at the taxpayer funded amount. Universal parental choice without the right to add on would wipe out mid-price range formal schooling options. It would limit private spending to after-school programs, tutoring, and premium schooling (i.e., elite prep schools).

If add-ons are illegal, tuition levels can reflect only political forces. The resulting price uniformity and inflexibility greatly diminishes specialization opportunities and the potential to offer new programs that, like any innovation, are often quite costly when first introduced. Add-ons funded by the wealthy will foster educational innovations that otherwise would never get off the drawing board. The prospect of temporary high profits motivates innovation, and purchases by the wealthy allow new products to get through the costly developmental stage of the product life cycle. Then, innovations can mature into widely affordable, well-known practices. "Throughout history, innovations and improvements that have started out benefiting the wealthy have ended up with the poor as the major beneficiaries."[29]

The debilitating effects of banning add-ons are far too high a price to pay for a symbolic and futile pursuit of equality or particular definitions of equity and fairness. The answers to complaints that low-income families cannot send their children to the best schools are scholarships for academically superior low-income children. With the non-discriminatory, high minimum level of taxpayer funding per child recommended throughout this book in place, scholarships need only finance add-ons. A particular level of scholarship funding would support many more children than it can now.

Redistribution isn't the only way to define equity and fairness. There is also the benefit principle. Accordingly, since school taxes exist for the benefit of children, everyone with children is entitled to benefit from the revenue. There are also practical reasons to keep policy making from becoming preoccupied with fear of "wicked windfalls for the wealthy."[30] A top reason is that very few families are so wealthy that thousands of dollars per child per year in tuition is a negligible expense.[31]

It is foolish to diminish the benefits of the majority just to deny benefits to a small minority—in effect, to spite the most successful members of society. Limiting parental choice reduces education purchases and preempts genuine competition. In addition, there are solid political reasons, including a significant array of controversial government programs, to believe that programs restricted to the poor are poor programs, if not immediately, then eventually for lack of influential political support.

Providing the same public support to virtually every child also avoids the administrative cost of means testing.[32] William Clune said there is growing support for such an approach.[33] A high nondiscriminatory, publicly funded minimum—this book's proposed approach to equity—was the mainstream position at least as early as 1905. Elchanan Cohn said that Elwood Cubberly "set down basic values and goals for the distribution of school funds by the states."[34]

> *All* [emphasis added] children of the State are equally important and are entitled to the same advantages; practically this can never be true. The duty of the State is to secure for all [emphasis added] as high a minimum of good instruction as is possible, *but not reduce all to this minimum* [emphasis added].[35]

However, there are two key differences between Cubberly and this book's proposed approach. High-income families earn (they are "entitled" to provide) additional advantages for their children. This is true because of the near equivalence of the terms *income* and *earnings*, but whether or not some children are entitled to better schooling is a largely moot issue because, as Cubberly points out, society cannot afford to provide every child the education level some families want to provide their children. In addition, unless we ban tutoring, high-income families cannot be stopped from investing in their children. The second difference is much more significant. This book uses "all" literally. Cubberly's comment was a reaction to interdistrict differences in per pupil funding of "public" schools, so his definition of "all" didn't include children enrolled in private schools.

This book's proposed approach to equity does not eliminate the redistributive effect of taxation. The children from low-income families will still receive education services that cost more than their parents' school tax payments. Allowing higher-income families some direct benefit from their school taxes, no matter what kind of school they choose for their children is just, and it ensures a broader base of political support and, therefore, better programs.

The next chapter, on diversity issues, closes out the debate issues section of this book. It describes the significant differences between the status quo, allegations about the restriction-laden programs that dominate the parental choice debate, and the probable outcomes of a competitive education industry.

NOTES

1. Laurie Bergner, "Work for Education Equity," *San Antonio Express-News* (November 30, 1993).

2. Jonathan Kozol, *Savage Inequalities: Children in America's Schools* (New York: Harper Perennial, 1992).

3. For example, David C. Berliner and Bruce J. Biddle, *The Manufactured Crisis* (Reading, Mass.: Addison-Wesley, 1995), p. 178, explain how new teachers start at the least desirable schools and transfer out as soon as they have enough seniority.

4. For example, see Therese A. McCarty and Harvey E. Brazer, "On Equalizing School Expenditures," *Economics of Education Review* 9, no. 3 (1990): 251–64.

5. Marilyn Stewart, "Voucher Bill Discriminatory, Misleading," *San Antonio Express-News* (March 5, 1999).

6. Wendy Wagenheim, legislative affairs director of the Michigan ACLU, gave a rare public defense of the pay twice requirement (Mackinac Center for Public Policy, "ACLU Hypocritical on School Choice, Critics Charge," *Michigan Education Report* [Fall 1999]: 5). She said paying for "public" schools while using private schools was the same as having to help pay for police even if you hired a private security service. The two are not comparable. A private education is a substitute for a "public" one. A private security service supplements and complements police services; it is not a substitute for them.

7. Private school tuition on top of school taxes is a trivial expense for only a tiny fraction of

the population. According to 1996 Census Bureau data, it only takes an income of $75,316 to place a family in the top 20 percent of income earners, an amount that certainly does not make a family "rich," especially if they live in a major city. The *average* family income of the top 20 percent is $125,627.

8. Camilla Benbow and Julian C. Stanley, "Inequity in Equity: How Equity Can Lead to Inequity for High-Potential Students," *Psychology, Public Policy, and Law* 2 (1996): 249–92; Barbara Kantrowitz and Pat Wingert, "Failing the Most Gifted Kids," *Newsweek* (November 15, 1993): 67; Ingrid Eisenstadter, "A Stupid Way to Treat Gifted Children," *Wall Street Journal* (July 12, 1995).

9. Hyman G. Rickover, *Education and Freedom* (New York: E. P. Dutton and Co., 1959).

10. Rexford G. Brown, *Schools of Thought* (San Francisco: Jossey-Bass, 1993), p. 109.

11. Frederick M. Hess, "Courting Backlash: The Risks of Emphasizing Input Equity Over School Performance," *The Virginia Journal of Social Policy & the Law* 6 (Fall 1998): 41.

12. Texas Education Agency, *Academic Excellence Indicator System: 1996–97 State Performance Report* (1997).

13. Bob Richter, "Special Students Lost in a Murky System," *San Antonio Express-News* (May 21, 2000).

14. Benbow and Stanley (1996): 249–92, found that there is an insistence that every student be taught from the same curriculum at the same level.

15. "ADD a Campaign Issue," *Wall Street Journal* (March 27, 2000): "10% of the small male population is currently under the influence of Ritalin, a sort of cure-all for fidgety children."

16. "That there is a single best pedagogy" is a typical "faulty assumption," William S. King, "A Simpler Conclusion," *Phi Delta Kappan* 78, no. 2 (October 1996): 180.

17. Andrew P. Dunn, "What's Wrong with Special Education?" *Education Week* (May 17, 2000): 36, 39.

18. Barry McGhan, "Choice and Compulsion," *Phi Delta Kappan* 79, no. 8 (April 1998): 610–15.

19. Benbow and Stanley (1996), 249–92.

20. Kantrowitz and Wingert (November 15, 1993), 67.

21. Eisenstadter (July 12, 1995).

22. Benbow and Stanley (1996), 249–92.

23. Dunn (May 17, 2000), 36, 39.

24. Public K–12 education spending per "public" school student exceeds $7,000. Children already enrolled in private schools are also entitled to public funding. That expense, plus the money for Federal Law 94-142, oversight and enforcement, data set maintenance, and K–12 education policy evaluation, will leave at least $5,000 per child.

25. After some time to establish new schools.

26. David Boaz and R. Morris Barrett, "What Would a School Voucher Buy? The Real Cost of Private Schools," *Cato Institute Briefing Papers* #25 (March 26, 1996). Because of a relatively few expensive, elite private schools, the median private school tuition is quite a bit lower than the average. The average private elementary school charges less than $2,500.

27. John Coons and Stephen Sugarman, *Education by Choice* (Troy, N.Y.: Educator's International Press, 1999), pp. 190–92.

28. "Any choice plan must secure equal family opportunity to attend any participating school," Coons and Sugarman, 1991, p. 191. The parental choice policy proposed here may satisfy Coons and Sugarman, since they seem willing to accept a program if "the amount of the voucher were so large as to preempt all interest in spending for [formal] education by all but an insignificant number of families." Their view would seem to depend on how small a number is "insignificant" and whether "all interest" could be softened to allow for the kinds

of modest add-ons the vast majority of families can afford. Recall that low income families are waiting in line to supplement privately funded, partial tuition vouchers with their own money. The vast majority of families can afford some add-on.

29. Milton Friedman in Alan Bonsteel and Carlos Bonilla, *A Choice for Our Children* (San Francisco: ICS Press, 1997), chapter 27.

30. See the skillful assault on the paranoia about "wicked windfalls for the wealthy" in Quentin L. Quade, "Watch Your Step! If School Choice Is So Great, Why Don't We Have It?" *Network News and Views* (January/February 1996).

31. See note 7; consistent with a Tax Freedom Day in early May (delineates how much of a year the average American must work just to pay their state, local, and federal taxes—see the Tax Foundation Web site at *TaxFoundation.org* for more details), assume that taxes consume 35 percent of the income of the top 10 percent average family. That leaves disposable income of $81,657. Even for such a wealthy family, tuition for two children to attend private schools would consume around 10 percent of their disposable income.

32. Two examples of arguments for means testing: Caroline Hoxby in Helen F. Ladd, *Holding Schools Accountable* (Washington: Brookings Institution, 1996); Paul Wyckoff, "A New Case for Vouchers," *Journal of Policy Analysis and Management* 10, no. 1 (1991): 112–16.

33. William Clune, "The Shift from Equity to Adequacy in School Finance," *Educational Policy* 8 (1994): 376–94. Clune's title implies that equity means equality. Since equality can only be approximated at levels below what some parents would like to spend, I don't agree with Clune's implicit assumption. See McCarty and Brazer (1990): 251–64, for a more detailed discussion of implications of "equalization."

34. Elchanan Cohn, *Economics of State Aid to Education* (Lexington, Mass.: D. C. Heath, 1974), p. 14.

35. Elwood P. Cubberly, *School Funds and Their Apportionment*, Contributions to Education No. 2 (New York: Columbia University Teachers College, 1905), p. 17.

CHAPTER 11

Diversity Issues

Choice opponents frequently assert that government-run school systems increase the interaction of children from different backgrounds, and that such systems are the best way to establish and maintain the appropriate collectively chosen common set of values. Neither assertion has much theoretical or empirical support, and the desirability of a politically chosen common body of beliefs is anything but obvious.[1]

Choice advocates do not refute those claims adequately; therefore, choice opponents still claim that parental choice will produce various forms of segregation and will cause our society and political system to crumble for lack of an appropriate common set of core values.[2] Some choice opponents even claim that choice will cause the proliferation of extremist schools. In contrast, it is actually the status quo and its achievement deficit, lack of choice, and absence of competition that threaten the integrity of the political process and our national unity. Extremism occurs on many "public" school campuses.[3]

The current system forces the political process to address divisive issues that individuals could resolve for themselves.[4] One reason for the system's inefficiency is that: "energized factions will waste resources trying to dominate that monopoly that could be much better spent on the education of their kids."[5] In addition, "The majoritarian assumption transformed the public schools into a battleground for determining public orthodoxy. By requiring that the majority decide how all children should be socialized we in effect require that people contest the most intractable issues of individual conscience [through the political process]."[6] Religion is a prime example. Choice opponents insist that the government's required neutrality on religion means that public funds can only support secular instruction. Choice advocates' claim that church-run school participation is critical to parental choice expansion is just as questionable. A competitive education industry can function—the conditions described in chapter 2 can be established—even if the courts decide that church-run schools cannot receive indirect taxpayer subsidies through vouchers or tax credits.

The dominant practice of defining parental choice policies as tools to shuffle children among the schools in the current system sustains and exaggerates the segregation issue. Choice advocates' mistakes are a major part of the problem. Their rebuttal of choice opponents' claim that choice will increase segregation is little more than a comparison of private and "public" school enrollments. The segregation issue persists largely because the rebuttals are inadequate and almost entirely defensive. Much more than a stronger rebuttal is possible; choice advocates can and should argue that a competitive education industry will maximize the interaction of children from different backgrounds.

LIMITED CHOICE EFFECTS, AND CORRELATION VERSUS CAUSATION

There is no explanation, much less a respected theory, of how choice without financial penalty, or a requirement to relocate, would homogenize the racial, ethnic, or socioeconomic makeup of a school's student body. Choice advocates must point that out and correct the myths that lend credibility to choice opponents' false allegations.

"White flight" from the inner city is probably the phenomenon that lends credibility to assertions that whites will not voluntarily attend a school with a large minority population. Prejudice certainly contributed to white flight, but income was probably the most important factor. Andrew Coulson reached the same conclusion: "What is not so well known is the fact that the 'white' in the 'white flight' refers more accurately to the color of people's collars than to the color of their skin. That is to say, money, not race, is the best predictor of who fled."[7] Though sorting by income was the dominant factor, prejudice certainly motivated some people. Prejudice still influences some families, but it is a much less important decision-making criterion now than when the white flight phenomenon was in full bloom. The correlation between income and minority membership exaggerated the perception of past prejudice.

Since there is a natural tendency for neighborhoods to contain people of similar incomes, the correlation between income and race produces racial homogeneity in many neighborhood schools. That's a result of exercising school choice the only way most people can afford to—by changing where they live. Property taxes were once an even larger source of funding than they are now, so it was obvious that upscale neighborhoods had better-financed schools. When higher-income families move, they leave behind a more homogenous low-income neighborhood. The current system promotes residential separation according to income.

Though prejudice can increase such behavior, residential sorting will occur even in the absence of prejudice. That is evident in comments by Angie Garcia, Texas director of the League of United Latin American Citizens (LULAC): "Those who had enough money have left our inner-city neighborhoods to buy homes in better school districts. This has weakened our inner-city communities, both financially and culturally."[8]

If everyone could exercise penalty-free choice without moving, parental choice would increase racial and ethnic separation only when a major academic specialty area was highly correlated with racial, ethnic, or socioeconomic characteristics— in other words, quite rarely. For example, modern stereotypes suggest that a school specializing in science might attract a disproportionately Asian student body, and schools with an emphasis on athletics might attract a disproportionately African-American student body.

The only other way choice could create greater homogeneity is if the composition of the student body mattered more to parents than any other differences among schools. That would take a sharp rise in prejudicial attitudes—the opposite of what seems to have occurred—or tiny differences between school practices and policies. The trivial differences among existing "public" schools, especially ones in the same district, exaggerate the importance of prejudice. When parents compare school attendance zones, the composition of the student body often is the only easily discernible difference between the schools. Student body composition will influence choice to the extent that restrictions on parental choice prevent choice from changing the school system and fostering specialization.

In a competitive education industry, the differences that result from specialization will matter a lot. Only for the most devout racists will the racial or ethnic makeup of the student body matter more than schools' program and pedagogical characteristics. Even if devout racists are a lot more common than they appear to be, choice will increase homogeneity only if schools violate the law and cater to those preferences by excluding minority children.

THEORY AND REALITY

Kevin Smith and Kenneth Meier, two typical choice opponents, claimed that choice would lead to segregation and religious indoctrination, and that "democratic institutions will seek to ensure such demands are not met."[9] Smith and Meier offered no theoretical or empirical support for the alleged single-minded intolerance of individuals, their idealistic view of the political process, or the implied private-public decision-making schizophrenia implied by the combination of the two. Since only evidence to the contrary comes to mind, the failure to support their bold assertion is not surprising. Terms like *segregation* and *indoctrination* imply the use of force, and force is the essence of government.[10] A thorough refutation of the Smith and Meier claim is another book. The less ambitious rebuttal that follows includes some theoretical arguments, and one especially relevant example from the U.S. education system.

Segregation

Choice can produce separation, but not segregation. Segregation implies the use of force—i.e., codified policy. Choice can produce some geographic sorting of people, but the sorting factor is not necessarily race, ethnic origin, or even income. Sorting would occur by chance or through business decisions that violate the law. Individuals do not control the sorting factor. For example, the neighborhood near a sports arena might contain the city's most rabid sports fans. Sorting criteria amount to segregation only when the government enforces a doctrine like the longtime separate, but equal policy, or when it ignores clearly discriminatory behavior.

In sharp contrast to Smith and Meier's claim about the political process, segregation by race was a longtime official policy of many "democratic"[11] institutions, including entire states and countries. U.S. history contains several examples of institutional favoritism and discrimination, including separate and supposedly equal "public" schools. Separate but equal education facilities were an official policy in many states until they were struck down by the U.S. Supreme Court in 1954. The states had actively sought to disenfranchise a large segment of the population, but that's part of the point. Political majorities use democratic institutions to dominate and oppress political minorities. Democratic institutions don't automatically do the right thing, even in the rare instances where the public interest is clearly defined. Democratic institutions don't automatically reflect the will of the people, for better or worse.[12] Term limits for legislators are good examples. Limits are rare, even though they enjoy overwhelming public support. The reality of the political process differs greatly from the idealized, high school civics version of politics. Wishful thinking—hope triumphing over experience—seems to underlie advocacy of government-run schooling and much of the opposition to parental choice.

Though the 1954 Supreme Court's *Brown v. Board of Education* decision ended officially mandated segregation, its symptoms persist.[13] Despite expensive, controversial policies like busing and court takeovers, the student bodies of many schools, perhaps most, is much more homogenous than the population of their regions.

The "public"school system decreases the interaction of children with widely differing backgrounds. For multischool, multineighborhood towns, there is every reason to expect that result. As early as 1966, Christopher Jencks observed that neighborhood schools would keep children from different socioeconomic backgrounds from mixing.[14] Daniel Akst's typical story shows how "lack of choice in schooling has helped segregate our cities and keeps them segregated."[15] According to Angie Garcia, Texas director of LULAC: "Our schools are still segregated, not because the government dictates it, but because of flight from low-performing, often unsafe inner-city schools."[16] Relocations bid up the price of homes in the attendance zones of better schools, thereby creating a barrier to lower-income households. The resulting increase in the property tax base of the better schools reinforces the income barrier. In the 1970s, the federal government's predecessor to the cabinet-level Department of Education said that parental choice would help advance racial diversity because choice would diminish the importance of neighborhood homogeneity.[17]

Attendance zones reduce the interaction of children from different backgrounds by shrinking the area from which schools can draw students. The official attendance zones of "public"schools do not overlap. If official attendance zones did not exist, the areas that contained each school's students would overlap, and neighbors would attend different schools more frequently. Then more children would interact with one set of children in their neighborhoods, and another set in their school of choice.

Indoctrination

Fear that democratic institutions would support indoctrination was a primary, well-founded reason for the first amendment to the U.S. Constitution. The founding fathers were excellent political scientists. They knew that governments are often intolerant of minorities, especially minorities defined by skin color, ethnic origin, or religious conviction. Such intolerance was a significant source of immigration to the New World. When a governing majority coalition is stable—when the majority coalition is about the same for every important decision—members of the majority are especially tyrannical, extracting tribute from the political minority to reward members of the majority constituencies for supporting those in power. As *Brown v. Board of Education* demonstrated, the courts, the least "democratic" part of the government, are often the only way to eliminate discriminatory policies.

Many people argue that a prevailing misinterpretation of the first amendment only changed the indoctrination message. They argue that politics and the first amendment cause "public"schools to produce indoctrination in secular humanism, an antireligious dogma.[18] Indoctrination also occurs through the highly political textbook selection and development process.[19] Politically correct textbooks and curricula impose a collective view by definition.

The Common School Myth

The claim that government-run school systems will establish and maintain the most appropriate common body of knowledge fails on several grounds. The most compelling reason to reject that claim is the ineffectiveness of "public"schools. The dubious claim that democratic institutions will create and convey a curriculum that contains well-defined, uncontroversial critical elements is irrelevant if the schools can't convey the material effectively.

Charles Sykes describes how politics infects curriculum development, and the textbook production and selection process.[20] Political correctness—the imperative to placate numerous special interests, each with its own view of what each course and book must include and omit—severely distorts and dilutes content. The curriculum development and textbook selection process is a glaring example of the difference between the naïve theory of people working together to define common values, and the reality of a contentious political process that yields "negoti-ated and compromised values"[21] and forces significant omissions to achieve agree-ment.

Especially devastating effects occur in subject areas such as history and social studies that matter most to unity and respect for democratic values. Consider the recent attempt to develop a national history standard. The National Governors Association's blue ribbon panel had considerable difficulty reaching an agree-ment. Finally, the association "brought forth a politically correct screed [informal piece of writing] that was denounced by professional historians, and rejected by a Senate vote of ninety-nine to one."[22] Even subject areas like math and physical sci-ences, which don't seem to have any political content, are not immune to the po-litical correctness disease.

THE INADEQUATE REBUTTAL

A big part of the segregation issue is the narrow definition of parental choice that pervades the debate. As already noted throughout the book, choice advocates are largely to blame. The typical definition of parental choice leaves most of the key elements of the status quo intact, which leaves little basis to argue that student body composition will become a less significant choice-making factor. It forces choice advocates into the difficult defensive position of having to assert that stu-dent composition would be a trivial choice-making factor with little in the way of school system change for support. Then the rebuttal of claims that more parental choice will increase segregation rests on the reasonably diverse makeup of exist-ing private schools and the current uses of restriction-laden versions of choice to pursue racial diversity goals. Those facts are important, but they are just a start-ing point for a counterattack on the segregation issue. Choice advocates must ar-gue that parental choice in a competitive education industry will make student body composition into a less significant choice-making factor.

Diversity Comparisons

James Coleman was among the first[23] to note the racial diversity of private schools.[24] Diversity was greater than in a typical "public" school, despite some sep-aration by income and considerable grouping by religion. Since private school users must pay tuition on top of their school taxes, income is actually a surpris-ingly small private school attendance factor. The high demand for privately funded *partial* low-income vouchers has shown that many low-income families can find money for private school tuition. The religion factor exists because church-run schools dominate the United States' tiny private school sector. The re-ligion factor is exaggerated by the many parents who send their children to church-run schools despite their religion content, not because of it.[25] Many parents tolerate religion courses because they prefer the academics, discipline, and safety of the church-run school over their neighborhood school.

Church-run schools probably will have a much smaller share of the larger private sector that a competitive education industry would establish. Many parents who can afford the relatively low tuition still don't use church-run schools. In a competitive education industry those parents would keep their children in a "public"school or choose a secular private school. Church-run schools would gain children currently kept away by tuition costs; however, church-run schools would lose students who attend only because a secular private school was not available.

Evidence From Hypocrisy

Choice opponents say that parental choice will increase separation, but they use choice to pursue court-ordered racial diversity targets.[26] Jim Carl said that a noteworthy feature of parental choice in the United States "was the use of parental choice as a strategy to racially integrate urban school systems."[27] Since the alternative was busing, limited choice "was a politically advantageous response to school desegregation orders."[28] Magnet schools started as a way to recruit white, non-Hispanic children for schools in minority areas, and that's still the primary purpose of many of these schools. Cambridge, Massachusetts, implemented controlled choice among "public"schools[29] to improve the racial diversity of its schools. District officials encouraged the schools to establish their own identities through unique programs, but to fulfill racial quotas, the authorities who had the final word on each child's school created many mismatches between schools and children's interests and capabilities. District officials denied some parents all of their top choices, because the political process assigned a particular version of racial diversity a higher priority than the best possible match between a school's programs and a student's academic characteristics. The children forced into a mismatch are lucky that the "public"school system cannot achieve much specialization.[30]

FROM REBUTTAL TO COUNTERATTACK

Inside the intellectual prison bars of the status quo and misinterpreted experience, "uncontrolled" choice that includes private schools can seem counterproductive.[31] When choice is seen as something that just shifts a few students from "public"schools to already existing private schools, a competitive education industry's positive effect on integration through increased specialization beyond what the political process will allow is not taken into account. Prejudice-related criteria are going to be decisive more often for "public"school choice because "public"schools lack significant program or pedagogical differences. State constitutions (e.g., Wisconsin) sometimes even prohibit significant differences.

Elimination of "public"school attendance zones would further reinforce the other positive effects of a competitive education industry. Since school specialization has been minimal, and remains so, experience with parental choice through relocation left the impression that parents assign separation a much higher priority than they actually do.[32] That kind of thinking led to the empowerment of district officials to overrule selections and eliminate any statistical appearance of separation through quotas or by manipulating controlled choice.

Desegregation Through Specialization

Parental choice can increase separation only if it makes schools more homogeneous than the population of their immediate neighborhood. If it were something to aspire to, it would be quite a challenge. The rationale underlying magnet schools and Cambridge's controlled choice program is that most people care more about program differences than integration[33] or the separation of certain groups. The increased diversity produced by the choice part of controlled choice will reflect the expected priority of academics over racial or ethnic homogeneity.

By maximizing competitive pressures, and by minimizing the influence of politics, a competitive education industry maximizes school specialization. Large program and pedagogical differences would reduce the student homogeneity of schools, and the academic differences would discourage prejudice-motivated behavior. For example, some families unfortunately will prefer more racially homogeneous schools. However, if the most homogeneous school is not a good academic match for their child, the prejudice factor probably will yield to academic considerations for most of them. It is against the law for schools to favor any groups. Therefore, unless racial, ethnic, or socioeconomic group membership is correlated with a school's program or pedagogical specialty area (very unlikely), schools will enroll a student body with similar academic interests that reflects the population of the neighborhoods close enough to the school to access reasonable transportation arrangements.

Borderless, Overlapping Attendance Areas

No school policy will completely eliminate neighborhood or student body separation by socioeconomic background, but a competitive education industry will minimize separation. In a competitive education industry, many schools will have informal, borderless, overlapping attendance areas determined by transportation costs. The pressure to specialize could force government-owned schools to eliminate attendance areas, so it could easily be all schools. In comparison, 80 percent of children now attend an assigned "public" school with a small, exclusive attendance area.[34]

Elimination of official, exclusive attendance areas would reduce family income differences of student bodies, but some systematic differences are unavoidable. Efforts to eliminate student body income differences completely will fail, and such efforts can do more harm than good. Private-public tuition sharing, such as through voucher add-ons, would cause some separation by income, but flexible prices are much too important to consider banning add-ons. The effect of add-ons on separation by income class is minimized if the level of public funding per child is high enough so that a large number of schools will accept it as nearly full payment; a practice strongly recommended here.

Smaller Income Differences

Since market forces produce significant specialization and competitive behavior, schools would improve everywhere. The improvements would be greatest in the inner city, where the worst schools and the least advantaged children live. Therefore, a competitive education industry would gradually shrink the inverse correlation between family income and racial/ethnic minority membership, which would reduce the extent to which natural sorting by income produces separation by racial or ethnic group in schools or in neighborhoods. In such a future, socioeconomically homogeneous neighborhoods would be less racially or ethnically homogeneous than they are now.

Reduced separation through a competitive education industry would accelerate the rate of improvement. In the political arena, diversity produces bland compromises, acrimony, and deadlock. Eugene Smoley[35] and the Twentieth Century Fund[36] cited electoral and special interest diversity as a major reason why school boards performed so poorly. However, in a market setting, diversity is an asset. Through the freedom that parental choice entails, "the great cultural diversity of urban schools—so often cited as an excuse for failure—could be turned into a tremendous asset."[37]

CHURCH AND STATE

The contention that the U.S. Constitution prohibits public support for church-run institutions is quite new, and limited almost completely to K–12 schooling. For example, public funds flow to church-run day-care centers, and veterans have attended sectarian universities under the GI Bill for more than half a century. "Well into the 20th century, students read bibles and sang religious songs in the public schools."[38]

Government support of church-run schools was an issue in the first half of the 19th century. That debate produced the common school movement that was the origin of today's government-run school system. However, concerns about church-state entanglement did not motivate the movement's leaders. Several scholars have pointed out that the aim of "the movement was to deny public funds to Catholic schools."[39] Government support was constitutional, even though it was much more direct than this book's proposal to base allocation of taxpayer funding on parental choices. "Common school reformers did not claim it was unconstitutional to spend public funds in Catholic schools. Instead they passed state laws to prevent it."[40] Public aid to church-run schools was "commonly accepted until then but, of course, until then, the schools' religious orientation had been overwhelmingly Protestant."[41]

Neutrality, Not Hostility

The history recounted above is consistent with some of the latest thinking about the first amendment. The federal government shouldn't oppose the exercise of religious beliefs. The appropriate government posture is neutrality. When the State of New York attempted to use something akin to a voucher to channel aid to a particular church-run operation, the U.S. Supreme Court struck it down. When the government observed neutrality, such as with the GI Bill and other voucher-like instruments, the U.S. Supreme Court allowed church-run operations to receive public funds.

Constitutionality

Legal scholars as diverse as Clint Bolick and Lawrence Tribe believe the U.S. Supreme Court will allow church-run schools to cash publicly funded vouchers as long as parents can use the vouchers to purchase schooling from a broad array of providers.[42]

The outlook is not as favorable for some states. At the height of the 19th century's common school movement, "James G. Blaine [Speaker of the U.S. House of Representatives] proposed an amendment to the U.S. Constitution that would have prohibited public aid to religious schools."[43] Congress said no, indicating "that the members not only agreed there was no barrier to such aid, but objected to putting one in place."[44] Blaine and his supporters had better luck with state constitutions. Many state constitutions contain so-called Blaine Amendments. In those states, it will probably take a constitutional amendment to allow public support for children enrolled in church-run schools.[45]

Significance

Recall from chapter 6 that many people, including prominent parental choice advocates, mistakenly believe that: "Little Blaine Amendments were added to the constitutions of about half the states. It is these provisions, not the [U.S. Constitution's] First Amendment, that pose the greatest legal obstacles to school choice proposals today."[46]

And:

In the end, the fate of school choice will turn on the willingness of the Supreme Court to impose its own constitutional guidelines upon the States in order to protect the free exercise rights of individuals.[47]

The [U.S.] Supreme Court could decide, once and for all, the constitutionality of school choice in the near future.[48]

Fortunately, each is technically false. The authorities can establish the key elements of a competitive education industry even if parents who use a church-run school cannot receive assistance from the government. However, while church-run school participation is not technically necessary, it may be politically necessary. A competitive education industry may not be politically feasible without the support of the church-run schools and the parents who prefer them.

The remaining chapters address political feasibility concerns and strategy: what mistakes are occurring, how to correct them, and where little recognized opportunities exist that would hasten implementation of a competitive education industry.

NOTES

1. Mary A. Raywid, "Choice Orientations, Discussions, and Prospects," *Educational Policy* 6, no. 2 (June 1992): 112–13. According to Raywid, libertarians and some conservatives believe that putting education practices in the domain of politics puts freedom in jeopardy, a sentiment famously expressed by John Stuart Mill (1859).

2. Dan D. Goldhaber, "School Choice as Education Reform," *Phi Delta Kappan* 79, no. 2 (October 1997): 143.

3. For example, the recent spate of school shootings and the arguments for school uniforms.

4. Robert Rector, "The Importance of Vouchers for Social Health," in *Colorado in the Balance* (Denver: Independence Institute, 1995).

5. Richard Sherlock, "Choice v. Conflict in Education," Sutherland Institute Public Policy Perspective (August 27, 1996).

6. Stephen Arons, "Educational Choice: Unanswered Question in the American Experience," in M. E. Manley-Casimir (ed.), *Family Choice in Schooling* (Lexington, Mass.: Lexington Books, 1982), pp. 24–25, 30.

7. Andrew Coulson, *Market Education* (New Brunswick, N.J.: Transaction Publishers, 1999), p. 137. Coulson based his claim on S. James Zafirau, and Margaret Fleming, *A Study of Discrepant Reading Achievement of Minority and White Students in a Desegregating School District: Phase IV* (Cleveland, Ohio: Cleveland Public Schools, Department of Research and Analysis, 1982).

8. Angie Garcia, "Vouchers Not Edgewood's Real Problem," *San Antonio Express-News* (December 6, 1998).

9. Kevin B. Smith and Kenneth J. Meier, *The Case against School Choice* (New York: M. E. Sharpe, 1995).

10. See Thomas Sowell, "Governments Have Fostered Discrimination," *The Des Moines Register* (August 5, 1995): 7, for more discussion and examples.

11. In fact, we live in a republic. Few public policies are the result of "democracy." As is common

elsewhere, the term *democratic* is used to denote the participatory process of choosing and lobbying representatives, and less frequently choosing and deciding ballot propositions.

12. Frederich A. Hayek, *The Road to Serfdom* (Chicago: The University of Chicago Press, 1994), p. 42.

13. A *Newsweek* cover story (Joe Klein, "The Legacy of Summerton," *Newsweek* [May 16, 1994]: 26–31) made that case, largely through the example of a particular, supposedly typical, example. It included this statement: "Recent studies show that most school systems remain as profoundly segregated as those in Summerton, and those in the inner cities seem far more desperate (p. 27)." According to Robert L. Carter, an NAACP lawyer who helped argue *Brown v. Board of Education*: "More black children are in all or virtually all black schools today than in 1954," "Civil Rights Leaders Wear Scars of Controversy," *Washington Times*, (May 17, 1994). According to James Coleman, *Public and Private Schools* (New York: Basic Books, 1987), "They ["public" schools] tend to be the most exclusive and segregated schools."

14. Christopher Jencks, "Is the Public School Obsolete?" *The Public Interest* 2 (1966): 18–27.

15. Daniel Akst, "Why Liberals Should Love School Choice," *Wall Street Journal* (April 6, 1998).

16. Garcia (December 6, 1998). Empirical evidence to support Ms. Garcia's assertion, and that the Akst story is not unique: Denis Doyle and Douglas Munro, *Reforming the Schools to Save the City* (Baltimore: The Calvert Institute, 1997).

17. Paul G. Wyckoff, "A New Case for Vouchers," *Journal of Policy Analysis and Management* 10, no. 1 (1991): 112–16.

18. Several prominent lawsuits are discussed in Charles Glenn, *The Myth of the Common School* (Amherst: University of Massachusetts Press, 1988).

19. Charles J. Sykes, *Dumbing Down Our Kids* (New York: St. Martins Press, 1995).

20. Ibid.

21. Raywid (June 1992): 113.

22. Paul Gray, "Debating Standards," *Time* (April 8, 1996): 40.

23. More recently, a similar finding comes from Jay P. Greene and Nicole Mellow, "Integration Where It Counts: A Study of Racial Integration in Public and Private School Lunchrooms," September 1998 Conference of the American Political Science Association Meeting in Boston.

24. James Coleman, *Public and Private Schools* (New York: Basic Books, 1987). The racial diversity of private schools was noted more recently by John Chubb and Terry Moe, "The Private vs. Public School Debate," *Wall Street Journal* (July 26, 1991).

25. A poll of the New York City parents seeking privately funded scholarships to attend Catholic schools indicated that the first concern of 85 percent of the parents was academic quality. Only 38 percent cited religious instruction as their primary motivation. Ed Feulner, "Is School Choice a Bad Idea?" *Heritage Member News* (Autumn 1998).

26. Amy S. Wells, *Time to Choose* (New York: Hill and Wang, 1993).

27. Jim Carl, "Parental Choice as National Policy in England and the United States," *Comparative Education Review* 38, no. 3 (August 1994): 297.

28. Raywid (June 1992): 111.

29. Edward B. Fiske, *Smart Schools, Smart Kids* (New York: Simon and Schuster, 1991).

30. According to Tony Wagner, a prominent educator and a resident of Cambridge, "The majority of the 13 [Cambridge K–8 schools] seem virtually interchangeable and are mediocre," "School Choice: To What End?" *Phi Delta Kappan* 78, no. 1 (September 1996): 71.

31. Wells, 1993.

32. A recent poll supports the view that academics are much more important to parents than diversity. The differences between non-Hispanic white parents, and minority families were small. About three-fourths of each group wanted schools to aim for academic excellence over diversity. The Public Agenda–Public Education Network-sponsored poll was reported in "Parents Prefer Academics to Integration," *School Reform News* (November 1998): 6.

33. See note 32.

34. National Center for Education Statistics Web site.

35. Eugene R. Smoley Jr., *Effective School Boards* (San Francisco: Jossey-Bass Publishers, 1999).

36. Twentieth Century Fund, *Facing the Challenge: The Report of the Twentieth Century Fund Task Force on School Governance* (New York: The Twentieth Century Fund Press, 1992).

37. Ann C. Lewis, "A Modest Proposal for Urban Schools," *Phi Delta Kappan* 78, no. 1 (September 1996): 5–7.

38. Diane Ravitch, "Somebody's Children," *Brookings Review* (Fall 1994).

39. Ibid. Several other scholars have reached the same conclusion: Derek Neal, "Religion in the Schools: Measuring Catholic School Performance," *The Public Interest* (Spring 1997): 81–93; David Kirkpatrick, *School Choice: The Idea That Will Not Die* (Mesa, Ariz.: Bluebird Press, 1997); Gerard V. Bradley, *Church-State Relations in America* (New York: Greenwood Press, 1987).

40. Ravitch (Fall 1994).

41. Kirkpatrick, 1997.

42. Karl J. Borden and Edward A. Rauchat, "Educational Choice: Making Even Good Schools Better," *A Constitutional Heritage Issue Paper* (1995): 12–13.

43. Kirkpatrick, 1997.

44. Ibid.

45. Joseph Viteritti, "Blaine's Wake: School Choice, the First Amendment, and State Constitutional Law" *Harvard Journal of Law and Public Policy* 21, no. 3 (Summer 1998): 657–718.

46. Michael W. McConnell, "School Choice in America," *The Weekly Standard* (December 21, 1998): 24.

47. Viteritti (Summer 1998): 657–718.

48. Nina Shokraii Rees, "School Choice 2000 Annual Report," *The Heritage Backgrounder*, No. 1354 (March 30, 2000).

3 Strategic and Tactical Issues

CHAPTER 12

Strategic and Tactical Fallacies

"It's time for major transformation of schools."

—Jeanne Allen, director of Center for Education Reform
Center for Edcuation Reform Newsletter 53 (May 1999): 1

Choice advocates talk about major reform, but nearly all of their proposals assume key elements of the status quo. They celebrate every new option for anyone, even when the proposals could delay or derail more meaningful reforms. For example, the *Center for Education Reform Newsletter* that contained Jeanne Allen's call for "major transformation of schools" also celebrated a Florida voucher bill that transforms nothing.[1] Voucher plans in Cleveland and Milwaukee evoke the same unrealistic hype.

In Florida, families assigned to schools guilty of long-term education malpractice can use *some* of the public money earmarked for their children to pay private school tuition. The schools' owner, the government, decides if any schools are failing; the "number could rise to as many as 170 as standards are raised."[2] That's only 6.1 percent of Florida's "public" schools, even though "half of the state's fourth-graders can't read at a basic level."[3] The nation is at risk because much more than 6.1 percent of its schools are not good enough.

Being among the 6.1 percent that can use a voucher still doesn't mean you can leave, or that the school will change in any way. The education malpractice that children must endure to become eligible for a voucher can mean that they've fallen so far behind grade level that they have to return to the "public" school that put them so far behind. Because private schools must accept the voucher as full payment, the voucher won't increase the private schools' money per student. Whether slightly larger and more numerous private schools enrolling a larger percentage of low achievers will improve the private sector is doubtful. It definitely will not transform the public sector. Only the small share of schools near the failure standard have any additional incentive to change, far less than the share of children below the National Assessment of Educational Progress's definition of basic reading and mathematics skills.

Choice advocates expect any parental choice to gradually evolve into their vision of universal choice, which is not always a competitive education industry. That vision of incremental change arose without any consistent evidence that major changes in the role of government can be implemented politically in stages. That means repeatedly revising and reenacting a policy, which is very different from a program phase-in. The latter only has to run the electoral and legislative gauntlet once, and it establishes a certain outcome at the outset. Choice advocates are so confident of incremental change that they act as if any improvement on the status quo guarantees that they eventually will achieve every political victory they need.

Choice advocates' own metaphors contradict the incremental change vision, and they ignore evidence that major reforms are best achieved in a cold turkey, blitzkrieg fashion.[4] In addition, some of the comparisons choice advocates make contradict the transformation goal. They enthusiastically support programs that transfer a few disadvantaged children to schools with fewer resources and leave the forsaken system intact with more money per child. Though the private sector also needs transformation, choice advocates act as if the transferees were rescued, and that reforms should put more children in schools like those currently in the private sector. Choice advocates compare "public" schools to the existing private schools, when they should compare different governance, funding, and incentive systems.

INCREMENTALISM?

Low expectations and ideological confusion lead to conclusions that progress must occur in "baby steps,"[5] or with "piecemeal reforms."[6] "They [choice advocates] have continued to seek out *margins* [emphasis added] on which they can press for change."[7] Unfortunately, piecemeal reforms can easily become longlasting stopping points, or even final destinations, rather than mileposts on the expressway toward a competitive education industry.

Even when policy improvements (restriction-laden programs) are small steps in the right direction, they don't reveal much about the final destination. Recall from chapter 3 that basing generalizations on experience with restriction-laden programs is a serious mistake. Ignorance is better than misinformation.

Right after Chester Finn (a Reagan administration Assistant Secretary of Education and prominent choice advocate) said he was "becoming more pragmatic [about choice advocacy]," he noted that "piecemeal reform often slows the course of revolution,"[8] an understatement since it can abort the revolution entirely. Low expectations lead to conclusions that we cannot restructure the education system because "we do not live in an ideal world,"[9] and that the public is just not ready for sweeping reforms. The resulting "less sweeping reforms than vouchers"[10] cannot produce, lead to, or reveal many effects of competitive market conditions. Chester Finn and Rebecca Gau are correct; choice strategies are "mutating,"[11] but not for the better, as implied by their upbeat tone. The first drastic strategy mutations[12] eliminated the critical features of Milton Friedman's original proposal,[13] and no parental choice program has come close to restoring market forces, including especially the critical elements of competition.

Also, recall from chapter 3 that choice opponents are attacking voucher proposals increasingly for their limited scope, which has become a common objection addressed by prochoice campaign literature.[14] It means incrementalism— stops on the "expressway"—may fortify, rather than reduce, resistance to parental choice by creating additional objections. The typical choice advocate response to that objection is not correct either. Advocates argue that lifeboat programs for low-income families or children enrolled in "low-performing" schools are appropriate or better than nothing. The correct response is that parental choice is the best way to allocate all public education funding to schools.

Lowered expectations also lead to half-measures like charter schools and choice limited to "public" schools. They are improvements over the status quo, but that doesn't mean they are steps in the right direction. Both are probably one-way detours off the road to universal, nondiscriminatory parental choice. The nation is at risk now; we don't have time to evaluate each baby step, and then hope to get restarted and pointed in the right direction again. Our country can't afford to neglect another generation of children, nor can it afford the repeated misinvestment of tax dollars in the current system. Progress toward a competitive education industry will require a sustained assault on those misconceptions. It won't be easy. The shortcomings of the current system are a major reason why those misconceptions are getting harder to correct. Most voters and their elected leaders attended "public" schools. Undereducation and miseducation, especially in economics,[15] makes it harder to make the case for a competitive education industry. It's another major source of urgency.

Bad Metaphor

John Hood said airline deregulation was a metaphor for gradual education reform. He said the "controlled choice" plan used to improve racial balance in Cambridge, Massachusetts, is an example of a good gradual reform starting point.[16] Though airline deregulation was not finished in one step, the first step was much bigger than Cambridge's controlled choice policy.

The poorly chosen metaphor illustrates several points. Hood unwittingly casts doubt on the assumed possibility of gradual reform. He admits that in the airline industry, there are "*lingering* [emphasis added] impediments to competition." He claims that airline deregulation is an example of gradualism, even though most of the regulatory changes were not gradual. The original airline reforms were quite extensive. Most of the changes that were achieved were in the original 1982 reform package. The subsequent changes were much less extensive. Entrenchment of the original changes created the "lingering impediments." Ostensible choice-based reform followed the same pattern.[17] The initial stages of restriction-laden reforms linger. The starting point of supposed gradual reform will strongly resemble the end point.

The airline industry conditions created by reform differ significantly from the controlled choice environment of Cambridge cited specifically by Hood, and the few somewhat less restrictive choice programs established since then (1991). The Cambridge program cited by Hood limited parents' new choices to government-owned schools. Most parents get their first choice, but school administrators have the final say. Fifteen percent don't get any of their top three choices. In contrast, air travelers are not told which airline to fly. With rare exceptions, choice-facilitated departures don't close schools or force ownership changes.[18] Even school employee terminations are rare, whereas many airlines dissolved or changed owners.

Stalled on a Detour

Chester Finn's statement about gradual reform needs more scrutiny. He conceded that "piecemeal reform often slows the course of revolution."[19] The risks are much greater. Detour hazards are plentiful; even small steps in the right direction can make a complete revolution less likely. A key reason is that leading proponents of school choice do not remind their supporters regularly of the appropriate destination (real competition). Many have never defined the key conditions that characterize it. If choice supporters aren't told where they're going, a hard-won victory will seem like a reasonable final destination to many. For example, though the key conditions of a competitive education industry are not present anywhere, the Center for Education Reform (CER) said "full school choice" already exists in Cleveland, Milwaukee, Vermont, Maine, and Southeast Delco, Pennsylvania.[20] In those places, only a few parents have a little bit of choice. The recent, much-heralded expansion of the Milwaukee program allows more participation than any other program the CER named, yet only 15,000 Milwaukee children out of an estimated 65,000 to 70,000 who meet eligibility requirements can participate. Another 30,000 to 35,000 children are not eligible.

In a recent upbeat survey article about "The New Ways of Education," Finn and Rebecca Gau act as if the final destination is close at hand, or that we're at least moving toward it quickly: "For all the noise around vouchers, public dollars already underwrite private school attendance in a variety of ways."[21] Every use of tax money, however trivial, that makes private schools more affordable is called a "virtual voucher." Finn and Gau do not explain the huge difference between where we are, with scattered, tiny "virtual vouchers," and an appropriate destination such as a universal choice program that would produce the competitive education industry the country desperately needs. Indeed, Finn and Gau do not mention competition, not even as an important force, much less an objective.

A similar example comes from George Clowes, editor of the *School Reform*

News. Clowes outlined five steps to his version of "full school choice." The Clowes version is only slightly less restrictive and discriminatory than the CER version. He defined it as a voucher system that includes church-run schools without financial penalty. Clowes says, "the Milwaukee Parental Choice Program now offers a full working model for the broadest form of school choice."[22] Limiting participation to 15 percent of the children, as the Milwaukee plan does, and unequal financial support of "public" and private school students with price controls (add-ons are forbidden in Milwaukee), must fall within his definition of "full school choice." Clowes does not mention competition either, and he implies that each step follows naturally from the previous one. In contrast, many programs, including Milwaukee's, skipped steps, and most stalled well short of Clowes's definition of "full school choice," often on their initial step. The five-step process outlined by Clowes is, at best, wishful thinking with a very modest wish. There is no reason you have to start with step one (intradistrict choice among "public" schools), and there is no reason to believe that each step is inevitably a temporary state of affairs that necessarily leads to the next step in a short amount of time.

DOES UNILATERAL COMPROMISE REDUCE RESISTANCE?

Will restriction-laden choice proposals face less determined organized opposition? History in general, as well as the specific political history of parental choice proposals, strongly suggests the answer is no.[23] One of Governor Gary Johnson's (R-NM) three key lessons for voucher supporters is "that [choice] opponents will fight you just as hard on a small choice plan as a large one."[24] Nevertheless, appeasement is common practice among parental choice advocates, in some cases right after acknowledging its futility. Consider this example. On page 5 of *Voucher Wars,* Daniel McGroarty correctly observes that "the full force of the education establishment will always be brought to bear to beat back any voucher experiment, no matter how limited in scope or small in size."[25] On page 24, McGroarty talks about a "Long March" and pursuing the ultimate objective of universal vouchers with a series of changes that are quite limited in scope and small in size. When you have to overcome the same opposition for any progress, and again for each additional increment, why not seek total victory from the outset? Universal, nondiscriminatory choice may not win right way, but the efforts will establish clearly what choice advocates stand for, and will focus the public debate on stronger proposals. Implement a determinate outcome in stages if necessary, but do not seek it in stages.

Futility understates the negative effects of appeasement. If the countries of Eastern Europe had tried such an incremental march from dictatorship to democracy, the Iron Curtain and many dictators would still be there. The former socialist dictatorship countries that are trying to implement competition in stages are far behind those that made the transition to full-fledged capitalism more abruptly. The incremental approach created many countries that are mired in a "no-mans-land" between socialism and capitalism.

Teacher unions, the primary opponents of parental choice, never promised to oppose weaker versions with less vigor. Still, choice advocacy groups expect unilateral compromise to reduce resistance. They celebrate tiny choice increments, even when such increments jeopardize more productive reforms. Modest proposals weaken parental choice advocacy by entrenching restriction-laden alternatives, creating potentially misleading evidence, and confusing the public about what choice advocates stand for.

A fight for a competitive education industry and weaker versions of parental choice will differ only in that the weaker versions contain debilitating restrictions that create additional grounds for criticism. In addition, weaker versions of choice leave more of the apologists for the status quo in positions of power from which they can cripple choice-based reforms, or undermine the reforms' political support by misrepresenting the effects.

Choice advocates abandon some of their strongest arguments by letting their relentless, no-holds-barred opposition define the terms of the debate. It's like hoping the enemy will be nicer if you let him pick the battlefield. Choice advocates accept restrictions that won't diminish the opposition, and choice advocates often seek validation through "the most challenging test case."[26] Many choice advocates apparently believe that parental choice will spread only if they demonstrate that it "works" under the most adverse conditions, including the absence of any genuine competition. Instead, choice advocates should attack the weakest point in the enemy line. If a genuinely competitive education industry arises, it will spread quickly.

Appeasement is a proven failed strategy. Every major ballot proposition contained provisions designed to appeal to proponents of the status quo. Traditional choice opponents still opposed them vehemently. Each proposition lost by a wide margin; in some cases by more than two to one. It is hard to imagine how reforms aimed at establishing a competitive education industry could do worse. By lobbying for reforms that would establish a competitive education industry, choice advocates will at least attack debilitating fallacies, and explain how universal, nondiscriminatory parental choice would address the "nation at risk" problem. That will pay off as people increasingly recognize that the typical reform proposals produce only disappointment.[27] In addition, many of the most politically effective previous criticisms of choice proposals do not apply to competition-friendly versions of parental choice.

Ostensible victories like the Florida and Milwaukee voucher programs illustrate how appeasement can gut programs. The Florida program will affect only a fraction of the state's children. The Milwaukee Public Schools (MPS) could join several other large urban systems[28] taken over by state authorities.[29] Governor Tommy Thompson backed off his June 2000 takeover threat, but since substantial improvements are not evident yet, the reprieve may only be brief. It appears that the alleged linkages between the voucher program and MPS behavior were unproductive, defensive reactions to embarrassment, rather than competitive responses. Even with the voucher program expansion approved by the Wisconsin Supreme Court in 1998, the Milwaukee low-income voucher program will not establish competitive conditions, and it may delay more extensive reforms. The voucher program achieves little more than a limited transfer to slightly more effective private schools, and the spin doctors of the status quo are trying to cripple choice advocacy with their versions of Milwaukee and the Cleveland data.

Corroboration of my explanation for the MPS reactions and failure to improve significantly—small, restriction-laden programs don't create meaningful competition—comes from the reaction to a privately funded voucher program in Albany, New York. District officials made major personnel and programmatic changes at troubled Giffen Elementary. According to the superintendent, "the real catalyst may not have been competition, but the subsequent media attention."[30] Again, there is no published evidence of academic gains as a result of the changes at Giffen. Angie Garcia, Texas director of LULAC, points out that "this ["spend more on public relations"] has been the first reaction of many public schools around the country that were faced with competition from charter schools and publicly and privately funded vouchers."[31]

SUPPORT ANYTHING CALLED SCHOOL CHOICE?

Parental choice organizations celebrate every favorable public mention of anything labeled choice. They proclaim victory, even when little is accomplished— sometimes a vague statement of support by a public official or a weak proposal with little chance of enactment. A Heritage Foundation report[32] begins with a typical example: ". . . nearly 32 states considered a school choice program *of some kind* [emphasis added] last year [1997]. At least 45 governors stated their support for different degrees of school choice or charter schools."[33] How many is "nearly" 32? Does "at least" 45 mean that there were unconfirmed rumors of support among the remaining governors? Closer examination of what actually was said (very little) and done (even less) reveals that most of the governors are just astute politicians trying to ride a popular issue (choice devoid of specifics) without doing or saying anything that would anger powerful special interests. Contrary to the Heritage report, none of the proposed reforms, much less enacted legislation, offered any significant steps toward "principles of free-market competition." By the 1998 election campaign, only 15 of the 36 states with gubernatorial contests had a major party candidate who supported any kind of parental choice. Only five supported voucher programs, mostly restriction-laden versions.

Another example is on page 12 of the March 1998 *School Reform News.* The headline proclaimed, "1997 a Banner Year for School Choice." The first line said, "1997 was a breakthrough year for market-oriented education reform." Again, the events of 1997 did not back that glowing headline. Changes that would establish a competitive education industry were not even proposed, much less implemented, in any state legislature, or by any ballot initiative. Relatively few children left their assigned "public" school, and the system's critical elements remain intact everywhere.

Mainstream parental choice advocates provide their opponents with significant opportunities to deceive the public about the nature of "vouchers" and the aims of parental choice advocates. Restriction-laden programs generate evidence that is easily distorted. A public perception of choice failure would have catastrophic political consequences. Even undeniable relative success with partial measures is not necessarily good. Widespread imitation will preclude more productive reforms.

PRIVATE SCHOOL-"PUBLIC" SCHOOL COMPARISONS?

Most differences in existing "public" and private schools are noteworthy only if we intend to leave the key elements of the status quo intact. Many analysts fall into the intellectual trap of assuming that current private school practices and outcomes are the alternative to "public" schools. Economists Masato Aoki and Susan Feiner used the existing private sector to assess procompetition arguments. Especially revealing was their conclusion that the chiefly religious character of the private sector "profoundly colors the argument for market choice."[34] Many choice advocates rest their case on the alleged superiority of existing private schools. Jay Greene said that parental choice could promote integration because in Cleveland, "private schools, on average, are better integrated than are public schools."[35] Joseph Viteritti thought it very important that "inner city parochial schools are more effective in meeting the educational needs of poor children than are typical public schools in the same neighborhood."[36] Prominent choice advocates John Chubb and Terry Moe said private school superiority was a cornerstone of choice advocacy: "if there are no differences between public and private schools, there is little reason to support educational choice of any kind, public or private."[37] They reached that conclusion, even though they acknowledged that "private schools generally have smaller [per pupil] budgets than public schools." They ignored the debilitating effect of having to charge much more for a much less expensive service. Unfortunately, the editors of the *Wall Street Journal* published the faulty Chubb and Moe analysis. Dan Goldhaber's article is a more recent, more extensive example of the same mistake.[38] All of them assumed that parental choice could not fundamentally change the public or private sector, that it could only change "public" and private market shares.

Failure to acknowledge the possibility of major private sector change is a big political mistake. The private schools of a competitive education industry would not look much like the low-budget, predominantly sectarian, nonprofit private schools that currently dominate the private sector. "Market forces are connected with profit-seeking, but 98% of America's private schools are not-for-profit institutions."[39] Some people mistakenly equate the private sector with elite prep academies, so claims that parental choice is a good idea because private schools are doing a better job creates dangerously unrealistic expectations, even for privately owned schools in a competitive education industry.

Unqualified comparisons of "public" and private schools can make parental choice look like an expensive, disruptive waste of time. Defenders of the status quo exploit that mistake by citing data that indicate that private school academic outcomes are similar to "public" school outcomes, at least in terms of readily measurable criteria such as standardized test scores. The proper interpretation of similar private and "public" school test scores is that the whole education system is broken.[40] The current system significantly handicaps most private schools. We need a competitive education industry, not to move some children to different schools, but to improve the entire school system, private schools included.

Comparisons of "public" and private schools have other negative consequences. By asserting that private schools produce better results, choice advocates probably give many teachers (more on this in chapter 14) and much of the general public the impression that parental choice is just an expensive new program that would operate within the current system. The low pay of existing private schools helps union leaders arouse rank-and-file support for the teachers' unions' vehement opposition to any meaningful parental choice.

Much-improved private schools, including many more profit-seeking firms, would be the alternative to government-owned schools unless parental choice is severely restricted, such as in capped programs like Milwaukee and Cleveland. Those restricted versions generate little or no competition, while simultaneously increasing taxpayer burdens.[41]

The next chapter examines the existing and potential linkages between privately funded voucher programs and efforts to establish a competitive education industry.

NOTES

1. Among others, so did "Victory in Florida," *School Reform News* (June 1999) and the Heritage Foundation (e-mail announcement of Florida Governor Bush appearance).

2. "Victory in Florida," School Reform News (June 1999): 1, 4.

3. Ibid.; *Education Week* (January 11, 1999): 137, reported the number of "public" schools in Florida.

4. Consider for example, the transformation of the Eastern Europe transition economies, and the slightly less demanding, but still major transformation of New Zealand.

5. Quentin L. Quade, "Strap on the Armor and Go: Never Give In!" *School Reform News* (June 1998): 16.

6. Chester Finn quoted in John Hood, "Educational Challenges: The Role of Choice," *Current* (December 1991): 11.

7. Douglas J. Lamdin and Michael Mintrom, "School Choice in Theory and Practice: Taking Stock and Looking Ahead," *Education Economics* 5, no. 3 (1997): 235.

8. Ibid.

9. John Chubb and Terry Moe, *Educational Choice* (San Antonio: Texas Public Policy Foundation, 1990), p. 21.

10. Ibid.

11. Chester E. Finn and Rebecca L. Gau, "New Ways of Education," *The Public Interest* (Winter 1998): 79.

12. See the discussion of the late 1960s voucher proposals of Christopher Jencks and Theodore Sizer in Joseph Viteritti, *Choosing Equality* (Washington: Brookings Institution, 1999), p. 55.

13. Milton Friedman, *Capitalism and Freedom* (Chicago: University of Chicago Press, 1962); Milton Friedman, "The Role of Government in Education" in Solo, R. A. (ed.), *Economics and the Public Interest* (New Brunswick, N.J.: Rutgers University Press, 1955).

14. For example, see Daniel McGroarty, *Voucher Wars: Strategy and Tactics as School Choice Advocates Battle the Labor Leviathan*, Issues in School Choice, no. 2 (April 1998), Milton and Rose Friedman Foundation, Indianapolis, Ind.; Dorman E. Cordell, "Answering Objections to School Vouchers in D.C.," *National Center for Policy Analysis Brief Analysis* 266 (May 22, 1998): 2.

15. Economic illiteracy is rampant: Dave Kansas, "Illiteracy about Economics Abounds among Americans, Survey Concludes," *Wall Street Journal* (September 11, 1992); Thomas Sowell, "Economic Literacy Escapes Most," *San Antonio Express-News* (January 4, 1995).

16. John Hood, "Educational Challenges: The Role of Choice," *Current* (December 1991).

17. The definition of entrenched is debatable. Most choice-based programs have changed very little. The least entrenched program is Milwaukee's low-income vouchers. Even so, it still took most of a decade to expand the program to 15 percent of the student population, and to give the majority of private schools a chance to be eligible. The remaining significant restrictions preclude the development of a competitive education industry, and Milwaukee's "public" schools are under threat of a state takeover.

18. Exceptions include some Giffen Elementary (Albany, N.Y.) employees who were fired after many parents responded to a privately funded rescue, and Harlem, District 4, where unpopular schools are closed.

19. Hood (December 1991): 11.

20. From CER's Web site *EDREFORM.com*.

21. Finn and Gau (Winter 1998), 79–92.

22. George A. Clowes, "Five Steps to Full School Choice," *School Reform News* (September 1998): 10–11.

23. McGroarty (April 1998).

24. Nina S. Rees, "Johnson's Voucher Vision," *School Reform News* (November 1999): 5.

25. McGroarty (April 1998).

26. Ibid.

27. Richard Omdahl and Jackie Ducote, *Education Accountability and the Role of School Choice*, Public Affairs Research Council of Louisiana, Inc., Analysis No. 299 (March 1999) describes how Louisiana reached that point: "Louisiana has tried almost every one of them ["reforms other than school choice"], from enhanced pre-schooling to finance reforms, during the period from 1975 to 1995.

28. Nineteen since 1988, including Baltimore, Boston, Chicago, Cleveland, Hartford, Newark, and Washington, D.C.: *School Reform News* (May 1999): 5.

29. Beth Reinhard, "Thompson Threatens a Takeover for Milwaukee," *Education Week* (January 28, 1998): 8.

30. Jeff Archer, "Voucher Proponents Claim Victory in Albany," *Education Week* (February 11, 1998): 5.

31. Angie Garcia, Vouchers Not Edgewood's Real Problem," *San Antonio Express-News* (December 6, 1998).

32. *Heritage Foundation F.Y.I.* (January 30, 1998).

33. Another *Heritage Foundation F.Y.I.* (April 21, 1997) makes almost identical claims about the previous years.

34. Masato Aoki and Susan F. Feiner, "The Economics of Market Choice and At-Risk Students," in William E. Becker and William J. Baumol (eds.), *Assessing Educational Practices* (Cambridge, Mass.: MIT Press, 1996).

35. Jay P. Greene, "Why School Choice Can Promote Integration," *Education Week* (April 12, 2000): 72, 52.

36. Joseph Viteritti, *Choosing Equality* (Washington: Brookings Institution, 1999), p. 15.

37. John E. Chubb and Terry M. Moe, "The Private vs. Public School Debate," *Wall Street Journal* (July 26, 1991).

38. Dan D. Goldhaber, "Public and Private High Schools: Is School Choice an Answer to the Productivity Problem?" *Economics of Education Review* 15, no. 2 (1996): 93–109.

39. Edwin G. West, "Autonomy in School Provision: Meanings and Implications—Review Essay," *Economics of Education Review* 11, no. 4 (1992): 423; more recently, Jack Klegg (interview in *School Reform News* [October 1998]: 20), says that fewer than 1,000 of the nation's 26,000 private schools are nonsectarian, for-profit schools.

40. The lack of significant differences between private school and government-run school test scores is repeated in national publications like the *Wall Street Journal* and *Newsweek* (Barbara Kantrowitz, Stryker McGuire, and Pat Wingert, "Take the Money and Run," *Newsweek* [October 11, 1999]: 65). "In national tests, there's not much difference between public and private school students from the same socioeconomic backgrounds."

41. Henry M. Levin and Cyrus E. Driver, "Costs of an Education Voucher System," *Education Economics* 5, no. 3 (December 1997): 265–83. Assuming a very restricted version of school choice, Levin and Driver estimate cost increases of up to 25 percent or more.

CHAPTER 13

Private Voucher Initiatives

The private voucher movement is the latest and most unorthodox strategic initiative intended to bring about a competitive education industry. There are two reasons why the initiative is hard to describe. First, it is a multipurpose program. It aims to help low-income children, and act as a catalyst to reform public policy. Specifically, the second motivation for the private voucher movement is:

> rooted in the belief that the programs could be a vehicle of revolutionary change. The reason: they would be working models that would show politicians and government officials the clear benefits of school choice. Furthermore, each new program would create a small but vocal constituency of parents and business executives who understood and valued school choice and whose collective voice could do more to alter public perceptions than could be achieved by even the most massive public relations campaign.[1]

Second, the dimensions of the program have changed significantly. The 1998 changes may prove to be critically important; however, it is too early to predict whether they will help or hinder progress toward a competitive education industry. All that is possible here is to summarize the program and discuss how it might help or hinder the pursuit of a competitive education industry.

The private voucher movement enjoyed a huge increase in scope in 1998. Some history and statistics provide some context.[2]

Momentum From a single program launched in Indianapolis in 1991, the private voucher movement expanded to 34 programs in 19 states and cities.

Students From an initial pool of 746 students in the 1991–92 school year, these voucher programs expanded to serve 12,684 students in 1997–98.

Families Virtually all families served by these programs are low-income, usually defined by eligibility for the school lunch program. All but a few are inner city residents. Many participating families have more than one child enrolled in the program.

Populations Private voucher programs serve families of all religious and ethnic backgrounds. Minorities are the dominant participants, but all types of backgrounds are well represented.

Schools The largest group of participating schools is Catholic, which is to be expected. They have the strongest presence in urban areas. However, other types of schools dominate in a number of markets, and participants include independent, Christian denominational and nondenominational, Muslim, and Afrocentric schools.

Awards Voucher awards for school tuition range from $150 to $4,000, and in most cases a family copayment is required. In the 1997–98 school year, the average award was $898, with almost $12 million committed nationwide that year.

Costs The typical participating school has a modest tuition, ranging from about $800 to $6,000. Administrative costs are negligible.

Demand There were over 64,000 voucher requests in the 1997–98 school year; about a 175 percent increase over two years earlier.

In 1998, the private voucher movement received a huge revenue increase and, with it, much greater visibility and bipartisan political support. The Children's Scholarship Fund (CSF) announced it had $100 million to help children seeking private schooling, available on a matching basis to local communities that raise funds for vouchers to begin in fall 1999. Ultimately, 1.25 million applicants competed for 40,000 4-year partial tuition scholarships.[3] The CSF and the older Children's Education Opportunity-type (CEO)[4] programs have similar requirements. Only low-income families are eligible; parents must demonstrate that their income does not exceed 185 percent of their area's poverty level; and they must pay part of the tuition, at least 40 percent, though services may be accepted in lieu of cash. K–8 children may receive four-year scholarships.

The major contributors to the CSF program are Theodore Forstmann and John Walton, a Wal-Mart family member. Forstmann was especially successful in getting an impressive array of business and political leaders to endorse the program and help raise funds. The support of President Clinton reflects the program's initial invulnerability to direct attack by teacher unions and other traditional choice opponents. The initial union reaction was a reluctant concession that philanthropists have the right to fund vouchers, regret that they did not try to strengthen "public" schools, and warnings that the program must not promote publicly funded vouchers. In other words, choice opponents were saying that tax dollars belong to the system. Children have the right to leave "public" schools, but they can't use elsewhere any of the money earmarked for their education.

CSF PROGRAM OBJECTIVES

The official objective of the CSF program is to help a small but significant number of children (50,000 nationwide) get a better education. Most of the individuals who actively support the CSF program are also advocates of universal choice; though sometimes versions of universal choice that lack key elements of a competitive education industry.[5] Like the supporters of the older CEO-type programs, they believe increased use of private schools may stimulate demand that political leaders eventually will accommodate. Paradoxically, Forstmann's success in lining up official endorsements may have compromised that possibility. To broaden the coalition of support to include President Clinton and other Democratic Party luminaries, CSF program literature could not mention any objective other than helping disadvantaged children.

Obstacles

Now that they have achieved significant visibility, CSF supporters are making the same mistakes described in chapters 3 and 12. The relative progress of voucher users is the evaluation criterion. Studies that will take years to complete rely on financially handicapped private schools to significantly outperform "public" schools in ways that available data will reflect. Then choice advocates must convince enough of the electorate that the findings from limited programs hint at equal or better outcomes from a competitive education industry, or hope that publicly funded, restriction-laden imitations gradually will shed those restrictions. The latter amounts to the incrementalism strategy critiqued in the previous chapter.

CSF officials have conceded that analyses of available data are always vulnerable to criticism. Choice opponents will continue to argue that apparent gains by voucher students are the result of selection bias; private schooling seekers able to help pay for it are more committed to educating their children than nonapplicants, so voucher children are going to perform better with or without the CSF program. Choice opponents will highlight every situation where improvements are not obvious.

As noted on several previous occasions, it is risky and misleading to base the case for a competitive education industry on the alleged superiority of the current system's private schools to "public" schools. Yet, that implicit assumption pervades the rhetoric of the CSF program and its founders. Transfers from "public" to private schools are seen as "rescues," even though private schools use the same education methods, but spend less money per student. Test scores are similar. Private school advantages—better incentive structures, working conditions, and safety—will suffer some erosion as class sizes rise, and they have to accommodate children who probably are behind their new classmates and may bring some bad habits from their former schools. Voucher student gains could be much smaller than CSF supporters expect.

In many cases, it will be difficult to gauge voucher students' gains. The voucher students will be scattered among hundreds of private schools in as many as 100 large school districts. CSF program officials argue that parental decisions will signal the success or failure of the program, and thereby create pressures to duplicate it. The political significance (persuasiveness) of parental satisfaction claims is unknown, but the kinds of disputes and distortions seen in Milwaukee are certain. For example, natural turnover that any program experiences (e.g., household relocation) was depicted as parental dissatisfaction. Many voucher program departures depicted as parental dissatisfaction were actually due to "public" school failings; some of the voucher recipients were so academically deficient that they could not cope with the private school curriculum.

Church-Affiliated School Issues

The Forstmann-Walton political vision may depend too much on church-affiliated, especially Catholic, schools to generate the critical mass of support for the publicly supported universal parental choice that CSF supporters seek. The older CEO-type programs are a good indication of what is likely to happen. In the 1997–98 school year, over half of the schools accepting students with CEO-type partial tuition vouchers were church-run schools, and more than 5,000 of the 12,684 CEO students were in Catholic schools. The numbers are somewhat uncertain because church-run schools often enroll students from families with other religious affiliations, but there is no question that church-run school enrollments dominate CEO-type programs. The CEO program does not favor church-run schools, but that's where most of the underutilized capacity is. That's also why some parents interested in alternatives to their assigned "public" school still have their children there—they want secular schooling. However, other parents use church-run schools despite their lack of interest in the religion content. For that reason, under-utilized space does not indicate lack of interest in private schooling, though choice opponents will claim that it does.

Furthermore, since for-profit schools will generate most of the improvements resulting from a competitive education industry, CSF and CEO-type programs will give us little insight into likely changes. There is very little under-utilized space in for-profit schools, and the private voucher movement isn't likely to prompt much expansion of the for-profit sector. The CSF program is only assured for four years, and the CEO-type programs are quite small. Entrepreneurs are creating small schools in existing buildings, but they are not likely to make major investments in new schools.

In the past, nonprofit schools have helped "public" school leaders block the expansion of schools for profit.[6] Therefore, because it will expand nonprofit school enrollments the most, the CSF program may slow rather than accelerate establishment of for-profit schools. The CSF does not seek that outcome, but it may contribute to it unwittingly. Leading officials of for-profit schools do not criticize the CSF program, but they are much less supportive of it than are nonprofit school leaders. They fear, rightly so I believe, that the CSF program will reinforce the mistaken perception that only the worst large urban school districts need parental choice.

The Impact of the CSF Program on School Costs and Teacher Pay

One of the major advantages of private schooling is the safety factor. Private schools are usually safer places to teach, and they have more authority to deal with unacceptable student conduct. The CSF program could erode that advantage. CSF program sponsors emphasize availability of space for voucher students, but they have not thought out fully the impact on teachers of filling that space. Many teachers accept as much as one-third less pay for the improved teaching conditions of private schools, so erosion of those conditions may increase private schools' labor costs. In addition, losses to nonvoucher private school users in the form of tuition increases and classroom deterioration may offset some of the benefits received by voucher students.

An Excuse for Delay

The CSF program may handicap the pursuit of a competitive education industry by providing fence-sitting politicians an excuse to defer action. Legislators could cite the CSF program as a reason to delay actions that would foster competition. Proponents of the CSF program have created a dilemma for themselves. If the program does not appear to produce significant gains quickly—which is likely—program supporters will have to argue that real reform takes time. Politicians on the fence will take refuge in that argument and delay reform agendas until the experiment produces more results.

The Safety Valve Problem

Several previous chapters questioned the assumption that progress toward a competitive education industry required a demonstration that parental choice produces significant academic gains among voucher children. Nevertheless, consider the CSF program from that perspective, and assume for the moment that such gains are documented.

The CSF program's political assumptions may be more suspect than its educational assumptions. Consider Albert Hirschman's classic study of responses to monopolies. He drew a distinction between profit-maximizing monopolies, and "lazy monopolies." Unlike profit-maximizing monopolies, "lazy monopolies" are more concerned with avoiding change in their comfortable, but inefficient ways. In Hirschman's words:

there are many cases where competition does not restrain monopoly as it is supposed to, but comforts and bolsters it by unburdening it of its more troublesome customers. As a result, one can define an important and too-little noticed type of monopoly tyranny: a limited type, an oppression of the weak by the incompetent, and an exploitation of the poor by the lazy which is more durable and stifling as it is both unambitious and escapable. The contrast is stark indeed with totalitarian, expansionist tyrannies or the profit-maximizing, accumulation-minded monopolies which may have captured a disproportionate share of our attention.

In the economic sphere, such lazy monopolies which welcome competition as a release from effort and criticism are frequently encountered when monopoly power rests on location and when mobility differs strongly from one group of local customers to another. If, as is likely, the mobile customers are those who are more sensitive to quality, their exit, caused by the poor performance of the local monopolist, permits him to persist in his comfortable mediocrity.

Those who hold power in the lazy monopoly may actually have an interest in creating some limited opportunities for an exit on the part of those whose voice might be uncomfortable. Here is a good illustration of the contrast between the profit-maximizing and the lazy monopolist: the former would engage, if he could, in discriminatory pricing so as to extract maximum revenue from its most avid customers, while the lazy monopolist would much rather price those customers out of the market entirely so as to be able to give up the strenuous and tiresome quest for excellence. For the most avid customers are not only willing to pay the highest prices, but are also likely to be the most demanding and querulous, in case of lowering standards.[7]

Hirschman's analysis suggests how the CSF program might weaken pursuit of a competitive education industry. The parents of the children who are in the CSF program may be less active advocates of publicly funded vouchers if their own preferences for private schooling are met through the program. Meredith Maran, author of the forthcoming book, *Class Dismissed* certainly believes such behavior is significant. "We must close the escape hatches through which those with privilege escape the universal fate. Until public schools have to be good enough for everyone, they won't be good enough for anyone."[8]

Will the CSF program merely provide a much-needed safety valve for the lazy monopoly known as the "public" school system? It is too early to assert that Hirschman's analysis applies to the CSF program, but its architects clearly did not consider that possibility.

ADVANCING THE PURSUIT OF A COMPETITIVE EDUCATION INDUSTRY

The Forstmann strategy enjoys several advantages over conventional choice advocacy strategies. It has ample resources, imaginative leaders, insulation from union attacks, bipartisan political support (for now), a strong media base, prestigious endorsements, and undivided control over the major strategic decisions. Notwithstanding those advantages, and my determination to avoid the NIH (Not Invented Here) Syndrome, I conclude that the CSF will facilitate progress toward a competitive education industry only if it creates conditions that much more closely resemble those of a competitive education industry (see chapter 2); something that can be defended as a reasonably valid experiment.

The CSF strategists can create the conditions of a reasonably valid experiment by funding a large number of children in a few areas at high levels for a long time. In contrast, the current strategy apparently will support relatively few children in a large number of areas for a relatively short time, and only for about half of a low tuition level. A valid experiment would also lack means testing and allow add-ons. To hold costs down without compromising the validity of the experiment, CSF could limit the vouchers to grades K–5, or K–6, to concentrate the funds on a particular market sector.

To gain a better understanding of that proposal, consider the CEO program in the Edgewood District of San Antonio, Texas. Every applicant who meets the district residency and low-income requirements receives a full tuition voucher of up to $4,000 per year. Since nearly every district resident would meet the low-income requirement, the means test does not limit potential participation very much. Voucher users are free to add on—that is, to use them to buy a private education that costs more than $4,000.

The primary shortcoming of the Edgewood Program as a source of insight is that the ten-year funding commitment is quite short from a potential entrepreneur's perspective. The perception that privately funded programs are by nature temporary is an unavoidable shortcoming of such programs, but the scope of the problem could be smaller.

Another noteworthy but less significant problem is the low-income eligibility criterion. In Edgewood, the means test does not bar many families from the program, but it greatly reduces families' ability to add on, which reduces the incentive to open new and innovative schools. Though the facts ultimately may say otherwise, I do not believe a short-duration voucher program will produce much, if any, new construction or many major expansions.[9] If the CEO strategists had made a longer funding commitment—something that may have been beyond their means—the Edgewood voucher probably would be large enough to produce some significant new private schools.[10] If there were stronger incentives to open new private schools, the Edgewood vouchers would be a much more reliable test of whether a productive, competitive response is forthcoming from at least the tiny Edgewood District.

Below are the specific elements of a more credible CSF voucher experiment. In each place where the CSF makes a commitment:

1. As in the Edgewood program, set the size of the voucher well above the average private school tuition. That will encourage investment in new private schools, and allow existing private schools to increase tuition, which they must do to increase teacher pay and hire more teachers. The availability of additional resources will demonstrate that when "public" and private budgets are more comparable, typical private schools will be much better than the typical "public" or private school is now. Allow add-ons, so that private school set-up and development is not constrained by a price cap.
2. Unlike the Edgewood program, make a much longer funding commitment, preferably an indefinite one.
3. Like the Edgewood program, at least have sufficient funds to offer vouchers to a very large share of the students of a particular school district. The Edgewood program is large in relation to the Edgewood District, but tiny relative to the San Antonio area. Therefore, to get the most valid test bang for the buck, a better approach is to fund a large number of vouchers in a smaller (than San Antonio), multidistrict, urban county. With an entire multidistrict county, that approach would better test private and public sector responses to competitive pressures.
4. Unlike the Edgewood program, do not means-test voucher eligibility. If only low-income families can participate, the voucher amount acts a lot like a price ceiling at the voucher amount, even when add-ons are allowed.

I recognize that these conditions may not be achievable with existing private financial resources, but potential donors, strategists, and analysts must recognize the difficulties and political risks inherent in conditions with significant shortcomings.

Positive results from a valid voucher experiment will not eliminate opposition to the universal parental choice policy advocated here. Since the teacher unions will lead the opposition, choice advocates must weaken that opposition by making the strong case for a competitive education industry to teachers. That is the subject of the next chapter.

NOTES

1. CEO America Web site (*ceoamerica.org*), August 8, 2000.
2. The data are from the Children's Educational Opportunity (CEO) Foundation of America 1998 Survey.
3. Wendy Zellner, "Going to Bat for Vouchers," *Business Week* (February 7, 2000).
4. Many people will not recognize the new name. Late in 1999, the CEO America oversight and support organization for the numerous CEO-type, privately funded voucher programs changed its name to Children First America.
5. For example, some believe that voucher add-ons should be prohibited. That's a competition-killing restriction.

6. Myron Lieberman, *Public Education: An Autopsy* (Cambridge, Mass.: Harvard University Press, 1993).

7. Albert O. Hirschman, *Exit, Voice, and Loyalty* (Cambridge, Mass.: Harvard University Press, 1970).

8. Meredith Maran quote from the *San Francisco Chronicle* (August 27, 2000) cited in the August 28, 2000 Education Intelligence Agency Communique (*members. aol.com/educintel/ eia*).

9. Over half the voucher users attend four schools. One is new, and most of its students are voucher users.

10. I hope the preceding sentence will be seen as nothing more than one economist's opinion about market behavior. It definitely must not be seen as criticism of CEO Horizon supporters for not being generous enough!

CHAPTER 14

Teachers

> "We treat them [teachers] badly, so they leave in droves."
>
> —John Merrow, "The Teacher Shortage: Wrong Diagnosis, Phony Cures,"
> *Education Week* (October 6, 1999): 64

A competitive education industry will change teachers' lives significantly, and I believe most teachers will benefit. The current system treats teachers badly, so there is much room for improvement. Because teacher unions will lose members and revenue, strong opposition on their part is inevitable. However, equally strong, monolithic teacher opposition is not. That's the primary point of this chapter. There are abundant signs of significant teacher dissatisfaction with the status quo and abundant virtues of a competitive education industry well worth bringing to their attention.

Reduced teacher opposition to, even eventual teacher support for, a competitive education industry is a realistic goal. As the teacher unions of some other countries illustrate, unions sometimes grudgingly accept parental choice after it has been operating for awhile. Teacher union opposition is a major political barrier, so well-crafted appeals to teachers could improve the political feasibility of a competitive education industry significantly.

TEACHERS VS. TEACHER UNIONS

Presidential nominee Bob Dole's speech at the 1996 Republican National Convention contained an attack on teacher unions that explicitly differentiated between union leaders and the rank and file.[1] School choice advocates rarely give that distinction the considerable attention it deserves. Choice advocates' statements usually reflect a widespread belief that teacher opposition to competition is inevitable, and that union leader opposition just reflects that. For example, Joseph Bast and David Harmer said, "It is the system, not the people in it, that is evil. For those reasons, we find it possible to forgive government school teachers for opposing the voucher movement."[2] Teacher opposition to a competitive education industry is not inevitable. Only about 60 percent of the nation's "public" schoolteachers are union members, and some members oppose their union's political platform.[3] Many more are just passive supporters, including many who have little issue awareness.[4] The competitive education industry version of parental choice has much more to offer teachers, and fewer reasons for them to fear it, than the versions of parental choice that appear in the public debate most often.

David Kirkpatrick is a longtime educator and former teacher union leader and a leading supporter of school choice. His experience includes solid evidence of major differences between teachers and union leadership on school choice, including vouchers:

> I spoke to this effect [school choice issue] at a number of [union] meetings, and at no time was I criticized by a member of the [National Education] Association. Teachers are willing to consider new ideas and follow positive leadership. Unfortunately, such leadership is not forthcoming as officers or staff play to the weakest and most fearful of their members or adopt positions perceived to be in the interests of the organization, its officers and staff, rather than those of the rank-and-file membership.
>
> The first thing we [teachers] must do is stop defending a system we did not create, and which is not in the interest of our students or ourselves [teachers] to maintain. We have been victimized along with our students.[5]

According to Denis Doyle, "the most ardent opponents of private school vouchers are public school teachers,"[6] when, in fact, "union officials constantly complain about the lack of grassroots participation,"[7] in anti-choice campaigns.

Herbert Gintis made an even stronger misstatement: "It is well-known that teachers and their unions are virtually unanimous in opposing school choice."[8] Many teachers already support some forms of parental choice and many are eager to learn more. The key point, already made above but well worth repeating, is that a competitive education industry arguably is more likely to appeal to teachers than the kinds of parental choice programs that receive the most publicity. There is even a teacher organization that overwhelmingly supports (probably limited) vouchers. The Association of American Educators' 1997 membership survey[9] revealed that 62 percent thought vouchers were a good idea. Only 32 percent disagreed. Furthermore, there are many teachers in choice (however limited) schools. They "seem ripe for the picking as allies in the struggle for school choice, and as human rebuttals to the teachers' unions incessant anti-choice rhetoric."[10] The same is probably true of private school teachers in general. A competitive education industry would eliminate the need to choose between better-paying "public" schools and more teacher-friendly private schools.

Contrary to Eugenia Toma's inference, "public" schoolteachers are not the "suppliers of a monopoly product."[11] They just work for the "public" school monopoly. Monopolies don't appreciate competition, but their employees might.

Despite choice advocates' failure to depict reform alternatives properly, some teachers already speak out against the status quo and advocate major reform,[12] often even parental choice. But for fear of reprisals from their colleagues and employers, more probably would. Prominent teachers are among the vocal dissidents. They include John Gatto, a New York City and state teacher of the year;[13] Tracey Bailey,[14] the 1993 national teacher of the year; and Kevin Irvine;[15] a Colorado state teacher of the year.

CHOICE ADVOCACY OPPORTUNITY

No one has come close to exploiting the differences between the teacher union leadership and teachers. The National Education Association (NEA) and the American Federation of Teachers (AFT) lead the opposition to every parental choice proposal, so there is much to be gained from at least weakening that opposition. Choice advocates should at least be able to count on the "two out of five teachers that routinely vote Republican."[16]

Choice advocates aren't making a major effort to solicit teachers' support. Instead, choice advocates unwittingly harden teacher opposition. Choice advocates' restriction-laden proposals make "choice" look like a limited transfer of students and teachers to private schools. Teachers see "choice" as something that will cause more teachers to earn the lower salaries of existing private schools. That's a distasteful outcome for most teachers, despite many private schools' better working conditions. "Teacher unions oppose vouchers in part because the private schools they foster generally pay lower salaries than the public systems."[17] The current image of "choice" cutting teachers' income helps union leaders rally teacher opposition. A competitive education industry version of parental choice would not spread the conditions of existing private schools. The negative image of restriction-laden proposals inappropriately tarnishes proposals that would establish such an industry.

There is empirical evidence that teachers could become parental choice supporters. "A [1990] survey of 2372 teachers by the National Center for Education Information shows 53 percent say schools would be better if students could attend the school of their choice."[18] Even if it is only choice among "public" schools, it is much more than the union leadership readily supports. Abroad, some teacher unions support school choice programs. Among 48 teacher unions in a dozen developed countries, 35 percent "are strongly in favor of choice or voucher programs."[19] Only 22 percent strongly oppose them.

MAKING THE CASE TO TEACHERS

Sources of teacher dissatisfaction with the status quo are a good starting point. The benefits teachers will realize from a competitive education industry are the appropriate end point. Certain benefits include a more competitive teacher labor market, opportunities to specialize more, increased mobility, linkage between productivity and compensation, and opportunities to become school entrepreneurs.[20] Better relations with parents are a likely effect of parents choosing schools, rather than assigning children to them. Because families can combine private and public funds, increased classroom spending is likely if public K–12 education spending is the same in the competitive education industry as it is now.

Teacher Dissatisfaction with the Status Quo

Like Merrow at the beginning of this chapter, Joseph Murphy describes his findings succinctly: "Conditions of employment for teachers are unprofessional and stifling."[21] Plenty of young people still seek teaching careers, but teaching experience prompts a growing number to ask: "Who would want to become a technician [teacher] in such a field [teaching]?"[22] High teacher turnover is one of the two devastating effects of those conditions. San Antonio's news media have displayed some of the concerns and deep dissatisfaction. A TV news report featured a teacher saying, "I'm doing a tough job with two hands tied behind my back." A June 1, 1997, San Antonio *Express-News* Sunday Insight section, titled "Schoolhouse Blues," described some of the underlying causes of discontent. The titles of the articles speak volumes: "I need to be in my classroom."[23] "Treat teachers as professionals."[24] "Good teachers tired of battling the system."[25] The alleged teacher shortage is a retention, not a recruiting problem, and it would be much larger but for the numerous teachers teaching outside their fields of expertise.

The "Schoolhouse Blues" articles noted that constantly changing programs create panic, low morale, and burnout, the second devastating result of the stifling, unprofessional conditions teachers endure. "Teachers are in a virtual state of panic, caught between crushing district mandates and the need to raise standardized test scores."[26] Scholar Gary Dworkin says the burnout effect is a widely researched topic. Most of the burned out teachers stay in their jobs because they lack comparable career opportunities.[27] A longtime Milwaukee teacher said, "Very common are teachers who at one time were good, but after years of bureaucratic nonsense and dwindling morale, do not much like their job anymore."[28] Such strong signals of dissatisfaction with the system represent opportunities to weaken union opposition to parental choice.

Signs of dissatisfaction exist even in union-sponsored publications and advertisements. A 1998 Today's Unions commercial said that unions gain teachers their employers' respect. School management respect (fear?) for union power differs from respect for teachers, and the fear of union power has many harmful side effects. Respect for union power discourages the dismissal of bad teachers and reduces accountability. Both are significant sources of the teacher-bashing that teachers resent.

By forcing nearly equal treatment of diverse teachers, unions discourage superior performance. At the same time, teacher unions make it more difficult to fire bad teachers. As a result, it is not surprising to read statements like this in such national publications as *U.S. News & World Report*: "Teachers' unions seem to be driving good teachers out, coddling bad ones, and putting bureaucracy in the way of quality education."[29] In spite of what the teacher unions claim they do in the name of enhancing teachers' professional image, there is no broad-based movement toward greater professionalization (teacher autonomy). Anecdotal evidence, including teacher complaints, points toward increasing micromanagement. Difficulty defining and consistently measuring professionalization and autonomy hinders systematic study.

Choice advocates need to exploit "public" schoolteachers' frustrations with the system. Discussion of the widespread so-called teacher-bashing phenomenon could increase teacher support significantly all by itself. Seymour Sarason said it just right. If a large number of people "conclude that almost all people in a particular role are inadequate, should one not ask what there is about the system that makes or sustains such failures?"[30]

The reasons why teachers underachieve demonstrate why the current system causes teacher bashing. Political and administrative processes distort textbook content and micromanage teaching methods and the curriculum, often through insulting "teacher-proof"[31] materials. Teachers are the "victim of job reduction and job simplification, prescriptive laws, the growing specter of legal liability and malpractice suits, and seniority rules."[32] "Policies that determine textbooks, course content, and even the style by which information is delivered are also removed from teacher's control."[33] Longtime AFT President Albert Shanker agreed that teachers had little say in policies, books, standards, or curriculum.[34]

The inability of parents to choose, and the resulting inability of schools or teachers to specialize much, creates unnecessary tension between overextended teachers and unhappy, trapped parents. As a result of forced, rather than chosen, teacher-parent, connections many teachers dread speaking to parents so much that they'd forgo substantial raises if it meant they'd never have to speak to a parent again.[35] Among the flood of people leaving teaching, many cite lack of support from parents as a major cause for their decision.[36]

The post-1983 reforms accelerated erosion of teachers' working conditions. "Ever since *A Nation at Risk* appeared in the early 1980s, schools have responded by evolving . . . into institutions that prescribe top down management control of every aspect of the teaching process."[37] Professors Aldo Bernardo and Marianne Jennings said, "big government is moving in on education," and "what is happening is not a dumbing down process, but [much worse] the emasculation of the American educational system."[38] "While reformers lip-sync homilies about creativity, empowerment, and involvement, they institute reforms that empower bureaucracies, reduce teachers to paraprofessionals, and marginalize parents."[39] More than ever, K–12 education suffers from "academically trained bureaucrats who believe that once they find the proper regulatory formula, they can make the world work properly."[40] According to Gary Dworkin and Merric Townsend, "Texas is implementing site-based management, but the mandate involves micromanagement of this implementation at higher levels. The effect has been a greater sense of powerlessness among teachers."[41] Policy makers "want teachers to become technicians who will be able to follow directions very well."[42] In almost every state, "education reform has had the effect of removing management of the classroom to the highest state levels. In most instances, the legislatures have micro-managed the school districts, campuses and classrooms."[43] Each so-called reform increased teachers' paperwork and frustration.

Teachers have to break the rules to educate children. They must endure fear of exposure and punishment and expend time and energy to hide their efforts and misrepresent their work. "A majority of public school teachers responding to a series of surveys conducted in Houston between 1977 and 1991 agreed or strongly agreed that school rules are so rigid and absurd that good teachers have to break them or ignore them."[44] New York State teacher of the year John Gatto said he became "an active saboteur."[45] David Kearns and Denis Doyle found that "superb teachers share a trait not widely talked about: they are canny outlaws, system beaters, and creative and responsible rule benders. They have to be 'outlaws' to succeed in most districts—especially the large ones—the deck is stacked against the creative, imaginative, and entrepreneurial teacher."[46] Former Milwaukee Public Schools Superintendent Howard Fuller agrees that teachers have to break the rules to succeed. Principals are often in the same situation. Tom Luce, an education reform activist and former candidate for Texas governor, said, a "principal must be an academic leader who knows how to get around the system."[47] A Heritage Foundation Study described by Samuel Carter said that effective principals are "mavericks who buck the system."[48] The same study found that the effective principals "found a way to free themselves from many of the personnel regulations, line-by-line budget requirements, and curricular mandates that hamstring most public school principals."

The system traps teachers to at least the same extent as parents. Teaching credentials have little value outside teaching. Teachers forfeit most of the investment in their skills if they leave teaching. "Public" schoolteachers have very little choice of where they work, because district administrators choose each teacher's campus.

Principals' inability to hire or fire creates additional friction with teachers. Principals must accept district-approved candidates, and sometimes they receive only one. Since they can't fire them, principals often conspire to make them miserable so they'll leave. A much better match would result if teachers and principals chose each other directly.

Ambitious, fairness-conscious teachers resent that their earnings reflect only credentials and time served. There is "no other profession where compensation and contract renewal are so largely divorced from evaluations of performance as they are in public school teaching."[49] G. Carl Ball and Steven Goldman found that "an excellent teacher who rocks the boat can receive poorer evaluations than less competent but 'safe' teachers."[50] Consider, for instance, the typical compensation policy. The single salary schedule is the way most school employees, both teachers and educational support personnel, are paid. The salary schedule is based on two criteria: experience and training.

In the current system, teacher salary incentives are a mixed blessing. They can motivate innovation and spur creativity, but they can also create tension among teachers.[51] Increased productivity doesn't raise a "public" school's merit pay funding or even its total budget. More money for one teacher means less for others. Since someone else's good evaluation is bad for them, teachers become more reluctant to share ideas and materials or to work in teams.

"Public"-private comparisons yield more empirical evidence of teacher dissatisfaction with "public" school working conditions. Ballou and Podgursky found that private schools had no difficulty filling openings, even though the average private school starting pay was 73.5 percent[52] of "public" school pay.[53] I agree with Dan Peters that "the extra amount that public school teachers get is combat pay."[54] Salary differentials for similar teachers are a good measure of a large number[55] of teachers' willingness to sacrifice income for better working conditions. A teacher quoted by Hugh Pearson said: "I'd rather teach here [private turned charter] than in the [regular] public schools because I have a lot more latitude in what I teach, and how I teach it."[56]

A survey of Indianapolis "nonpublic" schoolteachers found considerable dissatisfaction with the work environment of "public" schools.[57] Only about 20 percent, mostly younger teachers, said they would accept one of the higher-paying jobs in a suburban "public" school. About two-thirds of them took their current teaching job because a better-paying suburban position was not available. Only 10 percent of veteran teachers would take the higher-paying job in a "good" suburban "public" school. Only 2 percent of the "nonpublic" schoolteachers in the sample would leave their current job for a much higher-paying job in (an inner city) Indianapolis Public School. Typical comments were "no amount of money," "you've got to be kidding," and "maybe for a million dollars." Half the nonpublic schools in the sample were urban. Many teachers make a large financial sacrifice to leave "public" schools.

Fewer private schoolteachers have teaching certificates, but more have a degree in the subject they teach and more come from selective, prestigious universities, factors that correlate much more highly with student achievement than certification.[58] Most teachers prefer the higher salaries of "public" schools to the better working conditions of private schools, but many teachers are competing for the lower-salary, largely union-free private school openings. The much better-paying "public" school openings fill slowly.

The preferred conditions (except pay) of many private schools exist, even though most of them spend much less money per student. Since the competitive education industry described throughout this book would eliminate the funding gap, the already superior working conditions of many private schools would improve further. Therefore, the current salary gap understates the value to teachers of the improvement in working conditions they can expect from a competitive education industry.

Collective Bargaining Is Expendable

Will teachers regret the decline in union power that a competitive education industry will cause? A few will, but it's hard to miss something that produces many headaches and few benefits. The spread of collective bargaining did not produce noteworthy, general increases in teacher salaries.[59] "The American Legislative Exchange Council in Washington, DC released a report card on American education in September, 1994. This report found that since 1972, teacher salaries had gone up 3.5% in real dollars. Everything else in education other than teachers' salaries has gone up 90%."[60]

Many teachers are already willing to sacrifice the $5,000 difference between starting salaries for "public" and private teachers for the better working conditions that exist in many current private schools despite their major financial handicaps.[61] More teachers would pay less than $5,000, and a competitive education industry would improve those conditions. Generalizations don't apply to every teacher, but the mixed evidence of collective bargaining gains means there can't be many teachers receiving thousands per year in net benefits from it.

Another headache is the time and money cost of union membership. Previous studies omitted these costs, yet some still found that collective bargaining left teachers worse off. The omitted membership costs might exceed the estimated net benefits that some studies found. Teachers like Michael Fischer describe their belief that collective bargaining harms teachers in articles with strong titles like "A Betrayal of Teachers by Their Union."[62] An article with a similar title[63] includes another example—pension fund mismanagement—of divergence in union leadership and teacher interests and the fact that the former usually takes precedence.

Teachers in a Competitive Education Industry

The schools of a competitive education industry will not have externally imposed budget caps. Entrepreneurs could still cause some of the "public" school merit pay problems described earlier by allocating a fixed sum for merit raises, but market pressures will discourage that practice. Classroom achievements that please parents raise enrollments, budgets, and profits, thereby raising teachers' market value. Likewise, a reputation as a team player—someone who makes colleagues more productive with good ideas and useful materials—will raise a teacher's market value, which will increase the motivation for teachers to develop such reputations. Employers recognize merit or lose top teachers to competing school entrepreneurs. Since the flexible price requirement of a competitive education industry means that parents can supplement public funding with private funds (tuition add-ons), there isn't even a systemwide budget constraint. Teachers can increase the system's total funding and their earnings by improving the quality of education services.

When choice, rather than assignment, matches parents and schools and teachers and children, they will all get along better, and children will learn more. Assignment to a neighborhood "public" school creates frequent mismatches, often to the extent of culture shock.[64] It is not unusual to have middle-class teachers from suburban backgrounds start their teaching career assigned to a school in an urban, largely minority, working-class neighborhood. That's one of the major reasons why there are so many short teaching careers.

Parents' freedom to choose among diverse offerings will free schools and teachers to specialize in what they are best at. Schools will differ according to teaching styles, use of technology, governance structure, and subject emphasis, and some will focus on specific special needs. Teachers will enjoy increased productivity because they will work in the types of schools best suited to their particular skills and interests, and because they will teach children matched to their interests and instructional style. Teachers can make a bigger difference in the lives of children. "It [opening of the education market] is the one change that will permit teachers to emerge from the shadow of the bureaucracy and become professionals."[65]

Because school cartels, called districts,[66] hire most schoolteachers, local teacher labor markets are sometimes not competitive.[67] There is often little or no genuine competition for teachers. No current teacher labor market is as competitive as the teacher labor market in a competitive K–12 education industry. Analyses of data generated by "public" school district rivalry,[68] rather than competing profit-seeking entrepreneurs, understate the effects of competition, yet they still confirm the theoretically sound proposition that teacher salaries are higher in more competitive teacher labor markets.[69] Even if the "public" school sector of a competitive education industry still organizes itself into districts, expansion of the private sector still would greatly increase the number of self-managed campuses competing for teachers.

In a competitive education industry, more teachers would apply directly to the campuses where they want to work, thereby increasing teacher mobility and location choice and it would reduce teacher vulnerability to arbitrary or personal administrative decisions. Teachers in regions with few school districts (including some single-district, large urban areas) need such changes the most. Currently, teachers who run afoul of key administrators often have only unattractive alternatives. Termination usually is unlikely, but administrators can make teachers miserable. It may take a change of residence or a long commute to work in another school district. The only other choices are: a) leave the labor force; b) take a much lower-paying, nonteaching job; c) return to college for retraining; or d) take a lower-paying private school position if they can find one. A competitive education industry would have more independent employers, and private schools would receive as much public money per student as "public" schools. Even "public" schools probably would make more personnel decisions independently. Therefore, in a competitive education industry, a teacher seeking a new position has a much better chance of finding a good one without a big increase in commuting time.

If "public" schools receive public funds strictly through parental choice, rather than through budget allocations from their district, district administrators would have much less power. That would cause many district office functions to vanish, while others would shift to individual campuses and vendors. Districts in their current form could disappear completely. Funds saved by eliminating administrative overhead are available for teacher raises, and that's where those funds are most likely to go. Schools would have to compete for the best teachers to attract students. Except in the states that foolishly prohibit add-ons, an infusion of private funds would further increase the money available for teacher salaries.

PARTICULAR GAINERS AND LOSERS

Some effects of market forces are fairly certain. Other long-term effects are not as easily foreseen, but for some the likely key factors are identifiable. Some teachers would regret their weaker unions' reduced political clout. Salaries would reflect differences in teacher skills much more than now, an especially major change in the states with a single salary schedule. Lacking the captive audience of a "public" school, irretrievably burned out or incompetent teachers will become unpopular, perhaps to the point where no one will hire them. They will suffer unless they take advantage of the adjustment aid and transition incentives proposed below.

Since both supply and demand probably will increase, the size and direction of change in teacher salaries is uncertain. The entry of new teachers, return of former teachers, and long-term turnover reductions could be large. However, since the major changes will also drive many teachers into early retirement or other careers, a decrease in supply is possible. Demand is likely to rise because opportunities to supplement vouchers with private add-ons, and the improved quality that would result from stronger incentives and opportunities to specialize, will expand K–12 resources. However, that outcome is not certain. Technology applications may eliminate more teaching positions than they create, and the new positions may differ greatly from traditional teaching positions.

Certainly, the changes point to significant differences in the salaries of different kinds of teachers. A competitive education industry would replace the surpluses, shortages, and disguised exceptions to salary schedules based on general credentials and experience with market-based salaries based on subject area, technology skills, effectiveness working in teams, and popularity. Among the skilled and motivated, teachers in high-demand fields such as math and science would enjoy larger raises than teachers in traditionally low-demand fields such as history and English.

Lost Political Clout

Teacher unions are the single largest constituency in the Democratic Party: "The NEA/AFT form a political machine of unparalleled size and sophistication."[70] To the extent that teachers care about politics, and believe in the union's policy positions, they will regret the union's lost political clout. Dissident members will be glad that their association, and some of their dues, no longer supports policies they oppose.

Supply Changes

A competitive education industry will not accommodate every existing teacher, and some will not want to adjust. Irreconcilable mismatches between the skills school operators will want, and the skills existing teachers have or are willing to learn, would reduce the effective supply of teachers. Some teachers would have to change careers or retire early.

The attrition/mismatch effect, by itself, would raise salaries. However, the effect could be overwhelmed eventually by increased interest in a teaching career. The professionalization of teaching could increase interest in teaching careers among college students and former teachers. The increased size of the private sector, where certification matters less, would attract people interested in teaching as a second career who aren't willing to get the education degree and teaching certificate that "public" schools often require. It's only conjecture, but I believe that a competitive education industry would improve the teaching profession enough to greatly increase the supply of teachers. Such supply increases would reduce the salary increase caused by reduced spending on administration and parents' ability to supplement public spending on K–12 with privately funded tuition add-ons only to the extent that teaching jobs become more desirable.

Use of Technology

"Public" schools see technology as something to teach, much more than as a potentially superior way to teach some things to some children. "Chalk and talk" remains the dominant education process. The relentless pressure to improve quality and cut costs inherent in competitive industries may change that much faster than the current system would. The pressure could change significantly what a teacher does and the skills teachers need, as well as the total number of teachers school operators will want at the market price.

CRITICAL TRANSITION ISSUES

Choice advocates have an arsenal of powerful arguments, but uncertainty is a powerful enemy and the key to the status quo's defenses. A carefully crafted incentive package will fortify those arguments significantly, and increase the likelihood that teachers will accept the transition to a new system.

Assurances of pension portability are a must. Adjustment assistance measures, which are compassionate and politically astute, deserve serious consideration. Such assistance should include at least retraining assistance aimed at helping teachers to adapt to labor market changes within the newly evolving competitive education industry, or to begin new careers outside K–12 education. Other incentives, including severance payments for teachers in schools where ownership changes occur, are also worth considering.

A key political strategy and transition issue is choice advocates' ability to appeal to teachers without compromising the key elements of competitive education industries. Parental choice advocates must make the case, often and loudly, that teachers can prosper in a competitive education industry. Teachers have almost as much to gain from a competitive education industry as children do. How to get there is the subject of the final chapter.

NOTES

1. Elizabeth Gleick, "Mad and Mobilized," *Time* (September 9, 1996): 52.

2. Joseph L. Bast and David Harmer, *Vouchers and Educational Freedom: A Debate*, Policy Analysis Monograph #269 (Washington: The Cato Institute, 1997).

3. For example, in Milwaukee, a teacher opposed to the NEA position on school choice ran for school board against heavy NEA opposition: David Kirkpatrick, *School Choice: The Idea That Will Not Die* (Mesa, Ariz.: Bluebird Publishing, 1997), p. 110. The AFT and NEA endorsed Al Gore, but a nationwide survey of teachers by the Alexis de Tocqueville Institution (reported in a November 15, 1996 FAX) revealed that teachers' top three choices were "undecided," Bush, and McCain. Bush received more support than Gore and Bradley combined.

4. Education Intelligence Agency Communiqué, May 24, 1999. Nonparticipation follows from the low level of awareness of union representation. A survey of Alabama's NEA affiliate "revealed that only 2 percent of its members described the AEA as a labor union, and only 5 percent described the NEA as a labor union."

5. Kirkpatrick, 1997, p. 12.

6. Denis Doyle, "Lessons in Hypocrisy," *Wall Street Journal* (June 13, 1995).

7. Education Intelligence Agency, *NEA Confidential: A Practical Guide to the Operations of the Nation's Largest Teachers' Union* (1998).

8. Herbert Gintis, "The Political Economy of School Choice," *Teachers College Record* 96, no. 3 (Spring 1995): 508.

9. The 1997 Membership Survey of the Association of American Educators posted on the Internet at *www.aaeteachers.org/survey97.html.*

10. Deroy Murdock, "Teachers Warm to School Choice," *Headway* (April 1998): 20.

11. William Allen and Eugenia Toma, *A New Framework for Public Education* (Lansing, Mich.: Governor's Office, November, 1996).

12. Mackinac Center for Public Policy, "A Letter to the American People: From the Participants of the National Summit of Teachers for Education Reform," Mackinac Center for Public Policy Web site (*mackinac.org*); also described in *School Reform News* (December 1998): 3.

13. John Taylor Gatto, *Dumbing Us Down* (Philadelphia: New Society Publishers, 1992).

14. Drew Lindsay, "Turncoat, Part I," *Education Week* (May 7, 1997).

15. Ibid.

16. *Wall Street Journal* editorial board (July 7, 1998): A16.

17. Richard Lacayo, "They'll Vouch for That," *Time* (October 27, 1997): 74.

18. David Kirkpatrick, "School Choice Choir Has Broad Range of Voices," *School Reform News* (July 1999): 9, in *USA Today* (August 28, 1990).

19. Survey results reported in an Alexis de Tocqueville Institute FAX (November 15, 1996).

20. Richard K. Vedder, *Can Teachers Own Their Own Schools*, Independence Institute Policy Report (2000); Robert Maranto and Scott Milliman, "In Arizona, Charter Schools Work," *Washington Post* (October 11, 1999): A25. Maranto and Milliman found that Arizona's "best charter schools are started by entrepreneurial teachers who felt stymied by school administrators and school boards;" it's not a competitive situation, but a demonstration of entrepreneurial spirit.

21. Joseph Murphy, *The Privatization of Schooling* (Thousand Oaks, Calif.: Corwin Press, 1996): p. 151.

22. Paula M. Evans, "When I Grow Up, I Don't Think I Want to Be a Teacher," *Education Week* (June 2, 1999): 31.

23. Carolyn [last name withheld], "I Need to Be in My Classroom," *San Antonio Express-News* (June 1, 1997): 1J.

24. Joseph Powell, "Treat Teachers as Professionals," *San Antonio Express-News* (June 1, 1997): 1J.

25. Bill MacWhithey, "Good Teachers Tired of Battling the System," *San Antonio Express-News* (June 1, 1997): 1J.

26. Denis Udall, Letter to the Editor, *Education Week* (July 8, 1998): 41, 43.

27. A. Gary Dworkin, "Coping with Reform: The Intermix of Teacher Morale, Teacher Burnout, and Teacher Accountability" Bruce J. Biddle, Thomas L. Good, and Ivor F. Goodson (eds.), *International Handbook of Teachers and Teaching*, Volume 1 (Dordrecht, The Netherlands: Kluwer Academic Publishers, 1997), chapter 13.

28. Michael Fischer, "A Betrayal of Teachers by Their Union," *Wisconsin Interest* (Fall/Winter 1994): 35.

29. Thomas Toch, "Why Teachers Don't Teach," *U.S. News & World Report* (February 26, 1996): 62.

30. Seymour B. Sarason, *The Predictable Failure of Educational Reform* (San Francisco: Jossey-Bass Publishers, 1990), p. 15.

31. Dworkin, 1997, chapter 13; Diane Ravitch, *The Troubled Crusade* (New York: Basic Books,

1983), p. 233; Robert Chase, "Changing the Way Schools Do Business," *Vital Speeches* (May 1, 1998): 444. According to Ravitch, the rather demeaning term "teacher-proof" has its origin in the 1960s, and it has survived the power of teacher unions, and is even recognized by Robert Chase, current president of the National Education Association.

32. A. Gary Dworkin, *Teacher Burnout in the Public Schools* (Albany, N.Y.: SUNY Press, 1987), p. 15.

33. Dworkin, 1987, p. 69. A nearly identical statement is in G. Carl Ball and Steven Goldman, "Improving Education's Productivity," *Phi Delta Kappan* (November 1997): 230.

34. Albert Shanker on *The News Hour with Jim Lehrer* (August 22, 1996).

35. Sarason, 1990, pp. 25-26.

36. Alec M. Gallup, *Gallup Poll of Teachers' Attitudes toward the Public Schools* (Bloomington, Ind.: Phi Delta Kappa, 1985): 10; Stanley M. Elam, "Differences between Educators and the Public on Questions of Education Policy," *Phi Delta Kappan* (December 1987): 294–96.

37. *Teacher Magazine*, Unsigned Letter to the Editor, *Teacher Magazine* (November/December 1995).

38. *School Reform News*, "Professor: US Education Being Emasculated" *School Reform News* (December 1998): 3.

39. William S. King, "A Simpler Conclusion," *Phi Delta Kappan* 78, no. 2 (October 1996): 180.

40. George Melloan, "Global Finance: Some Day We'll Get Organized," *Wall Street Journal* (May 4, 1999). Melloan was referring to international finance bureaucrats, but it applies equally well to most bureaucrats.

41. A. Gary Dworkin and Merric L. Townsend, "Teacher Burnout in the Face of Reform: Some Caveats in Breaking the Mold," in Bruce A. Jones and Kathryn M. Borman (eds.), *Investing in U.S. Schools: Directions for Educational Policy* (Norwood, N.J.: Ablex Publishing Company, 1994), p. 77.

42. Evans (June 2, 1999), 31.

43. Ibid.

44. Dworkin, 1997, p. 463.

45. John T. Gatto, *Confederacy of Dunces: The Tyranny of Compulsory Schooling* (New York: John Taylor Gatto, 1992), p. 9.

46. David T. Kearns and Denis P. Doyle, *Winning the Brain Race: A Bold Plan to Make Our Schools Competitive* (San Francisco: ICS Press, 1991), p. 64.

47. Tom Luce, speaker at October 17, 1997, School Choice Conference sponsored by the Federal Reserve Bank of Dallas.

48. Samuel C. Carter, *No Excuses: Lessons from 21 High-Performing, High-Poverty Schools* (Washington: Heritage Foundation, 2000).

49. Dale Ballou and Michael Podgursky, *Teacher Pay and Teacher Quality* (Kalamazoo, Mich.: The Upjohn Institute, 1997), p. 81.

50. G. Carl Ball and Steven Goldman, "Improving Education's Productivity," *Phi Delta Kappan* (November 1997): 230.

51. Dworkin and Townsend, 1994, chapter 6.

52. Based on full-time teachers in the 1987–88 Schools and Staffing Survey.

53. Ballou and Podgursky, 1997.

54. Peters quoted in Murdock (April 1998), 20.

55. Teachers' willingness to pay for better working conditions (by accepting a lower salary than government schools offer) will diminish as the total number of teachers sought by the pri-

vate school sector increases. To greatly increase their market share (now about 10 percent nationally) private schools would have to reduce the private school-government school salary gap.

56. Hugh Pearson, "An Urban Push for Self-Reliance," *Wall Street Journal* (February, 7, 1996).

57. William Styring, "Teachers and School Choice," *American Outlook* (Spring 1998): 49–51.

58. Ballou and Podgursky, 1997.

59. Myron Lieberman, *The Teacher Unions* (New York: The Free Press, 1997).

60. Michael Fischer, "A Betrayal of Teachers by Their Union," *Wisconsin Interest* (Fall/Winter 1994): 33.

61. The 1987–88 starting salary gap between "public" and private schools was nearly $5,000: Ballou and Podgursky, 1997.

62. Ibid.

63. Stephen Glass, "A Pension Deficit Disorder: Teacher Unions Betray Their Members," *Policy Review* (Winter 1995): 71–74.

64. Dworkin and Townsend, 1994, p. 77.

65. Denis P. Doyle, "The Challenge, the Opportunity," *Phi Delta Kappan* (March 1992): 518.

66. A cartel is an association that reduces competition. The organization of schools into districts with centralized personnel policies eliminates competition among schools for students (customers) and for personnel. That lack of competition among schools within districts is especially significant for teachers because, except in areas like math and science, the significant investment in teaching skills has little value outside of teaching.

67. John Merrifield, "Monopsony Power in the Market for Teachers," *Journal of Labor Research* 20, no. 3 (Summer 1999): 377–91.

68. See the findings and literature review in ibid.

69. More competition probably will also produce better working conditions. Employees with options have to be treated better to retain them. Empirical support is harder to generate for this theoretically sound proposition because working conditions are not measured and quantified as easily in a consistent manner over time or among jurisdictions.

70. Lieberman, 1997.

CHAPTER 15
Outlook and Political Strategy

"I sense that we are on the verge of a breakthrough in one state or another, which will then sweep like wildfire through the rest of the country."

— Milton Friedman, *Washington Post* Weekly Edition (February 27, 1995)

"Without a change in tactics, school choice will be a permanent loser."

— John Miller, "Why School Choice Lost," *Wall Street Journal* (November 4, 1993)

Both of these statements are true. The outlook—what spreads and how fast—depends on the choice advocacy strategy. Many parental choice proposals are losers, if not politically, then as reform catalysts.

If the current choice advocacy strategy persists, the outlook is dismal. That's a major reason why this book was written. Shocking incidents of academic failure and exasperation with typical reform strategies will increase implementation of parental choice, but the public mindset and current advocacy practices probably will spread restriction-laden choice through so-called experiments and pilot programs that are not "tentative procedures" because they cannot transform the system. Only a subset of low-income families and/or students from government-designated low-performing schools will participate directly. Discrimination against taxpayers who use private schools will retard transformation of the private sector. It will take 20–30 years to realize that helping a few economically disadvantaged children will not produce widespread academic improvements. Another decade *may* be enough to convince the public that limited parental choice was an ineffective reform catalyst because of the limitations. Widespread economic illiteracy already makes that a hard sell, and it won't get any easier.

To replace that scenario with a more promising one, choice advocates must begin openly supporting parental choice programs that contain every key element of a competitive education industry. They must *loudly and visibly* subordinate movement within the system to system transformation. Small changes in the status quo should be left to legislatures where caution and compromise approaches are inevitable while political pressure builds for the necessary K–12 transformation.

However, cautious compromise policies must not be allowed to diminish that pressure. Programs that help thousands of children are great as long as they don't jeopardize reforms that would help millions. Choice advocates must articulate strong reservations when they support restriction-laden programs that lack key elements of a competitive education industry. Unless they do, incremental changes will often turn into lengthy detours.

Choice advocates must use opposition to deficient proposals to educate the public and define choice advocacy as the pursuit of universal opportunity and empowerment. Something like this is appropriate:

> Today, Governor X proposed a low-income voucher program wherein the state share of "public" school funding follows the children of successful applicants—up to Y% of district enrollment—to the school they prefer. We are deeply disappointed, because the state could do much more with the existing K–12 budget. Competition through universal parental choice would help all children by improving the entire system. When public support follows every child without regard to school ownership, schools will join the vast majority of service providers and become directly accountable to the people they serve. Market forces would produce the relentless improvement that characterizes most of the economy. Governor X's restrictions on choice continue the long-standing practice of assigning the comfort of "public" school employees—public servants—a higher priority than the education of children. School taxes exist to support children, so their welfare should be our top priority. While we continue our pursuit of universal choice and empowerment, we'll support X's proposal so that the school system's worst victims can attend schools that their parents believe are better for them.

With some smart political work, I believe we'll enact unbiased (public support per child doesn't depend on school ownership) universal parental choice within four to six years, and then it will spread like wildfire. The smart political work must address the following:

- Most suburbanites believe their schools are fine.
- Most states don't publish detailed, school-level, academic data or academic standards for each grade.
- Leaders of low-income groups, especially African Americans, take parental choice positions at odds with most of their constituents.
- Teachers, the cornerstone of choice opposition, have much to gain from a competitive education industry. Many teachers are conservative, and most only support the union position passively. The vast majority are apolitical, and don't understand the parental choice policy options.
- Except for changes in the finance and governance system that would create

competition, every potential reform strategy has been tried many times, and has produced only big expenditures and disappointment. "More-of-the-Same-Harder" hasn't worked.

- The public knows very little about the parental choice options, and most of the available information is wrong, misleading, or irrelevant.
- Increasing access to the best choices currently available can hinder transformation of the choices.
- Hardly anyone cares about competition per se, but most of the potential benefits of parental choice depend on it.
- Winning will be easier in some places.
- Policy essentials and key options of a competitive education industry.

WINNING IN THE SUBURBS

Blissful ignorance is a formidable opponent. Its victims won't seek the truth, and their ability to deny the truth is evident in the persistence of the myth that suburban schools are good in the face of frequently published evidence to the contrary. The propensity to deny is even apparent in the title—"Reality Check 2000"[1]—of a prominent piece of that evidence.

The words of a popular song—"Tell me lies, tell me sweet little lies"—are quite relevant. The truth could hurt property values. Households with no school-age children—the majority—probably have the strongest preference for "sweet little lies." Some families prefer living downtown, but move to the suburbs because the schools usually are better.[2] They will not readily accept a contention that the better school that helped attract them is still pretty bad.

Deeply ingrained myths are durable; they will survive single doses of overwhelming evidence. Resentment of the messengers will outlast the eventual, grudging acceptance of the message. However, the distastefulness of the task doesn't alter the fact that school system transformation will not begin until choice advocates destroy the myth that major academic deficiencies exist only in the low-income inner city. Suburban bliss is a major roadblock on the road to a competitive education industry.

Publication of detailed school-level data is the first step. The next step is to compare it to what children in each grade should know. Regional groupings of schools are appropriate. The top schools may still be pretty bad, so school rankings should be avoided. For large urban areas, it might be helpful to compare subgroups of schools to what children should know. Subgroups, such as "public" school districts or inner city vs. suburb, might be useful.

Choice advocates should not attack the myth one school at a time. That approach would maximize the property value effects. The outcry could undermine the process and divert attention away from the critical message that the whole system is broken, that relocating to another neighborhood or switching to a private school probably won't help much. Truly outstanding schools should be singled out so that users of other schools cannot cling to the widespread myth that problems exist in every school but their own.

WEAKENING THE OPPOSITION

Discord between labor and the poor, and between the poor (especially African Americans) and their leaders, could weaken parental choice opponents significantly. Labor and the poor are core constituent groups of politicians, mostly Democrats, who currently oppose all but the weakest forms of parental choice, and who would feel the same about a competitive education industry. Choice advocates must exploit such rifts in the opposition.

The teacher unions are the biggest opponents of parental choice, but they cannot stop choice on their own, and they confront several problems that parental choice advocates can exploit politically. Teacher union leaders must maintain the backing of teachers and fight to preserve an antiparental choice liberal coalition that supports public funding for many other kinds of choice. Liberals' discomfort with the contradiction between the teacher union position and other liberal causes was clearly evident in a Gore-Bradley debate (2000). Both were eager to change the subject, to flee what the *Wall Street Journal* correctly dubbed, a "piece of Democratic Kryptonite."[3] Choice advocates must use it to reform or defeat the "liberal superhero" position on parental choice.

The passionate opposition of teacher union leaders is not seen among teachers. Even though very few choice advocates vigorously solicit teacher support, few teachers show a strong interest in working to defeat parental choice. Most teachers fear the unions' definition of parental choice enough to support the union position, but they're not happy with the status quo. Teachers resent teacher bashing, which they see as condemnation for following orders and the mistakes of others. They don't like mandates, micromanagement, or teaching tests. Teachers don't like coping with parents who want out, but can't leave. They don't like mainstreaming everyone, including revolving-door discipline problems and special needs children who require specialized services. Many want linkage between compensation and genuine merit. Teachers want a transformation of the system, but not enough agree that genuine competition is the best way to do it. As teachers see more evidence that efforts to make the system work are painful acts of futility that often degrade their lives further, more of them will realize that a parental choice-based system is the only alternative. Choice advocates must accelerate that process.

Teacher union leaders can maintain rank-and-file support only if they can make parental choice look even worse than the current system. That's really tough. Since administrators and legislators will continue their frenzied efforts to make teachers succeed despite the system, maintaining teacher support for the union position will get tougher. Choice advocates can accelerate the erosion of teacher opposition to parental choice. It would help a lot if choice advocates would just stop enthusiastically supporting restriction-laden parental choice proposals and stop making the analytical errors that help union leaders frighten teachers. Because teachers see little else discussed, and because choice advocates so enthusiastically embrace restriction-laden programs, teachers probably think of parental choice as something that will extend to more teachers the existing opportunity to give up one-third of their income to escape the problems described above. Choice advocates must point out that a competitive education industry would do more than eliminate that trade-off. Other current disadvantages of the private sector, such as the scarcity of secular schools, would disappear, and government-run ("public") schools would either get better and more teacher-friendly or become increasingly scarce.

The poor, especially minorities, represent another political opportunity. According to a recent *Time* magazine article, "inner city blacks are beginning to join the Republican cry for vouchers to pay private school tuition."[4] "The Joint Center for Political and Economic Studies, a left-leaning think tank that focuses on African-American issues, found in its 1999 annual survey that 60 percent of blacks support school choice."[5] A recent Republican National Committee ad campaign targeting African American voters made the headlines.[6]

"School choice and charter schools are becoming the civil rights movement of the 1990s,"[7] and "over 70 percent of blacks under 35"[8] support parental choice. In a "1997 Delta Kappa/Gallup Poll between 62 and 72 percent of African-Americans expressed their support for vouchers."[9] Such polling data signal potentially "serious trouble for Democratic legislators and school choice opponents, given blacks' status as the most loyal of all Democratic constituencies."[10] The survey respondents probably understood "vouchers" to be restriction-laden vouchers worth less than the per pupil funding of the "public" schools. Therefore, I believe that the parental choice system advocated throughout this book—and properly explained in the survey instrument—would produce even better polling data. Unlike every existing voucher and tax credit program, the system advocated in this book would put all but the elite prep academies within reach of every family.

The situation presents enormous dangers and opportunities. The opportunities will come from the growing pressure on leaders of low-income groups to profess support for parental choice with public funding through vouchers or tax credits. The danger is that their proposals won't include the key elements of a competitive education industry. Reluctant, born-again choice advocates—leaders of low-income groups—will try to pile on the restrictions. They will do so to try and maintain the appearance of consistency with previous commitments, and to appease their longtime allies in the liberal coalition. They are more likely to get away with it if restriction-laden proposals continue to dominate the public debate;[11] a situation that choice advocates can avoid by repudiating incrementalism.

Light must accompany heat. Choice advocates must explain how each type of restriction hurts low-income groups.

DOCUMENTING FUTILITY

The authorities are under enormous pressure to improve K–12 education. Repeated failures to make the current system produce even satisfactory results, much less excellence, produces growing frustration and anger. The authorities have had enough time to try every conceivable elixir for the current system somewhere, and some reform strategy elements nearly everywhere.[12] Well-worn reform strategies resurface repeatedly in a never-ending triumph of hope over experience.[13] David Kearns and James Harvey said, "education reforms recycle"; they appear, "disappear, and then reappear again."[14] The MOTS-H approach[15] (more-of-the-same-harder) wastes time, money, and young minds. MOTS-H sounds like a long-standing definition of insanity: "Insanity is repeating something that doesn't work and expecting different results."[16] Better documentation can help reduce the repetition of costly acts of futility.

Some parental choice advocacy organization(s) must produce a report that catalogs those disappointments by major plan ingredient, things like teacher raises, merit pay, social promotion, and class sizes. The report should also reveal what each government tried. Such a report is an indispensable advocacy tool. It will comprise a cornerstone of the urgently needed campaign to convince reformers that a reform package will produce satisfactory results only if it fosters genuine competition.

Proper interpretation of findings is critical. For example, merit pay isn't a bad idea just because it has not produced significant improvements yet. It's a big advantage of a competitive education industry. Competition forces managers to reward true merit. Without genuine competition, managers are under much less pressure to recognize merit, and measurement is much more difficult. The point such a report must make is that the political process rarely enacts merit pay, and that the rare exceptions are predictably ineffective and even counterproductive at times. The report must argue that empirical evidence and theoretical reasons indicate that politically created merit pay is not likely to fare any better in the future. Parent/consumers voting with their feet and their money will reward and increase genuine merit much more than an administrator trying to allocate an externally fixed budget according to scheduled acting performances ("observations" of teachers) or test scores.

Similar points should be made about most of the other efforts to make the system work better, including, in particular, teacher raises, increased K–12 spending, and reduced class size.[17] For example, consider the political approach to class size. If enough vocal supporters believe class size reductions warrant the political price of higher taxes or cuts in other areas, class size is capped for certain grades. In contrast, profit-seeking entrepreneurs would find out exactly where class size reductions matter the most, advertise general class reductions, and minimize cost and maximize benefits by implementing the largest class size reductions where they would matter most, and smaller reductions, perhaps even some increases, where they mattered least. The political process cannot produce such an outcome because it would be seen as unfair. Again, it's not that teacher pay, class size, and K–12 spending don't matter. It's that the political process hasn't used them in a way that would bring about improvements, and that for theoretical, as well as empirical reasons, we should not expect it to do so in the future. Social promotion isn't a bad idea because failing students should advance. It's a bad idea because in the current system, ending social promotion means a repeat of the circumstances that led to failure. Choice advocates can summarize with a key generalization. Markets cause resources to flee failure, but in the government's share of K–12, failure often attracts additional resources.

Since a good story helps make any point, choice advocates also should pick out some especially noteworthy recent acts of futility. The California situation is likely to become one of those. Some of Governor Gray Davis's campaign statements will make it especially noteworthy. He said the current situation was "a disaster,"[18] and that his administration had to achieve significant improvements to be seen as successful. There is nothing in the package of so-called reforms enacted by the California legislature[19] that could achieve such improvements.

CHANGING BLISSFUL IGNORANCE

A summer 1999 Public Agenda opinion poll indicated that "a vast majority of the American public claims to have little or no knowledge about charter schools, education vouchers, or for-profit schools," but that "debate at the top levels of national leadership is crisp, and well-defined."[20] "On Thin Ice," the report of the survey results, and I view the survey findings much differently. Since the most critical public statements about parental choice are usually wrong, misleading, or irrelevant, Public Agenda's conviction that the top levels are on track is quite alarming, and the high degree of public ignorance is a blessing. It is much easier to inform people than to dispel their misconceptions.

The survey results also repudiate a key premise of the incrementalism strategy: That approach to some version of full school choice began with the premise that the public is not ready for radical changes in the status quo. Since a substantial segment of the public doesn't even know what choice advocates proposed, they are not necessarily against it. They are not ready for radical change because ignorance makes people more resistant to change and more gullible. Choice opponents skillfully exploit both. They usually have more money to get their message out, allowing them to get away with more emotion-evoking distortions.

A reality check, followed by relentless truth in labeling, is the only way out of the encumbrance of public ignorance and the more devastating mistaken beliefs of longtime participants in the school choice wars. The reality check should begin with what is really happening in places like Milwaukee and Cleveland. Restriction-laden low-income voucher programs are not tentative reform procedures. Choice advocates should celebrate each student transfer for exactly what it is—some additional freedom and academic progress—and remind policy makers and the public that each escape attempt is at least a rejection of comprehensive uniformity, and that tweaking the status quo is not good enough. Particular school managers, including the government, can best serve only a fraction of our diverse population.

Competition advocates must use words like *freedom* and *escape* loudly and frequently, especially when they condemn choice program restrictions, including the large number left behind[21] and the minimal effect on the system.[22] That's more important than celebrating the exhilaration of the escapees. The emotional reaction of many voucher recipients causes the word *rescue* to come to mind, but that term should be used sparingly. The term *rescue* may lead many people to believe that current private schools are in good shape, when in fact they have much room for improvement.

RECONCILING PRAGMATISM AND PRINCIPLES

A competitive education industry may not be politically feasible yet. In the meantime, the inevitable pursuit of lesser objectives must not conflict with that ultimate objective. In other words, choice advocates must push for a competitive education industry to effect systemic reform while efforts to provide some additional choices, and limited chances to use alternatives to "public" schools, continue in a manner that does not undermine the reform effort.

The key is truth in labeling. With truth in labeling, the limited choice escape valves that John Hood[23] mistakenly called "gradual reform" can continue without "the limitations and risks that entails" or the risk of being intellectually "right, but outmaneuvered" politically with a competitive education industry-or-nothing policy. Interim, limited victories are often necessary to maintain the morale of the key choice advocates, and they broaden support by publicly demonstrating political strength.

Truth in Labeling in Practice

Here's how advocates of a competitive education industry should have described the passage of the parental choice program enacted for Milwaukee, Wisconsin:

> Today, the State of Wisconsin decided to help 1 percent of the low-income students trapped in the reform-resistant Milwaukee Public Schools (MPS) attend certain private schools; nonsectarian schools willing to educate a child for about half as much as MPS spends. Only the children of low-income families will have the freedom to attend a private school with some of the tax money earmarked for their education. The families that pay most of the school taxes can't use their taxes to help them leave. Escape attempts represent complaints about the comprehensive uniformity forced

on public schools by attendance areas and about low quality, yet escapes give MPS more to spend on each remaining captive. The modest rise in MPS's per pupil funds will have no immediate impact on the remaining 99 percent of MPS captives, including many more low-income children stuck in the worst MPS schools. Because of the restrictions on private schools, the extremely low cap on participation, and the unequal funding of MPS captives and escapees, the escapes will produce no discernable competitive pressures. We can only hope that embarrassment[24] alone is enough to motivate some constructive reactions by MPS officials.

Advocates of a competitive education industry should have said something like this after all the initial applications for vouchers were in:

> The private schools can spend much less per child than MPS, yet many more parents want to shift their children to private schools than the excess capacity of the private schools will allow. Very few were deterred by MPS harassment, or by the legal cloud of uncertainty that hangs over the new program. But for some crippling restrictions, the private sector eventually could serve everyone who wants an alternative to MPS. The cap on participation and the ban on adding private money to the voucher are especially troublesome. In addition, the large voucher waiting list contains only low-income applicants. Some of the families that supposedly have enough money to pay for education services twice are so desperate for escape assistance that they risk punishment for filing false income statements.[25] The high demand for vouchers directly contradicts the claims of some choice critics that parents, especially low-income families, can't compare schools. Voucher applicants were so unhappy with their much better-funded MPS school that they greatly prefer a much leaner private school they have no personal experience with, even though such a move probably means some inconvenience and discomfort, such as separating their children from their friends, and transportation requirements. Right now, more children want to escape, and each departure saves taxpayers' money and increases the funding per "public" school user. If private school and MPS users had equal public funding, and a wider array of private schools could cash vouchers, the number of applications would be far greater. Citizens tax themselves to educate children by the best possible means, not to support school systems. Therefore, the authorities should make the program universal and eliminate the "public" school funding advantage. That would allow us to reap the benefits of competition.

COMPETITION–THE CRITICAL PROCESS

The Luntz Research Companies tested various K–12 reform and parental choice messages on focus groups. By testing the appeal of the word and concept, they concluded that "competition does not matter to anyone."[26]

Luntz and Castro overstated their findings. The people they talked to care about competition, whether they know it or not, because virtually all of the things that did matter depend on genuine competition. That's the correct message to choice advocates. Since citizens care about academic outcomes and fairness, not underlying processes, choice advocates must connect the outcomes to the critical process of competition.

The truly alarming but not surprising implication of the Luntz finding is that people do not make the connection on their own. Economic education is one of the most glaring defects of the current system. As Myron Lieberman pointed out, economic illiteracy makes choice advocacy more difficult: "Public education has flourished because it fails to educate effectively. Its failure to foster an understanding of market systems has led citizens to accept a larger public education sector than a more informed citizenry would permit."[27]

The parents of the escaping children and unsuccessful applicants are natural, politically active constituents for a competitive education industry. Since they already believe that the political process hasn't fixed "public" schools, it is especially important to mobilize them on behalf of a competitive education industry. Regular reminders of the difference between the benefits of a move within the system and system transformation are especially important. Unless they are convinced that a competitive education industry will make private schools much better, appreciation of the difference between a "public" school and the existing private school best suited to their child may make them complacent.

WHERE TO START THE WILDFIRE

For the sake of our children and our country, it would be great if competitive education industries could start up everywhere at the same time. They can't. Economic realities of limited resources and geographically uneven barriers to change require that we carefully choose the wildfire's ignition point. The first modern competitive education industry will not be an experiment. Competitive forces already have an impressive track record, even in education. The next competitive education industry will provide the modern demonstration that will ignite the wildfire.

Since any large town will do, don't wage political warfare in places like California, where choice opponents' money and media time advantages mean the most. Because of the way K–12 is funded, a small, conservative state could be ideal.

POLICY ESSENTIALS AND OPTIONS

The critical elements of a competitive education industry described in chapter 2, political pragmatism, and the recommendation of a high minimum level of support for every child, come down to some policy essentials and options. The policy essentials are:

1. State and local public funding of K–12 instruction must be entirely child-based so that parents' school choices exclusively decide each school's share of state and local government funding.

2. Each child's share of state and local K–12 instruction spending is the same, whether the child attends government-owned, private nonprofit, or private for-profit schools.
3. There must be no restrictions on private spending on K–12 instruction. Families must have the right to use private funds to help buy more instruction than the public funds will buy.
4. Child-based state and local public funding of K–12 must begin at the current K–12 funding level.
5. As required by existing federal law, federal K–12 funding must provide supplemental public support to special needs children on a case-by-case basis.
6. There must be a minimum enrollment to qualify an educator to receive public funding to educate children. This will deter fraud and extremist schools, and stop families from earning income by educating their own children.
7. There must be a way to verify the enrollment of each school.

The significant policy options are:

1. There are at least two possible public funding mechanisms. Vouchers are okay, but not necessary—a plus, given the "V-word" phenomenon discussed earlier. School enrollment is the only piece of information needed to send the appropriate government check to each school. Another option is a fully refundable tax credit. Then schools would bill parents, and the government would only have to issue checks to families with K–12 credits larger than their tax liabilities.
2. Providing the same level of public support to government and private school users does not preclude age-based or place-based differences in public funding per child. For example, private school tuition levels are now typically higher for high school grades than for elementary grades, an indication that it costs more to educate older children. Therefore, more public funding for, say, tenth graders than second graders may be deemed appropriate. Likewise, the authorities may decide that regional cost differences warrant regional differences in the public funding per child.
3. The administrative requirements of child-based K–12 funding are vastly smaller than and different from the administrative requirements of the current system. The authorities will have to decide how much of current government spending to allocate to instruction and how much to allocate to administrative functions. With child-based funding, the administrative requirements include enrollment verification, fund disbursal, and monitoring and enforcement requirements of regulations and potential fraud.

As long as there are no restrictions on private K–12 spending, the political tug-of-war over the appropriate age- and region-based differences and the issue of instructional vs. administrative spending won't be too damaging.

4. The government's role as an information provider and data generator—including standardized testing—must be defined. Test score comparisons will still matter to some parents, but with the specialized schools of a competitive education industry, such data won't matter as much as they do with the comprehensive uniformity that now dominates "public" schools.

States would have to define "school" to determine eligibility to receive public K–12 instructional funding. The definition that states use to enforce compulsory attendance laws will probably serve that purpose adequately, but there will be pressures to add regulations. They must be resisted. The market will resolve all of the other issues, things like personnel qualifications, textbooks, curricula, food service, and transportation services. Those are competition areas.

Market forces deter and punish mistakes more effectively than costly, stifling government regulations can prevent them. Choice and tolerance, not regulation, are the answer to disagreement over what schools should teach. One reason regulations would be counterproductive is the same as the demand for them—the ever-changing controversy over what the rules should require. The other reason is that they would hinder the relentless pursuit of improvement that characterizes competitive markets.

PROCESSES AND OUTCOMES

Most of the specific effects[28] of market forces are utterly unforeseeable, but a hypothetical example can illustrate key elements of the child-based funding process and connect the process to likely general effects. The effects that might stand out during a transition are especially noteworthy. Unless choice advocates prepare the public for a bumpy transition period, market forces could be stifled before they completely take hold.

Let's say a county with 100,000 K–12 age children implements the policy essentials described above for the 2003–2004 school year. For the sake of simplicity, assume that K–12 enrollment in that area will stay at 100,000, and that in the previous year, state and local public funding for K–12 was $600 million. For 2003–2004, the authorities must fund debt service, administer the child-based funding payment process, and monitor rule compliance. Now, let's say that debt service consumes $50 million a year, and that the administrative requirements of child-based funding consume another $5 million. For a margin of safety, in case federal funds are not enough of a supplement for special needs families, the county school authorities set aside another $20 million for that. In the first years of child-based funding, the authorities also should allocate money for severance and retraining support. Help for educators seeking new careers or trying to adjust to changing K–12 opportunities would produce significant economic and political benefits. Assume the authorities allocate $25 million per year for that. With the same state and local funding level in 2003–2004 as in 2002–2003, that will leave $500 million ($600 – $50 – $5 – $20 – $25) to allocate to schools according to parental choices; an *average* of $5,000 per K–12 child ($500 million ÷ 100,000 children). However, the level of support per child probably will vary by grade level, with more than $5,000 for older children and less for younger ones.

If the county is typical, and 12 percent of the students attended private schools or were home-schooled when public schools had their monopoly on public funding, child-based funding—ending the government's discrimination against private school users—will cause a 12 percent drop in government-owned schools' per pupil funding. Even though schools will be free to charge more than the average $5,000 public funding level, and child-based funding will eliminate some costs (see below), some people will cite potential hardship for low-income families to justify increased public spending on K–12, and they'll find ready allies in private school operators eager for opportunities to raise their prices. Charities can eliminate that justification for increased public funding by providing a low-income safety net, help for families that don't live near a school that will accept the $5,000 public funding as full payment and can't afford a required add-on. A true scholarship program that gives low-income families access to schools that demand large add-ons would have a great deal of economic and political value, as well.

Child-based funding would directly eliminate some costly tasks—some directly—and it would undermine the rationale for others. School budgets would depend on parents' choices, not the decisions of the district central office. That would weaken significantly the rationale for an expensive District Superintendent and the raft of associates, assistants, directors, and program coordinators. In addition, district administrators won't have to develop budgets or maintain, adjust, or enforce school attendance areas. Government-owned schools can maintain their district identity, but schools would perform many formerly district-provided services themselves. Personnel is a good example. School principals want to hire their own staff; they don't want district administrators to do it for them.[29] Because district schools would not benefit equally from district-provided support services, the schools would increasingly resist funding them. In addition, the changes that would come with the pressure to specialize require a wider range of service providers.

Ending government discrimination against private school users would increase the demand for private schooling. That would drive up private school tuition unless education entrepreneurs and existing private school owners have enough advance warning to provide additional capacity to handle the demand increase. Even if there is enough time to expand facilities and establish new schools, some schools will have more applicants than space. Since oversubscribed schools may not discover the problem until it is too late to change advertised prices for the upcoming school year, they will do exactly what choice opponents have warned they would: They will become more selective. But these shortages would be short-lived. Copycat entrepreneurs would quickly offer more of the most popular services. When explaining this facet of the transition to a competitive education industry, parental choice advocates also should point out that selectivity—school choice, by "public" school officials, rather than parents—already exists in the current system. However, the current system contains no mechanism to quickly eliminate space shortages in magnet schools, or in some states, charter schools.

Some people may fear that the large private school sector of a competitive education industry would become a second strong lobby for higher school taxes. That is not necessarily true, and any increase in lobbying pressure from the private sector would not offset the shrinking clout of "public" schools. Certainly, increases in public funding per child will produce price increases and higher short-term profits, but the education entrepreneurs may realize that higher short-term profits will attract additional competitors. If they don't, they will learn that lesson quickly. Additional competition will restore the rate of return to a level that is normal for businesses with comparable risks, in part by forcing some schools to reduce the add-on they demand. Many school operators will conclude that such a cycle of change is not worth lobbying for. Basic economics texts often discuss a phenomenon called *limit-pricing*, a practice whereby firms sacrifice short-term profit to avoid an intensification of competition and a possible decrease in long-term profitability. In the current system, school operators see no downside to across-the-board funding increases. A competitive education industry would produce much weaker pressures for government funding increases, and school operators cannot stifle the signals (like excess capacity) that can justify spending restraint.

MOUNTAINS AND TRENCHES AS METAPHORS

A fog enshrouded abyss lined with mountains is a good metaphor for the school choice wars. The highest summit is a competitive education industry (CEI). There is trench warfare on the lower slopes between the defenders of the current system and people desperate to fundamentally change it. Reformers can achieve the CEI summit that dominates all the others, but the premier summit is hard to see through the fog of war. Though every route is difficult—proponents of the current K–12 system will ferociously defend every inch of every route out of the status quo abyss—many of the routes lead to low subpeaks of the CEI summit. The subpeaks of the CEI summit are relatively small changes in the status quo like low-income vouchers, small tax credits, vouchers for children assigned to the worst schools, and public school choice, including even strong charter laws. Relative to the current battleground in the foothills, the subpeaks represent noteworthy improvements, but they are dead-end detours far below the CEI summit. Bruising battles can make any subpeaks feel like the summit or, at least, a significant milepost on the road to it, but sub-peaks are false summits—tempting objectives that increase the distance to the CEI summit. False summits can easily sap enough time and energy to put the CEI true summit out of reach, or push attempts to reach the true summit into the distant future.

False summits can become permanent detours. Government programs are difficult to change. Pursuit of every route that leads up—unqualified, enthusiastic support for every "choice" increment—divides the parental choice army, and confuses the troops and potential recruits. Many are acting lost. To reach the CEI summit, reform advocates need to know what the summit looks like (chapter 2), and develop a complete map (strategy), something not easily done in the trenches. This book makes some observations from behind the front lines. It aims to define the significant differences between the CEI summit and the subpeaks and chart the route to the summit. The competitive education industry outcomes of social justice and relentless pursuit of improvement are worth the difficulties that must be endured to reach them.

NOTES

1. "Reality Check 2000," *Education Week* (February 16, 2000): S1–S8.
2. Daniel Akst, "Why Liberals Should Love School Choice," *Wall Street Journal* (April 6, 1998): A14.
3. "No Choice for Democrats," *Wall Street Journal* (February 23, 2000).
4. Sally B. Donnelly and Tamala M. Edwards, "They'll Vouch for That," *Time* (October 27, 1997): 72–74.
5. Nina S. Rees, "Will the 106th Congress Promote School Choice?" *School Reform News* (April 2000): 3.
6. John Mintz, "GOP Woos Black Voters with Radio Ad Campaign," *Washington Post* (October 13, 2000).
7. Jodi Wilgoren, "Young Blacks Turn to School Vouchers as Civil Rights Issue," *New York Times* (October 9, 2000); Nina Shokraii Rees, "Free at Last: Black America Signs up for School Choice," *Policy Review* (November/December 1996).
8. Nina Shokraii Rees, "School Choice 2000 Annual Report," *The Heritage Backgrounder*, No. 1354 (March 30, 2000).
9. Rochelle Stanfeld, "A Turning Tide on Vouchers," *National Journal* (September 27, 1997): 1911.
10. Burdett Loomis, "The Politics of Vouchers" in *Vouchers and Related Delivery Mechanisms: Consumer Choice in the Provision of Public Services*. Conference (October 2–3, 1998) Papers (Washington: Brookings Institution, 1998), p. 80.
11. Stephen Talbot, "The Battle over School Choice," *PBS Frontline* (May 23, 2000). The hour-long TV special did not discuss competition or how parental choice might bring about a system transformation. The possibility of universal choice was not considered. Instead, the

program stated that there was "not much need for school choice in some places." Parental choice was presented strictly as a way for low-income families to escape bad "public" schools.

12. John S. Barry and Rea S. Hedeman, Jr., *Report Card on American Education: A State-by-State Analysis, 1976–99* (Washington: American Legislative Exchange Council, 2000).

13. Kevin Baker, "Promised Improvements Have Failed to Materialize," Bakersfield *Californian* (October 17, 2000).

14. David T. Kearns and James Harvey, *A Legacy of Learning* (Washington: Brookings Institution Press, 2000), p. 56.

15. Wayne B. Jennings, "Let's Ride the Wave of Change," *Enterprising Educators* 6, no. 2 (Spring 1998): 1.

16. G. K. Chesterton cited in Center for Education Reform *Newsletter* 60 (February/March 2000).

17. David W. Kirkpatrick, "Class Size Reduction: Costly and Ineffective," *School Reform News* (April 1999): 9.

18. California Governor Gray Davis quoted in David Broder, "Reforming Education a Tough Assignment," *San Antonio Express-News* (March 2, 1999): 7B.

19. "California's Tony Blair," *Wall Street Journal* (September 2, 1999).

20. Education Policy Institute, "New Poll Finds Public in Dark About Charters and Vouchers," *EPI-Update* (November 19, 1999).

21. "Fifteen Percent of Eligible Cleveland Public School Children Apply for Vouchers," *The Buckeye Institute for Public Policy Solutions* (June 1996). There is a huge excess demand for the latest CEO voucher offering.

22. Wisconsin Governor Tommy Thompson gives MPS ultimatum: improve significantly by June 2000, or be taken over by the state. Beth Reinhard, "Thompson Threatens a Takeover for Milwaukee," *Education Week* (January 28, 1998): 8.

23. John Hood, "Educational Challenges: The Role of Choice," *Current* (December 1991): 11.

24. Some MPS changes, such as increased school autonomy, have been attributed to embarrassment about the escapes. In Albany, New York, Viginia Gilder funded some low-income vouchers for students at woeful Giffen Elementary. The overwhelming response to the offer prompted some changes at Giffen. According to Albany Superintendent Lonnie Palmer, "The real catalyst may not have been competition, but the subsequent media attention."

25. Mark Walsh, "Audit Criticizes Cleveland Voucher Program," *Education Week* (April 15, 1998).

26. Frank Luntz and Bob Castro, "Dollars to Classrooms and Parental Choice in Education," Memorandum (April 14, 1998).

27. Based on a general observation by Mancur Olson in Myron Lieberman, *Public Education: An Autopsy* (Cambridge, Mass.: Harvard University Press, 1993), p. 160.

28. Size, number, and specialization area(s) of each school, typical modes of instruction; salary levels of different types of educators; market shares of government-owned, private for-profit, private nonprofit, church-run schools, etc.

29. Describing a typical urban school principal, Rexford Brown noted that "his greatest frustration is his inability to hire and fire his own teachers. You're the boss, but you're not able to hire and fire your own employees": Rexford G. Brown, *Schools of Thought* (San Francisco: Jossey-Bass, 1993), p. 104.

Bibliography

Akst, Daniel. "Why Liberals Should Love School Choice," *Wall Street Journal* (April 6, 1998): A14.

Allen, Jeanne. "Benefits of Choice," Letter to the Editor *New York Times* (November 8, 1993).

Allen, William, and Eugenia Toma. *A New Framework for Public Education* (Lansing, Mich.: Governor's Office, November 1996).

Alter, Jonathan. "Chicago's Last Hope," *Newsweek* (June 22, 1998): 30.

American Legislative Council. *You Can't Buy Higher Grades: 50-State Report Card on American Education Funds* (April 2000).

Aoki, Masato, and Susan F. Feiner. "The Economics of Market Choice and At-Risk Students," in William E. Becker and William J. Baumol (eds.). *Assessing Educational Practices* (Cambridge, Mass.: MIT Press, 1996).

Archer, Jeff. "Voucher Proponents Claim Victory in Albany," *Education Week* (February 11, 1998): 5.

———. "Chicago Catholics to Reform Their School Funding," *Education Week* (January 13, 1999): 1, 14.

———. "Huge Demand for Private Vouchers Raises Questions," *Education Week* (April 28, 1999): 1, 12.

Armor, David. *"Competition in Education: A Case Study of Interdistrict Choice"* (Boston: Pioneer Institute for Public Policy, 1997).

Arons, Stephen. "Educational Choice: Unanswered Question in the American Experience," in M. E. Manley-Casimir (ed.), *Family Choice in Schooling* (Lexington, Mass.: Lexington Books, 1982).

Ascher, Carol. "Performance Contracting: A Forgotten Experiment in School Privatization," *Phi Delta Kappan* 77, no. 9 (May 1996): 615.

Ascher, Carol, Norm Fruchter, and Robert Berne in *Hard Lessons* (New York: Twentieth Century Fund, 1996).

Ascher, Carol, and Richard Gray, "Substituting the Privilege of Choice for the Right to Equality," *Education Week* (June 2, 1999): 44, 33.

Avishai, Bernard. "Companies Can't Make Up for Failing Schools," *Wall Street Journal* (July 29, 1996).

Baker, Kevin. "Promised Improvements Have Failed to Materialize," *Bakersfield Californian* (October 17, 2000).

Ball, G. Carl. "In Search of Educational Excellence," *Policy Review* (Fall 1990): 54, 55.

Ball, G. Carl, and Steven Goldman. "Improving Education's Productivity," *Phi Delta Kappan* (November 1997): 231.

Ballou, Dale and Michael Podgursky. *Teacher Pay and Teacher Quality* (Kalamazoo, Mich.: W.E. Upjohn Institute for Employment and Training, 1997).

Barro, Robert J. "Can Public Schools Take Competition?" *Wall Street Journal* (March 10, 1997).

Barry, John S., and Rea S. Hedeman, Jr. *Report Card on American Education: A State-by-State Analysis, 1976–99* (Washington: American Legislative Exchange Council, 2000).

Bast, Joseph L., and David Harmer. "Vouchers and Educational Freedom: A Debate," *Policy Analysis Monograph* no. 269, The Cato Institute (1997).

Baumol, William J., John C. Panzar, and Robert D. Willig. *Contestable Markets and the Theory of Industry Structure* (New York: Harcourt Brace Jovanovich, Inc., 1982).

Beales, Janet R. "Educating the Uneducatable," *Wall Street Journal* (August 21, 1996).

Beare, H., and W. L. Boyd (eds.). *Restructuring Schools* (Washington: The Falmer Press, 1993).

Benbow, Camilla, and Julian C. Stanley. "Inequity in Equity: How Equity Can Lead to Inequity for High-Potential Students," *Psychology, Public Policy, and Law* 2 (1996): 249–92.

Bennett, William J. "School Reform: What Remains to Be Done," *Wall Street Journal* (September 2, 1997).

Bennett, William J., Willard Fair, Chester E. Finn Jr., Rev. Floyd Flake, E. D. Hirsch, Will Marshall, Diane Ravitch et al. "A Nation Still at Risk," *Policy Review* 90 (July/August 1998).

Bergner, Laurie. "Work for Education Equity," *San Antonio Express-News* (November 30, 1993).

Berliner, David C. "Mythology and the American System of Education," *Phi Delta Kappan* 74 (1993): 638.

Berliner, David C., and Bruce J. Biddle. *The Manufactured Crisis* (Reading, Mass.: Addison-Wesley, 1995).

Blumenfeld, Samuel. *Is Public Education Necessary?* (Boise, Idaho: The Paradigm Company, 1981).

Boaz, David. "Five Myths about School Choice," *Education Week* (January 27, 1993): 36.

Boaz, David, and R. Morris Barrett. "What Would a School Voucher Buy? The Real Cost of Private Schools," *Cato Institute Briefing Papers* #25 (March 26, 1996).

Bonsteel, Alan, and Carlos Bonilla. *A Choice for Our Children* (San Francisco: ICS Press, 1997): chapter 27.

Borden, Karl J., and Edward A. Rauchat. "Educational Choice: Making Even Good Schools Better," *A Constitutional Heritage Issue Paper* (1995): 12–13.

Borenstein, Severin. "The Evolution of U.S. Airline Competition," *Journal of Economic Perspectives* 6 (Spring 1992): 45–74.

Boston, Rob, and Steve Benen. "Vouchers Harm Public Schools, Violate Church-State Separation, National Watchdog Group Charges," *Americans United for Separation of Church and State Letter* (July 29, 1997).

Bowles, Erskine, and Jack Kemp. "An Offer Bush and Gore Can't Refuse," *Wall Street Journal* (June 15, 2000).

Bowman, Darcia H. "States Giving Choice Bills Closer Look," *Education Week* (March 1, 2000): 1, 24.

Boyd, William L. "Balancing Public and Private Schools: The Australian Experience and American Implications," *Educational Evaluation and Policy Analysis* 9, no. 3 (Fall 1987): 183–97.

Bradford, David F., and Daniel Shapiro. "The Politics of Vouchers," in *Vouchers and Related Delivery Mechanisms: Consumer Choice in the Provision of Public Services*. Conference (October 2–3, 1998]) Papers (Washington: Brookings Institution, 1998): 52.

Bradley, Ann. "Teachers' Pact Deters Achievement, Study Says," *Education Week* (October 1, 1997): 1, 13.

Bradley, Gerard V. *Church-State Relations in America* (New York: Greenwood Press, 1987).

Brandly, Mark. "Explosion in Home Schooling," *US News & World Report* (February 12, 1996): 57–58.

———. "Home Schooling Leaps into the Spotlight," *Wall Street Journal* (June 9, 1997).

Brimelow, Peter, and Leslie Spencer. "The National Extortion Association?" *Forbes* (June 7, 1993): 72.

Broder, David. "Reforming Education a Tough Assignment," *San Antonio Express-News* (March 2, 1999): 7B.

Brown, Byron W. "Why Governments Run Schools," *Economics of Education Review* 11, no. 4 (1992): 287–300.

Brown, Rexford G. *Schools of Thought* (San Francisco: Jossey-Bass, 1993), p. 137.

Bush, Jeb. "A Year's Worth of Knowledge in a Year's Time," *Heritage Lectures*, no. 648 (November 10, 1999): 3.

Carl, Jim. "Parental Choice as National Policy in England and the United States," *Comparative Education Review* 38, no. 3 (August 1994): 297.

Carnegie Foundation for the Advancement of Teaching. *School Choice: A Special Report*, (Princeton, N.J.: Author, 1992).

Carnoy, Martin. "Lessons of Chile's Voucher Reform Movement" in Robert Lowe and Barbara Miner (eds.), *Selling Out Our Schools* (Milwaukee, Wisc.: Rethinking Schools, 1996), pp. 26–27.

Carpenter, Polly, and George Hall. *Case Studies in Educational Performance Contracting: Conclusions and Implications*, Report #R-900/1-HEW (Santa Monica, Calif.: Rand Corporation, 1971).

Carter, Robert L. "Civil Rights Leaders Wear Scars of Controversy," *Washington Times* (May 17, 1994).

Carter, Samuel C. *No Excuses: Lessons from 21 High-Performing, High-Poverty Schools* (Washington: Heritage Foundation, 2000).

Cavazos, Lauro F. "Achieving Our National Education Goals: Overarching Strategies," *Harvard Journal of Law and Public Policy* 14, no. 2 (1991): 357.

Chase, Bob. "An Idea Conservatives Could Dislike," *The Beacon Journal* (September 19, 1997): A15.

———. "Changing the Way Schools Do Business," *Vital Speeches* (May 1, 1998): 444.

———. *Keynote Address to the NEA National Convention*, The Education Intelligence Agency (July 3, 1999).

Chesterton, G. K. cited in Center for Education Reform *Newsletter* 60 (February/March 2000).

"Choice Debate Is Over," *Wall Street Journal* (April 6, 2000).

"Choice Thunderclap," *Wall Street Journal* (June 11, 1998): A22.

Chubb, John and Terry Moe. *Educational Choice* (San Antonio: Texas Public Policy Foundation, 1990).

———. *Politics, Markets, and America's Schools* (Washington: Brookings Institution, 1990).

———. "The Private vs. Public School Debate," *Wall Street Journal* (July 26, 1991).

———. "After 15 Years, Nation is Still at Risk," *Intellectual Ammunition* (September/October 1998): 5.

———. "Five Steps to Full School Choice," *School Reform News* (September 1998): 10–11.

———. "The Dark Side of Suburban School Achievement," *School Reform News* (January 2000): 7.

———. "Interview with Andrew Coulson on Computers in K–12 Classrooms," *School Reform News* (April 2000): 10–11.

Clune, William. "The Shift from Equity to Adequacy in School Finance," *Educational Policy* 8 (1994): 376–94.

Coats, Dan. "The Bell Is Sounding for School Choice: DC Example Shows Why Support for It Is Growing Inside Congress," *Roll Call* (June 2, 1997): 10.

Cobb, C. W. *Responsive Schools, Renewed Communities* (San Francisco, Calif.: The ICS Press, 1992).

Cohn, Elchanan. *Economics of State Aid to Education* (Lexington, Mass.: D. C. Heath, 1974).

Coleman, James. *Public and Private Schools* (New York: Basic Books, 1987).

Collinge, Robert A., and Ronald M. Ayers. *Economics by Design* (Upper Saddle River, N.J.: Prentice Hall, 1997).

Cookson, Peter, in Edith Rasell and Richard Rothstein (eds.). *School Choice: Examining the Evidence* (Washington: Economic Policy Institute, 1993), p. 252.

———. "Response to Bruce Cooper's Review of the Choice Controversy," *Journal of Education Finance* 19 (Fall 1993): 223–25.

Coons, John, and Stephen Sugarman. *Education by Choice* (Troy, N.Y.: Educator's International Press, 1999).

Cordell, Dorman E. "Answering Objections to School Vouchers in D.C.," *National Center for Policy Analysis Brief Analysis* 266 (May 22, 1998): 1–2.

Coulson, Andrew J. "Are Public Schools Hazardous to Public Education?" *Education Week* (April 7, 1999): 36.

———. *Market Education* (New Brunswick, N.J.: Transaction Publishers, 1999).

Cubberly, Elwood P. *School Funds and Their Apportionment*, Contributions to Education No. 2 (New York: Columbia University Teachers College, 1905).

Cutler, Ira M. "This Card-Carrying Liberal Endorses School Choice," *Education Week* (October 30, 1996).

Danitz, Tiffany. "Private Vouchers are Going Public," *Insight* (September 8, 1997): 14–16.

Danzberger, J. P., M. W. Kirst, and M. D. Usdan. *Governing Public Schools* (Washington: Institute for Educational Leadership, 1992).

Davis, Bob. "Dueling Professors Have Milwaukee Dazed over School Vouchers," *Wall Street Journal* (October 11, 1996): A1.

Diehl, Kemper. "Setting Out to Slay the TEA Dragon," *San Antonio Express-News* (December 12, 1993).

Dilulio, John J., Jr. "My School Choice: Literacy First," *The Weekly Standard* (October 19, 1998): 26.

Dixon, A. P. "Parents: Full Partners in the Decision Making Process," *NASSP Bulletin* (April 1992): 15–18.

Donnelly, Sally B., and Tamala M. Edwards. "They'll Vouch for That," *Time* (October 27, 1997): 72–74.

Dougherty, J. Chrys, and Stephen L. Becker. *An Analysis of Public-Private School Choice in Texas* (San Antonio: Texas Public Policy Foundation, 1995).

Doyle, Denis P. "The Challenge, the Opportunity," *Phi Delta Kappan* (March 1992): 518.

———. "Lessons in Hypocrisy," *Wall Street Journal* (June 13, 1995).

———. "Why Vouchers Are Needed for Poor Children," *Heritage Foundation Committee Brief* (May 10, 1996).

———. "Vouchers in Religious Schools," *The Public Interest* (Spring 1997): 89.

Doyle, Denis, and Douglas Munro. *Reforming the Schools to Save the City* (Baltimore: The Calvert Institute, 1997).

Drury, Darrel W. "Vouchers and Student Achievement," *Policy Research* (Summer 2000).

Dunn, Andrew P. "What's Wrong with Special Education?" *Education Week* (May 17, 2000): 36, 39.

Dworkin, A. Gary. *Teacher Burnout in the Public Schools* (Albany, N.Y.: SUNY Press, 1987).

———. "Coping with Reform: The Intermix of Teacher Morale, Teacher Burnout, and Teacher Accountability" in Bruce J. Biddle, Thomas L. Good, and Ivor F. Goodson (eds.), *International Handbook of Teachers and Teaching*, Volume 1 (Dordrecht, The Netherlands: Kluwer Academic Publishers, 1997).

Dworkin, A. Gary and Merric L. Townsend. "Teacher Burnout in the Face of Reform: Some Caveats in Breaking the Mold," in Bruce A. Jones and Kathryn M. Borman (eds.), *Investing in U.S. Schools: Directions for Educational Policy* (Norwood, N.J.: Ablex Publishing Company, 1994).

Economic Policy Institute. *School Choice: Examining the Evidence* (Washington: Author, 1993)

Education Intelligence Agency. *NEA Confidential: A Practical Guide to the Operations of the Nation's Largest Teachers' Union* (1998).

Education Policy Institute. "New Poll Finds Public in Dark About Charters and Vouchers," *EPI-Update* (November 19, 1999).

Eisenstadter, Ingrid. "A Stupid Way to Treat Gifted Children," *Wall Street Journal* (July 12, 1995).

Ekelund, Robert B., and Robert D. Tollison. *Microeconomics: Private Markets and Public Choice*, 5th ed. (Reading, Mass.: Addison Wesley Longman, Inc., 1997).

Elam, Stanley M. "Differences between Educators and the Public on Questions of Education Policy," *Phi Delta Kappan* (December 1987): 294–96.

Elmore, Richard, Gary Orfield, and Bruce Fuller. *School Choice: The Cultural Logic of Families, the Political Rationality of Institutions* (New York: Teachers College Press, 1995).

Epple, Dennis, and Richard E. Romano. "Competition between Private and Public Schools, Vouchers, and Peer Group Effects," *American Economic Review* 88 (March 1998): 33-62.

Esack, Steve. "Seeking a School, Finding Jail," *Philadelphia Enquirer* (September 21, 2000).

Evans, Paula M. "When I Grow Up, I Don't Think I Want to Be a Teacher," *Education Week* (June 2, 1999): 31.

Farwell, Kamrhan. "Money Doesn't Always Equal High Test Scores," *The Press Enterprise* (August 10, 1998).

Feldman, Sandra. "Not All Credit to Bush," *Wall Street Journal* letter (August 11, 2000).

Feulner, Ed. "Is School Choice a Bad Idea?" *Heritage Member News* (Autumn 1998).

Fikac, Peggy. "Bullock Defends Pro-Voucher Role," *Austin American-Statesman* (November 12, 1997).

Fine, Michael. "Democratizing Choice," in Edith Rasell and Richard Rothstein (eds.), *School Choice: Examining the Evidence* (Washington: Economic Policy Institute, 1993).

Finn, Chester E., Jr. "The Schools," in N. Kozodny (ed.), *What to Do About . . .* (New York: HarperCollins, 1995).

Finn, Chester E., and Rebecca L. Gau. "New Ways of Education," *The Public Interest* (Winter 1998): 79.

Finn, Chester E., Bruno V. Manno, Louann A. Bierlein, and Gregg Vanourek. *Charter Schools in America Project: Final Report, Part 2* (Indianapolis: Hudson Institute, 1997).

Finn, Chester E., Jr., Bruno Manno, and Gregg Vanourek. *Charter Schools in Action: Renewing Public Education* (Princeton: Princeton University Press, 2000).

Finn, Chester E., Jr., and Michael J. Petrilli. "Washington versus School Reform," *The Public Interest* (Fall 1998): 63.

Fischer, Michael. "A Betrayal of Teachers by Their Union," *Wisconsin Interest* (Fall/Winter 1994): 35.

Fiske, Edward B. *Smart Schools, Smart Kids* (New York: Simon and Schuster, 1991).

Fiske, Edward B., and Helen F. Ladd. *When Schools Compete: A Cautionary Tale* (Washington: Brookings Institution, 2000).

Fondy, Albert. *School Vouchers in Pennsylvania: Bad Education Policy, Worse Public Policy* (Philadelphia: Pennsylvania Federation of Teachers, 1998).

Fossedal, Gregory. "Help for Schools? Try Deregulation," *Wall Street Journal* (March 27, 1996).

Fox, Michael. "Remarks of Ohio State Representative Michael Fox," *State Legislator Guide to Teacher Empowerment* (Washington: American Legislative Exchange Council, February 1997): 17.

"Free to Grow," *Wall Street Journal* (September 3, 1996).

Freiwald, Leo. "Recognizing the Horses," *Phi Delta Kappan* 78, no. 2 (October 1996): 180.

Frey, Donald E. "Can Privatizing Education Really Improve Achievement? An Essay Review," *Economics of Education Review* 11, no. 4 (1992): 427–38.

Friedman, Milton. "The Role of Government in Education" in R. A. Solo (ed.), *Economics and the Public Interest* (New Brunswick, N.J.: Rutgers University Press, 1955).

———. *Capitalism and Freedom* (Chicago: University of Chicago Press, 1962).

———. "The Only Solution Is Competition (interview with George Clowes)," *School Reform News* (December 1998): 20, 16–17.

Howard Fuller. "A Research Update on School Choice," *Marquette University Current Education Issues* 97, no. 3 (October 1997): 1.

Fuller, Howard L. "The *Real* Evidence: An Honest Research Update on School Choice Experiments," *Wisconsin Interest* (Fall/Winter 1997).

Fuller, Howard L., and Sammis B. White. *Expanded School Choice in Milwaukee: A Profile of Eligible Students and Schools* (Thiensville, Wisc.: Wisconsin Policy Research Institute, 1995).

Gallup, Alec M. *Gallup Poll of Teachers' Attitudes toward the Public Schools* (Bloomington, Ind.: Phi Delta Kappa, 1985), 10.

Garcia, Angie. "Vouchers Not Edgewood's Real Problem, *San Antonio Express News* (December 6, 1998).

Gatto, John T. *Confederacy of Dunces: The Tyranny of Compulsory Schooling* (New York: Author, 1992).

Gatto, John Taylor. *Dumbing Us Down* (Philadelphia: New Society Publishers, 1992).

Gibbs, Nancy. "Schools for Profit," *Time* (October 17, 1994): 48.

Gintis, Herbert. "The Political Economy of School Choice," *Teachers College Record* 96, no. 3 (Spring 1995): 503.

Glass, Stephen. "A Pension Deficit Disorder: Teacher Unions Betray Their Members," *Policy Review* (Winter 1995): 71–74.

Gleick, Elizabeth. "Privatizing Lives," *Time* (November 13, 1995): 88.

———. "Mad and Mobilized," *Time* (September 9, 1996): 52.

Glenn, Charles. *The Myth of the Common School* (Amherst: University of Massachusetts Press, 1988).

Glenn, Charles L. "Where Public Education Went Wrong." *Family Policy* 11, no. 5 (September/October 1998).

Goenner, James N. "Charter Schools: The Revitalization of Public Education," *Phi Delta Kappan* 78, no. 1 (September 1996): 32–34.

Goldberg, Bruce. "A Liberal Argument for School Choice," *The American Enterprise* (September/October 1996): 26, 29.

Goldhaber, Dan D. "Public and Private High Schools: Is School Choice an Answer to the Productivity Problem?" *Economics of Education Review* 15, no. 2 (1996): 93–109.

———. "School Choice as Education Reform," *Phi Delta Kappan* 79, no. 2 (October 1997): 143.

———. "School Choice: An Examination of the Empirical Evidence on Achievement, Parental Decisionmaking, and Equity," *Educational Researcher* (December 1999): 16–25.

Goldwater Institute. *The Top Ten Myths about School Choice* (Phoenix, Ariz.: Author, 1994).

Gray, Paul. "Debating Standards," *Time* (April 8, 1996): 40.

Greene, Jay P. "Why School Choice Can Promote Integration," *Education Week* (April 12, 2000): 52, 72.

Greene, Jay P., and Nicole Mellow. "Integration Where It Counts: A Study of Racial Integration in Public and Private School Lunchrooms," September 1998 Conference of the American Political Science Association Meeting in Boston, Mass.

Greene, Jay P., Paul Peterson, and Jiangtao Du. *The Effectiveness of School Choice: The Milwaukee Experiment* (Cambridge, Mass.: Program in Education Policy and Governance, Harvard University, 1997).

Greene, Jay P., Paul Peterson, and William Howell. *Test Scores from the Cleveland Voucher Experiment* (Cambridge, Mass.: Program in Education Policy and Governance, Harvard University, 1997).

Grusendorf, Kent (R). "Test Vouchers before Flunking Them," *San Antonio Express-News* (April 29, 1995).

Hakim, Simon, Paul Seidenstat, and Gary Bowman (eds.). *Privatizing Education and Educational Choice* (Westport, Conn.: Praeger Publishers, 1994).

Hanushek, Eric A. "School Resources and Student Performance," in Gary Burtless (ed.), *Does Money Matter?* (Washington: Brookings Institution, 1996).

———. "Why True Reform of Schools Is So Unlikely," *Jobs and Capital* (Winter 1997): 23–27.

———. "Incentives: the Fundamental Problem in Education," *School Reform News* (January 2000): 17.

Harmer, David. *School Choice* (Washington: Cato Institute, 1994).

Hayek, Frederich A. *The Road to Serfdom* (Chicago: The University of Chicago Press, 1994).

Hayes, Kathy J., and Lori L. Taylor. "Neighborhood Characteristics: What Signals Quality to Homebuyers?" *Federal Reserve Bank of Dallas Economic Review* (4th Quarter 1996).

Heritage Foundation F.Y.I. (April 21, 1997).

Heritage Foundation F.Y.I. (January 30, 1998).

Hess, Frederick. *Spinning Wheels: The Politics of Urban School Reform* (Washington: Brookings Institution, 1999).

Hess, Frederick, Robert Maranto, and Scott Milliman. "Coping with Competition: How School Systems Respond to School Choice," Working Paper (1999).

Hess, Frederick M. "Courting Backlash: The Risks of Emphasizing Input Equity Over School Performance," *The Virginia Journal of Social Policy & the Law* 6 (Fall 1998).

Hill, Paul T. "The Innovator's Dilemma," *Education Week* (June 14, 2000): 33.

Hirsch, E. D., Jr. *The Schools We Need* (New York: Doubleday, 1996).

Hirschman, Albert O. *Exit, Voice, and Loyalty* (Cambridge, Mass.: Harvard University Press, 1970).

Holmes, Kim R. "In Search of Free Markets," *Wall Street Journal* (December 12, 1994).

Hood, John. "Educational Challenges: The Role of Choice," *Current* (December 1991): 11.

Hoxby, Caroline, in Helen F. Ladd, *Holding Schools Accountable* (Washington: Brookings Institution, 1996).

Hoxby, Caroline. "What Do America's Traditional Forms of School Choice Teach Us about School Choice Reforms?" FRBNY *Economic Policy Review* 4 (March 1998): 47–59.

Hume, Jerry. "In Search of Educational Excellence," *Policy Review* (Fall 1990): 55.

Hutchinson, Peter. "The Five C's," *Education Week* (September 17, 1997.): 37, 39.

Jacobsen, Susan. "School Choice: It's a Seller's Market," *Education Week* (October 1, 1997).

Jencks, Christopher. "Is the Public School Obsolete?" *The Public Interest* 2 (1966): 18-27.

Jennings, Wayne B. "Let's Ride the Wave of Change," *Enterprising Educators* 6, no. 2 (Spring 1998): 1.

Judson, Jeff. *The True State of Texas Education* (San Antonio: Texas Public Policy Foundation, 1998).

Kansas, Dave. "Illiteracy about Economics Abounds among Americans, Survey Concludes," *Wall Street Journal* (September 11, 1992).

Kantrowitz, Barbara, and Pat Wingert. "A Dismal Report Card," *Newsweek* (June 17, 1991): 65.

———. "Failing the Most Gifted Kids," *Newsweek* (November 15, 1993): 67.

Kearns, David T., and Denis P. Doyle. *Winning the Brain Race: A Bold Plan to Make Our Schools Competitive* (San Francisco: ICS Press, 1991).

Kearns, David T., and James Harvey. *A Legacy of Learning* (Washington: Brookings Institution Press, 2000).

King, William S. "A Simpler Conclusion," *Phi Delta Kappan* 78, no. 2 (October 1996): 180.

Kirkpatrick, David. *School Choice: The Idea That Will Not Die* (Mesa, Ariz.: Bluebird Publishing, 1997).

———. "Class Size Reduction: Costly and Ineffective," *School Reform News* (April 1999): 9.

———. "School Choice Choir Has a Broad Range of Voices," *School Reform News* (July, 1999): 9.

Kiviat, Joy. "Vouchers Improve Academic Outcomes" *School Reform News* (April 2000); 6–7.

Klein, Joe. "The Legacy of Summerton," *Newsweek* (May 16, 1994): 26–31.

———. "Parochial Concerns," *Newsweek* (September 22, 1996): 27.

Kloehn, Steve. "Protestants Take Aim at School Voucher Programs," *Chicago Tribune* (November 11, 1998).

Kozol, Jonathan. *Savage Inequalities: Children in America's Schools* (New York: Harper Perennial, 1992).

Kronholz, June. "School Voucher Drive Bolstered by Court Action," *Wall Street Journal* (June 11, 1998): A24.

———. "In Michigan, Amway Chief and Wife Give School Vouchers a Higher Profile," *Wall Street Journal* (October 25, 2000).

Lacayo, Richard. "They'll Vouch for That," *Time* (October 27, 1997): 74.

Lamdin, Douglas J. and Michael Mintrom. "School Choice in Theory and Practice: Taking Stock and Looking Ahead," *Education Economics* 5 no. 3 (1997): 235.

LeConte, Joe. "Schools Learn That Vouchers Can Have a Hidden Cost," *Wall Street Journal* (January 26, 1999).

"Lessons on Vouchers from Milwaukee," *School Reform News* (May 1999).

Levin, Henry M. "The Economics of Educational Choice," *Economics of Education Review* 10 (1991): 137–58.

Levin, Henry M., and Cyrus E. Driver. "Costs of an Education Voucher System." *Education Economics* 5, no. 3 (December 1997): 265–83.

Levine, Arthur. "Why I'm Reluctantly Backing Vouchers," *Wall Street Journal* (June 15, 1998).

Levine, Arthur, and Jeannete S. Curetin. "Collegiate Life: An Obituary," *Change* (May/June 1998): 14–17, 51.

Lewis, Ann C. "A Modest Proposal for Urban Schools," *Phi Delta Kappan* 78, no. 1 (September 1996): 5.

Lieberman, Joseph, quoted by Nina H. Shokraii. "What People are Saying about School Choice" *The Heritage Foundation Backgrounder* 1188 (June 2, 1998).

Lieberman, Myron. *Public Education: An Autopsy* (Cambridge, Mass.: Harvard University Press, 1993).

Lieberman, Myron. "The School Choice Fiasco" *The Public Interest* (Winter 1994): 29.

Lieberman, Myron. *The Teacher Unions* (New York: The Free Press, 1997).

Lieberman, Myron, and Charlene Haar. *The Real Cost of Public Education* (in press).

Lindsay, Drew. "Turncoat, Part I," *Education Week* (May 7, 1997).

Loomis, Burdett. "The Politics of Vouchers" in *Vouchers and Related Delivery Mechanisms: Consumer Choice in the Provision of Public Services.* Conference (October 2–3, 1998) Papers (Washington: Brookings Institution, 1998): 80.

Lott, John R., Jr. "Why Is Education Publicly Provided? A Critical Survey," *Cato Journal* (Fall 1987): 475–501.

Lowe, Robert, and Barbara Miner in Robert Lowe and Barbara Miner (eds.). *Selling Out Our Schools* (Milwaukee, Wisc.: Rethinking Schools, 1996), p. 3.

Luce, Tom, at October 17, 1997, School Choice Conference sponsored by the Federal Reserve Bank of Dallas.

Lund, Jami. "How Much Bureaucracy Is Carried by Classroom Teachers?" *Policy Highlighter* 9, no. 5 (Evergreen Freedom Foundation, March 31, 1999).

Luntz, Frank, and Bob Castro. "Dollars to Classrooms and Parental Choice in Education," Memorandum (April 14, 1998).

Lutz, Robert, and Clark Durant. "The Key to Better Schools," *Wall Street Journal* (September 20, 1996).

Manno, Bruno V. "The Real Score on the SATs," *Wall Street Journal* (September 13, 1995).

Maranto, Robert, and Scott Milliman. "In Arizona, Charter Schools Work," *Washington Post* (October 11, 1999): A25.

McCarty, Therese A., and Harvey E. Brazer. "On Equalizing School Expenditures," *Economics of Education Review* 9, no. 3 (1990): 251–64.

McConnell, Michael W. "School Choice in America," *The Weekly Standard* (December 21, 1998): 24.

McGhan, Barry. "Choice and Compulsion," *Phi Delta Kappan* 79, no. 8 (April 1998): 610–15.

McGroarty, Daniel. "School Choice Slandered," *Public Interest* (Fall 1994): 95–96.

———. *Break These Chains* (Rocklin, Calif.: ICS Press, Prima Publishing, 1996).

————. "Hope for Milwaukee," _Report Card_ (May–June, 1996).

————. "Voucher Wars: Strategy and Tactics as School Choice Advocates Battle the Labor Leviathan," _Issues in School Choice_, #2 (Milton and Rose Friedman Foundation, Indianapolis, Ind.: April 1998).

Meier, Deborah W. "The Little Schools That Could," _The Nation_ (September 23, 1991): 1, 338.

Melloan, George. "Global Finance: Some Day We'll Get Organized," _Wall Street Journal_ (May 4, 1999).

Merrifield, John. "Monopsony Power in the Market for Teachers," _Journal of Labor Research_ 20, no. 3 (Summer 1999): 377–91.

Merrifield, John, and Robert Collinge. "Efficient Water Pricing Policies as a Municipal Revenue Source," _Public Works Management and Policy_ (October 1999): 119–130.

Miller, D. W. "The Black Hole of Education Research," _Chronicle of Higher Education_ (August 6, 1999).

Miller, John. "Opting Out," _The New Republic_ (November 30, 1992): 12–13.

————. "Why School Choice Lost," _Wall Street Journal_ (November 4, 1993).

————. "GOP Woos Black Voters with Radio Ad Campaign," _Washington Post_ (October 13, 2000).

Mobilization for Equity (newsletter), February 1998.

Moe, Terry, in "Responses to a Harvard Study on School Choice: Is It a Study at All?" Pioneer Institute for Public Policy Research _Dialogue_ (1995): 6.

Molnar, Alex. "School Reform: Will Markets or Democracy Prevail?" in Robert Lowe and Barbara Miner (eds.), _Selling Out Our Schools_ (Milwaukee, Wisc.: Rethinking Schools, 1996).

Morrison, Linda. _The Tax Credits Program for School Choice_ (Mackinaw, Mich.: National Center for Policy Analysis Policy Report #213, March 1998.

Morrison, Steven A., and Clifford Winston. "Empirical Implications and Tests of the Contestability Hypothesis," _Journal of Law and Economics_ 30 (April 1987): 53–66.

Munk, La Rue G. _Collective Bargaining: Bringing Education to the Table_ (Midland, Mich.: Mackinac Center for Public Policy, 1998).

Murdock, Deroy. "Teachers Warm to School Choice," _Headway_ (April 1998): 20.

————. "Will Reinvented Gore Embrace Vouchers?" _Wall Street Journal_ (June 21, 1999).

Murphy, Joseph. _The Privatization of Schooling_ (Thousand Oaks, Calif.: Corwin Press, 1996).

Murray, Frank B. "What's So Good about Choice?" _Education Week_ (January 27, 1999): 52.

Nathan, Joe (ed.). _Public Schools by Choice_ (St. Paul, Minn.: The Institute for Learning and Teaching, 1989).

National Commission on Excellence in Education. _A Nation at Risk: The Imperative for Educational Reform_ (Washington: U.S. Department of Education, 1983).

Neal, Derek. "Religion in the Schools: Measuring Catholic School Performance," _The Public Interest_ (Spring 1997): 81–93.

Nelsen, Frank C. "Parental Choice: Will Vouchers Solve the School Crisis?" _Christianity Today_ (August 19, 1991): 29.

Newman, Joseph W. "Bribing Students out of Public Schools," _Education Week_ (January 27, 1999): 76, 53.

"No Choice for Democrats," _Wall Street Journal_ (February 23, 2000).

Norton, James H. K. "Solution or Problem?" _Education Week_ (March 29, 2000): 47.

OECD. _Education at a Glance: OECD Indicators_ (Paris: Author, 1995).

Olson, Lynn. "Policy Focus Converges on Leadership," _Education Week_ (January 12, 2000): 1, 16–19.

Omdahl, Richard, and Jackie Ducote. "Education Accountability and the Role of School Choice," Public Affairs Research Council of Louisiana, Inc., Analysis No. 299 (March 1999).

"Overcoming Opposition to School Choice," _School Reform News_ (December 1998): 11.

Pearson, Hugh. "An Urban Push for Self-Reliance," _Wall Street Journal_ (February 7, 1996).

Peterkin, Robert. "Choice and Public School Reform," in Robert Lowe and Barbara Miner (eds.), *Selling Out Our Schools* (Milwaukee, Wisc.: Rethinking Schools, 1996).

Peters, Tom. "In Search of Educational Excellence," *Policy Review* (Fall 1990): 57–58.

Peterson, Paul E. "A Report Card on School Choice," *Commentary* (October 1997): 29–33.

Peterson, Paul E., Jay P. Greene, and Chad Noyes. "School Choice in Milwaukee," *The Public Interest* (Fall 1996): 38–56.

Pfaff, Leslie G. "The Right to Choose," *The New Jersey Monthly* (September 15, 2000).

Pierce, R. K. *What Are We Trying to Teach Them Anyway?* (San Francisco: Institute for Contemporary Studies, 1993).

Pogrow, Stanley. "Reforming the Wannabe Reformers," *Phi Delta Kappan* 77, no. 10 (June 1996): 656–67.

Price, Hugh B. "Establish an Academic Bill of Rights," *Education Week* (March 17, 1999): 54–55, 76.

"Professor: U.S. Education Being Emasculated," *School Reform News* (December 1998): 3.

Public Agenda Public Education Network. "Parents Prefer Academics to Integration," *School Reform News* (November 1998): 6.

Quade, Quentin L. "Watch Your Step! If School Choice Is So Great, Why Don't We Have It?" *Network News and Views* (January/February 1996).

———. *Financing Education* (New Brunswick, N.J.: Transaction Publishers, 1996).

———. *The National Education Association vs. America's Parents*, mimeograph, Marquette University, Marquette, Wisc., 1997.

———. "Strap on the Armor and Go: Never Give In!" *School Reform News* (June 1998): 16, 20.

———. "Must Tax Dollars Kill School Independence?" Blum Center Web site, *www.marquette.edu/blum/taxkill.html* (August 8, 2000).

Rasell, Edith, and Richard Rothstein (eds.). *School Choice: Examining the Evidence* (Washington: Economic Policy Institute, 1993): xii.

Raspberry, William. "Let's at Least Experiment With School Choice," *The Washington Post* (June 16, 1997).

———. "The Historical Case for School Choice," *Washington Post* (August 17, 1998): A19.

Ravitch, Diane. *The Troubled Crusade* (New York: Basic Books, 1983): 233.

———. "Somebody's Children," *Brookings Review* (Fall 1994).

Raywid, Mary A. "Choice Orientations, Discussions, and Prospects," *Educational Policy* 6, no. 2 (June 1992): 112–13.

"Reality Check 2000," *Education Week* (February 16, 2000): S1–S8.

Rector, Robert. "The Importance of Vouchers for Social Health," in Independence Institute, *Colorado in the Balance* (Denver: Independence Institute, 1995).

Rees, Nina S. "Public School Benefits of Private School Vouchers," *Policy Review* (January/February 1999): 16–19.

———. "Fighting for a Good Education," *A Heritage Foundation Op-Ed* (September 7, 1999).

———. "Johnson's Voucher Vision," *School Reform News* (November 1999): 5.

———. "School Choice 2000 Annual Report," *The Heritage Backgrounder*, No. 1354 (March 30, 2000).

———. "Will the 106th Congress Promote School Choice?" *School Reform News* (April 2000): 3.

———. "Free at Last: Black America Signs Up for School Choice," *Policy Review* (November/December 1996).

Reese, Charley. "Vouchers Are a Bad Idea," *The Orlando Sentinel* (November 19, 1998).

Reinhard, Beth. "Thompson Threatens a Takeover for Milwaukee," *Education Week* (January 28, 1998): 8.

Republican Main Street Partnership. *Defining the Federal Role in Education: A Republican Perspective* (Washington: Author, 2000).

Richman, Sheldon. *Separating School and State* (Fairfax, Va.: The Future of Freedom Foundation, 1994).

Richter, Bob. "Special Students Lost in a Murky System," *San Antonio Express-News* (May 21, 2000).

Rickover, Hyman G. *Education and Freedom* (New York: E. P. Dutton and Co., 1959).

Roberts, Donald J. *Policy Review* (Fall 1990): 58.

Rockwell, Llewellyn. "Costly Initiative Will Hurt Private Schools," *Human Events* (August 28, 1993): 10.

———. "School Vouchers: An Enemy of Religion," *The Wanderer* (September 1998).

Rothbard, Murray. *Free Market* (January 1994): 1.

Rouse, Cecilia E. *Private School Vouchers and Student Achievement: An Evaluation of the Milwaukee Parental Choice Program* (Washington: National Bureau of Economic Research, 1996).

Salganik, Laura H. "The Rise and Fall, of Education Vouchers," *Teachers College Record* 83 (1981): 263.

Sanchez, Rene. "Riley Launches Attack on School Vouchers," *Washington Post* (September 24, 1997): A6.

Sandham, Jessica L. "Florida OKs 1st Statewide Voucher Plan," *Education Week* (May 5, 1999): 1, 21.

Sarason, Seymour B. *How Schools Might Be Governed and Why* (New York: Teachers College Press, 1997); p. xii.

———. *The Predictable Failure of Educational Reform* (San Francisco: Jossey-Bass Publishers, 1990).

Savas, Emanuel S. *Privatizing the Public Sector* (Chatham, N.J.: Chatham House, 1982), p. 102.

———. *Privatization: The Key to Better Government* (Chatham, N.J.: Chatham House, 1987).

Sawhill, Isabel V., and Shannon L. Smith. "Vouchers for Elementary and Secondary Education" in *Vouchers and Related Delivery Mechanisms: Consumer Choice in the Provision of Public Services* (Washington Conference: Brookings Institution, October 2–3, 1998), p. 150–54.

Shleifer, Andrei. "State Versus Private Ownership," *Journal of Economic Perspectives* 12, no. 4 (Fall 1998): 133–50.

Schnaiberg, Lynn. "Firms Hoping to Turn Profit from Charters," *Education Week* (December 10, 1997): 14.

———. "Charter Schools Struggle with Accountability," *Education Week* (June 10, 1998): 1, 14.

Schneider, Mark, Paul Teske, Melissa Marschall, and Christine Roch. "School Choice Builds Community," *The Public Interest* (Fall 1997): 86–90.

"School Reform Blooms," *Wall Street Journal* (May 5, 1999).

Schundler, Brett. "Public Money for the Public," *Michigan Education Report* (Fall 1998): 12.

Segal, Troy. "Saving Our Schools," *Business Week* (September 14, 1992): 70–78.

Shanker, Albert, and Bella Rosenberg in Simon Hakim, Paul Seidenstat, and Gary Bowman (eds.) *Privatizing Education and Educational Choice* (Westport, Conn.: Praeger Publishers, 1994).

Shapiro, Walter. "Tough Choice," *Time* (September 16, 1991): 55.

Sherlock, Richard. "Choice v. Conflict in Education," *A Sutherland Institute Policy Perspective* (August 27, 1996).

Shlaes, Amity. "The Next Big Free-Market Thing," *Wall Street Journal* (July 9, 1998).

———. "Voucher Program Passes Its Test," *Wall Street Journal* (October 30, 1998).

Shleifer, Andrei. "State Versus Private Ownership," *Journal of Economic Perspectives* 12, no. 4 (Fall 1998): 133–50.

Shokraii, Nina H. "What People are Saying about School Choice," *The Heritage Foundation Backgrounder* 1188 (June 2, 1998): 3–4.

Shokraii, Nina H., and John S. Barry. "Two Cheers for S. 1: The Safe and Affordable Schools Act of 1997," *The Heritage Foundation Issue Bulletin* 232 (May 14, 1997): 5.

Silva, Mark. "House Approves Bush's Program for Public Schools," *Miami Herald* (April 29, 1999).

Singal, Daniel J. "The Other Crisis in American Education," *The Atlantic Monthly* (November 1991): 59–74;

Smith, Kevin B., and Kenneth J. Meier. *The Case against School Choice* (New York: M. E. Sharpe, 1995).

Smoley, Eugene R., Jr. *Effective School Boards* (San Francisco: Jossey-Bass Publishers, 1999).

Solmon, Lewis C., Michael K. Block, and Mary Gifford. *A Market-Based Education System in the Making* (Phoenix, Ariz.: Goldwater Institute, 2000).

Sowell, Thomas. "Economic Literacy Escapes Most," *San Antonio Express-News* (January 4, 1995).

———. "Governments Have Fostered Discrimination," *The Des Moines Register* (August 5, 1995): 7.

Stanfeld, Rochelle. "A Turning Tide on Vouchers," *National Journal* (September 27, 1997): 1911.

Stecklow, Steve. "SAT Scores Rise Strongly after Test Is Overhauled," *Wall Street Journal* (August 24, 1995): B1, B12.

Steurle, C. Eugene. "Common Issues for Voucher Programs," in *Vouchers and Related Delivery Mechanisms: Consumer Choice in the Provision of Public Services.* Conference (October 2–3, 1998) Papers (Washington: Brookings Institution, 1998): 15.

Stevenson, Harold W. "Learning from Asian Schools," *Scientific American* 267, no. 6 (December 1992): 70–76.

Stewart, Marilyn. "Voucher Bill Discriminatory, Misleading," *San Antonio Express-News* (March 5, 1999).

Styring, William. "Teachers and School Choice," *American Outlook* (Spring 1998): 49–51.

Sykes, Charles J. *Dumbing Down Our Kids* (New York: St. Martins Press, 1995).

Talbot, Stephen. "The Battle over School Choice," *PBS Frontline* (May 23, 2000).

Testa, William A., and Surya Sen. "School Choice and Competition (A Conference Summary), *Chicago Fed Letter* #143a (July 1999).

Texas Education Agency, *Academic Excellence Indicator System: 1996–97 State Performance Report* (1997).

Texas Federation of Teachers, "The Choice Issue," undated.

"Third International Mathematics Study," *School Reform News* (April 1998): 1.

Thomas, Cal. "No Brainer to See Education Is Failing," *San Antonio Express-News* (July 15, 1996).

———. "School Choice Saves Children," *San Antonio Express-News* (June 15, 1998): 11A.

Thompson, Bruce R. "School Choice: Changing the Vision for Public Education" (interview, May 1999).

Tiebout, Charles. "A Pure Theory of Local Expenditures," *Journal of Political Economy* 64 (October 1956): 416–24.

Tirozzi, Gerald. "Vouchers: A Questionable Answer to an Unasked Question," *Education Week* (April 23, 1997): 64–65.

———. "Vouchers for Some Harm the Rest," *Education Week* (February 10, 1999): 37.

Toch, Thomas, "Why Teachers Don't Teach," *U.S. News & World Report* (February 26, 1996): 62.

———. "The New Education Bazaar," *U.S. News & World Report* (April 27, 1998): 34–36.

Trevino, Julian H. "Education Goal Is to Provide Choices," *San Antonio Express-News* (June 15, 1998): 11A.

Totty, Michael, and Anne Reifenberg. "Fear of TAAS Scores Has Prep Firms Booming," *Wall Street Journal* (April 29, 1998): T1, T3.

Trujillo, Anthony. Interview, "Wall-to-Wall, for All Children," *School Reform News* (February 1999): 20, 16.

TSTA/NEA. *Our Public Schools: The Best Choice for Texas,"* mimeograph, Austin, Tex., 1994.

Twentieth Century Fund. *Facing the Challenge: The Report of the Twentieth Century Fund Task Force on School Governance* (New York: The Twentieth Century Fund Press, 1992).

"Two School Chiefs Talk about Vouchers," *School Reform News* (January 2000): 10.

Udall, Denis. Letter to the Editor, *Education Week* (July 8, 1998): 41, 43.

Unsigned Letter to the Editor. *Teacher Magazine* (November/December 1995).

Vanourek, Greg. "The Choice Crusade," *Network News and Views* (December 1996).

Vedder, Richard K. "Can Teachers Own Their Own Schools?" Independence Institute Policy Report (2000).

Viteritti, Joseph. "Blaine's Wake: School Choice, the First Amendment, and State Constitutional Law," *Harvard Journal of Law and Public Policy* 21, no. 3 (Summer, 1998): 657–718.

———. *Choosing Equality* (Washington: Brookings Institution, 2000).

Voliva, Sharon G. "Public Support for Nonpublic Schools," *PrairieNet.org* (accessed August 26, 1999).

"Voucher Advocate Says 'Milwaukee Plan' Should be Exported," *Church and State* (May 1992): 16–17.

Wagenheim, Wendy. "Why Public Money Shouldn't Go to Private Schools," *Michigan Education Report* (Fall 1998): 12.

———. "ACLU Hypocritical on School Choice, Critics Charge," *Michigan Education Report* (Fall 1999): 5.

Wagner, Tony. "School Choice: To What End?" *Phi Delta Kappan* 78, no. 1 (September 1996): 71.

Walberg, Herbert J. "Market Theory of School Choice," *Education Week* (July 12, 2000): 49.

Walsh, Mark. "Vouchers Face Key Legal Test in Wisconsin," *Education Week* (March 11, 1998).

———. "Audit Criticizes Cleveland Voucher Program," *Education Week* (April 15, 1998).

———. "Vouchers Yield Mixed Results, Report Says," *Education Week* (December 2, 1998): 3.

———. "Giuliani Proposes a Voucher Program for New York," *Education Week* (January 27, 1999): 3.

———. "Ground Zero for Vouchers," *Education Week* (March 17, 1999): 46–51.

Weinschrott, David J., and Sally B. Kilgore. "Educational Choice Charitable Trust: An Experiment in School," Hudson Institute Briefing Paper #189, 1998.

Wells, Amy S. *Time to Choose* (New York: Hill and Wang, 1993).

Wenman, Cosmo. "Choice Cuts: The Real Impact of Milwaukee's Vouchers," *Reason* (December 1996).

Wessel, David. "The Outlook," *Wall Street Journal* (November 19, 1998): A1.

West, E. G. "Autonomy in School Provision: Meanings and Implications—Review Essay," *Economics of Education Review* 11, no. 4 (1992): 417–25.

———. *Education and the State*, 3rd ed. (Indianapolis: Liberty Fund, 1994).

———. *Education Vouchers in Practice and Principle: A World Survey* (Washington: Human Capital Development Working Paper #64, February 1996).

Wheelan, Charles. "Turning the Tables on School Choice," *New York Times* (May 25, 1999): A31.

White, Kerry A. "Ahead of the Curve," *Education Week* (January 13, 1999): 34.

Wilgoren, Jodi. "Young Blacks Turn to School Vouchers as Civil Rights Issue," *New York Times* (October 9, 2000).

Williams, Joe. "MPS Guarantees Help for Poor Readers," *Milwaukee Journal Sentinel* (December 23, 1998).

Wirt, Frederick, and Michael Kirst. *The Political Dynamics of American Education* (Berkeley, Calif.: McCutchan, 1997).

Witte, John F. *The Market Approach to Education: An Analysis of America's First Voucher Program* (Princeton: Princeton University Press, 2000).

Witte, John F., and Mark E. Rigdon. "Education Choice Reforms: Will They Change American Schools?" *Publius: The Journal of Federalism* (Summer 1993): 95–114.

Witte, John F., Andrea B. Bailey, and Christopher A. Thorn. *Third-Year Report, Milwaukee Parental Choice Program* (Madison, Wisc.: Department of Political Science and The Robert La Follette Institute of Public Affairs, University of Wisconsin, December, 1993).

Wolk, Ronald. "What is Best for the Children?" *Education Week* (November 4, 1998): 47.

Wyckoff, Paul G. "A New Case for Vouchers," *Journal of Policy Analysis and Management* 10, no. 1 (1991): 112–16.

Yergin, Daniel, and Joseph Stanislaw. *The Commanding Heights* (New York: Simon and Schuster, 1998).

Zafirau, S. James, and Margaret Fleming. *A Study of Discrepant Reading Achievement of Minority and White Students in a Desegregating School District: Phase IV* (Cleveland, Ohio: Cleveland Public Schools, Department of Research and Analysis, 1982).

Zellner, Wendy. "Going to Bat for Vouchers," *Business Week* (February 7, 2000).

Index

About the Author

John Merrifield is a senior research fellow of the Education Policy Institute and a member of the economics faculty at the University of Texas at San Antonio, a position he has held since 1987. He has published *The School Choice Wars* and more than 30 articles in his primary teaching and research fields of education economics, international trade, the environment, natural resource management, urban and regional economics, and public choice. Dr. Merrifield received a B.S. in natural resource management from Cal Poly San Luis Obispo in 1977, a M.A. in economic geography from the University of Illinois in 1979, and a Ph.D. in economics from the University of Wyoming in 1984.

Dr. Merrifield is a first-generation German immigrant. He accompanied his mother, Dr. Doris Merrifield-Leffingwell, to the United States in 1960 at the age of five. He lives in downtown San Antonio, Texas, with his wife, Gayla, and their three four-legged sons, canines Bob and Buddy and feline Charlie. Additional details are available at *www.business.utsa.edu/faculty/jmerrifi/*.